if
TEARS
COULD
SPEAK

KAY STAUBLE

IF TEARS COULD SPEAK

ISBN: 0-9723806-2-0

Published by Turnkey Press in conjucntion with
Candelabra Publishing, Austin, Texas.

TurnKey
press

2525 West Anderson Lane, Suite 540
Austin, Texas 78757

Tel: 512.407.8876
Fax: 512.478.2117

E-mail: info@turnkeypress.com
Web: www.turnkeypress.com

Childhood experiences influence our choices...
and ultimately our life's journey.

Introduction

My mind was clouded that hot July evening as I steered my Oldsmobile deliberately toward the chapel grounds. Earlier that day, veils of steam rose from the street where a brief shower graced my cul-de-sac with welcome relief from the heat.

The Texas coast is humid in the summer with temperatures often reaching one hundred degrees. Everything seemed to float in slow motion–chemical plants, buildings, gas stations, billboards, and stoplights. I arrived at the hallowed house in a hypnotic state. Except for four cars near the front entrance, the parking lot was empty. I drove out of sight behind the building and parked next to the giant dumpster.

I eased the gearshift into park, grabbed my purse, and checked my appearance in the rear view mirror before opening the door. I inhaled the last stages of the orange sunset in the distance and let the quietness of the moment soothe me. Nausea overwhelmed me as I anxiously approached the door. My heels clicking against the pavement signaled a conductor's queue to the crickets that chimed in unison to a deafening crescendo. I paused to listen, wanting any excuse to delay going in. My crepe dress fell softly against the modest curves of my body to just below my knees. My only jewelry was a pair of tiny pearl earrings and a gold wedding band. At twenty-six, I had been married eleven years and was the mother of three. Still, the years had been kind to me; I had my schoolgirl figure, and my features were still soft.

Inside the building a peculiar feeling stopped me. The place was usually a haven for me-comfortable, warm, reassuring, and safe-but not tonight. My gaze moved slowly toward the ceiling, then down the walls and floors of the hushed hallway. The empty corridors seemed to whisper my name with a doomed sorrow. In the foyer, I saw light beneath the bishop's door. I sat on a bench, searching for comfort in an atmosphere that yielded none. I stood and paced the floor.

The muffled sound of voices came from the bishop's office. I took a handkerchief from my purse and squeezed it tightly. The door opened and Bishop Monroe, a short, bald man with a kind smile, walked toward me. Just behind him in the office were three other men.

"Hello, Sister," he said, extending his hand to shake mine. "We'll be just a few more minutes. Do you mind waiting?"

"No, Bishop, I don't mind."

"Are you okay?"

"Yes, thank you. I'm fine." He put his arms around me and hugged me before returning to the office. His warmth comforted me. This was going to be as difficult for him as for me. I knew that he felt the clamminess of my fingers when he touched my hand. I waited, subdued and apprehensive.

Bishop Monroe was four years my senior, the same age as my sister. We had known each other since we were children. We all attended church together in the small church before the new one was built. Now he was our bishop. Although a young man, he was a mountain of strength in his testimony of Christ, devoted to our congregation in every way. He received no pay for his administrative duties as Father of the Ward. The Mormon Church has an unpaid ministry, and all members share Church duties. Bishop Monroe worked forty hours a week as a security guard at a nearby chemical plant to support his family and performed his Church duties after regular working hours. One responsibility was to conduct disciplinary councils when members broke moral covenants.

In the Mormon Church (Church) disciplinary councils may be held for transgressions such as rape, sexual abuse, adultery, fornication, homosexual relations, child abuse, and spousal abuse. All those transgressions seemed disgraceful to me. There was a time when I judged others summoned to a disciplinary council. How could they dare commit such sin? Now I stood at the door awaiting trial. At that time, the courts' decisions were shared with the priesthood. Although they were not to disclose the information, some men inevitably told their wives, who told other women in strictest confidence.

The purpose of a disciplinary council is threefold: to save the soul of the transgressor, to protect the innocent, and to safeguard the Church's purity, integrity, and good name. Decisions of the council are made following divine inspiration from a bishop and two counselors, with a ward clerk recording the proceedings. A council can reach one of four conclusions: no action, formal probation, dis-fellowship, or excommunication. Excommunication is the most severe. The person excommunicated loses the privileges of membership, including temple worship and the payment of tithes and offerings. They may attend public church meetings, but their participation is limited. Excommunicated persons are encouraged to repent and live so they may be re-baptized.

The council takes many factors into consideration such as: whether marriage covenants have been violated; the frequency, seriousness, and magnitude of the transgression; and evidence of repentance. Councils meet in the spirit of love; retribution is not the objective, but rather helping the offender make changes necessary to stand clean before God.

The door to the bishop's office opened. "Rose, we are ready for you now."

I clutched the handkerchief, now damp, and walked to the only vacant chair as each man shook my hand. The Bishop smiled in an effort to abate the awkwardness of his task. I regretted being the cause of the council, their most difficult duty in the Church. I suppose they thought me incapable of committing acts sufficient to warrant a trial. Until tonight, they watched me attend church with my growing family week after week, year after year, participating in programs, engaging in missionary work, leading the women's group, and teaching little children. Now they braced themselves to hear me confess something personal and deeply imprudent. I had already discussed my sin with the bishop, but he had only just informed the counselors of the reason for the court.

The bishop opened the council with a prayer. Then he looked at me and said, "I have already explained to these gentlemen that we are convened to consider a case of moral transgression, Rose. Are you comfortable discussing the case?"

"Yes, sir."

"Why don't you start by telling us where this all began."

"Where it all began?" I asked.

"Yes, Rose. How did this whole thing start?"

I lay my head against the wall and tried to remember where it started. I closed my eyes and bit my lip. Where *did* it all start? I asked myself as tears welled up. I put the handkerchief over my eyes to keep the tears from streaming down my face. How could I possibly explain it to them? They wouldn't understand. I didn't understand myself. How could I begin to say where it all began? Like a motion picture playing in reverse, I thought back five, ten, eleven years, until I saw myself as a child bride eloping in a secret marriage and hiding it for three months. Perhaps, I should start there, but that isn't where it all began. It began long before that. Twenty years back, to my childhood, maybe that would be a good place to begin. How could I explain my pitiful childhood, when I didn't understand it myself? And I couldn't understand my childhood, until I understood my parents. Twenty years later I could answer, but I would not have those answers until I was forty-seven years old.

I didn't tell them that it started with loveless parents who shared only fists of fury with one another and their children, nor did I explain the child abuse and neglect that permeated my upbringing. I neither knew love as a child nor with my husband. The only love I knew was my love for my children. Maybe it started with the need to escape my childhood to survive mentally. I didn't tell them how miserable I was married to someone I didn't love or even like. I kept quiet about the many times Bud pushed, shoved, kicked, elbowed, or knocked me around. I didn't explain that my sick marriage was at the core of my predicament. During this hour of dread, I would make no excuses for my behavior. I alone was accountable for my choices. Even under the worst circumstances, I should never have sinned against my Lord. But if I had known then what I now know, I would have gone back at least fifty years to my parents' childhoods-before Vietnam, before World War II, to the Depression.

PART I, CHAPTER I

Wanda and Henry

"I wan' a tan-o-toe-toe," little Wanda demanded. The grocer laughed and asked my mother to repeat her mispronunciation for others in the store to hear.

"She means that she wants a can of cocoa," her little sister, Pearl, explained as Wanda ran from the store crying.

My mother, Wanda, told us the story many times. She often spoke of the mistreatment, neglect, and humiliation she knew as a child, but we never took it seriously. In fact, we often laughed at her stories of misfortune. Not until I became an adult did I try to look at her life and search for answers. I meditated on her surroundings as a child and thought of all the stories she told us. I closed my eyes and hypnotically went into her mindset, went back in time, remembering her stories. I lived in the Great Depression, in her house, with her family. I played in her yard, wore her clothes, her brother's shoes, attended her school, slept in her bed. I was no longer Rose. I became Wanda . . .

When I got home from the grocery store in tears and told mother of my embarrassment, far from consoling me, she found my humiliation amusing. She thought it was funny that my sister, four years my junior, spoke more clearly than I. Pearl got all the compliments. I was the home-liest of my siblings, who often teased me about my speech impediment. Nobody could understand me because I was tongue-tied. When Mom needed something from the store, she sent me with a written note for the

6

grocer so I wouldn't have to speak, or she sent Pearl as my interpreter.

I had two older brothers, one older sister, one younger. William, the eldest, was eleven years older than me. Although he spoke clearly by the time I was born, he had the same speech impediment when he was younger. We were also the only towheads in the family. Everyone said I looked like William. My older sister Sarah was popular, petite, and cute, and could dance better than any other girl in the county. My younger sister Pearl was the family darling. Mom doted on her, adorned her curly hair with pretty ribbons, made her lace petticoats, and decorated her homespun dresses with colorful cords and bows. She was partial to Sarah and Pearl, while I was left out, ignored, and never commended. I could not compete with my sisters' looks, talent, or personality.

My brother Crumley, only two years older, fought with me almost every day. When he smashed my face into the ground and made me eat dirt, Mom chuckled and did nothing to protect me or stop him. I was considered a perfect child until Pearl was born when I was four years old. After that, I was no longer the baby of the family. I was jealous of her because she got all the attention and became the family pet. She only got one whipping in her entire life, and that was for digging up Dad's elephant ear plant in the front yard. I laughed at her for getting that spanking. I bet that was one whipping the family pet will never forget! I became mean, ornery, and devilish, prompting Mom to take the switch to me.

I wet my bed until I was almost a teen. Pearl was potty trained by age two. One winter when I lost my shoes, Mom made me wear Crumley's tennis shoes to school. When I stretched my legs in front of me to play jax my shoes looked as tall as my torso. The other children laughed at me and called me Bozo the Clown, but I refused to cry. Instead, I got angry. My sisters never had to wear those shoes to school or suffer such humiliation.

Sarah accidentally threw me into a bath of scalding water burning my backside terribly. I was so sore I could hardly walk. Mom bandaged my hips with gauze so I couldn't remove the bandages to go to the bathroom and sent me to school like that. By the end of the day I had peed and pooped in the bandages and had to remain at school in that smelly condition which brought on ugly remarks from the other children.

One Christmas, Mom made me a pretty red coat. I was proud of the coat, because it was nicer than Pearl's. I wore it to the picture show and left it on the seat when I went to the candy counter. Two older girls took the coat and stuffed it into a dirty toilet bowl in the girl's room and ruined it. I went without a coat the rest of the winter. I seemed always to be the target of nasty jokes and devilish gags.

Dad ran around with other women and was often away from home. When he couldn't be found, William filled in for him at work by oiling the rigs so he wouldn't lose his job. Dad barbered on the side, and when I was six years old he cut my hair like Crumley's-but he left my two sisters' curly locks intact. The family thought my new look was hilarious. Mom took a picture of Crumley and me that day; both dressed in overalls with boyish haircuts. I wore a scowl of humiliation on my face. That haircut so tormented me that I wore an old aviator's cap for months until my hair grew out. I called my dad Mr. Young after he cut my hair like a boy's. By the time I was thirteen, Dad divorced my mother to be with his long-time mistress, and I quit wetting the bed. That is when William became the father figure in our family, at least for the three youngest children, Crumley, Pearl, and me. William was good to us.

I was born in Texas in 1926, in the same hospital as Henry Weaks. The same doctor delivered us just four days apart. We grew up in large families during the Great Depression. Life was hard, especially since our fathers abandoned us, albeit differently. They both worked in the Texas oil fields, and both had destructive vices. My dad had a weakness for women, Henry's, a weakness for the bottle. He was rarely home, but when he was, his paycheck was already spent on gambling and cheap liquor. Henry's home was an unheated shack with a rotten roof so full of holes the children didn't have to look out a window to wish upon a star. They couldn't afford decent shoes and wore rags for clothes. When the soles of his shoes wore through, Henry stuffed newspaper into them. When that didn't work any more, he went without. Henry and I went to elementary school together, and he was usually barefoot. I would have sooner gone barefoot than wear Crumley's tennis shoes.

While my life wasn't easy, I knew Henry's was even harder. His mother warmed rocks over the stove, wrapped them in cloth, and stuffed them in the children's covers to warm their feet. He and his brothers played with snuff bottles in the dry dirt under their house and pretended the bottles were little cars. Sometimes, Henry had only mustard biscuits *for his lunch. I felt bad for him when he stuck his head into his lunch sack so the other children couldn't see his scanty meal. Henry told me on the playground that when his dad came home he was usually drunk and often beat him for no reason. When he was fourteen, his drunken father made him strip naked, then beat him horribly with a leather strap. Henry showed me the marks on his back. He said his dad couldn't remember what he had done the next day.*

We both dropped out of school in the tenth grade and dated a little before he left for the Army. While he was gone, I went to California to live with my sister and work as a waitress. I never loved Henry, but Mom talked me in to courting him again after he came home. She said he would be a good provider since he had a job at a Refinery in Texas City, Texas. When he proposed to me, I really didn't want to marry him, but I let Mom talk me into it. We married in 1949, and I joined him in Texas City, where we made our new home and started a family.

When I came out of the meditation, I understood that both my parents had inferiority complexes. Teased, humiliated, neglected, and mistreated as children, both were convinced they were bad children and deserved the mistreatment they got. Others intimidated them and made them feel they didn't deserve good things. Nothing they ever did was good enough to earn their parents' approval. My parents knew little about affection, but ridicule and mockery they had gathered in abundance. Consequently, they lived with a constant feeling of shame that translated into contempt–and contempt needs an outlet to vent its passage.

CHAPTER II

The City That Would Not Die

Texas City, Texas, my hometown, occupied a grassy flatland void of trees, flowers, hills, or creeks. Plats called neighborhoods covered a pasture of sandy loam, with force-fed Saint Augustine grass. Black crows and buzzards visited frequently, while blue jays and redbirds kept their distance and nested elsewhere. Between Houston and Galveston, Texas City borders Galveston Bay, a location both desirable and undesirable.

Storms and tragedy have battered the Texas Gulf Coast repeatedly since the turn of the 20th century. Beginning with the 1900 hurricane, the "Storm of the Century," which took more lives than any other natural disaster in American history, Galveston County seemed destined for doom. Another hurricane in 1915 tested the newly built seawall and claimed 275 lives. That storm destroyed the Army camp in Texas City, which relocated out of the area. But nothing in its history so devastated Texas City as the events of the morning of April 16th, 1947. The freighter *Grand Camp*, berthed in the Texas City harbor, fully loaded with a cargo of ammonium nitrate fertilizer destined for war-torn Europe, caught fire and set off more than fifty explosions. Just after 9:00 a. m. The *Grand Camp* itself exploded, and columns of smoke rose over two thousand feet. Ten seconds later a violent shock wave struck. Within moments the Monsanto Chemical plant was in flames. As entire buildings collapsed trapping people inside, fires spread quickly to the refineries that made up the Texas City industrial complex. The city became an inferno. A tidal wave caused by the return of bay water driven out by the explosion rushed back in and drove over 150 feet inland, inundating the docks and sweeping away everything in its path.

The *High Flyer*, another freighter loaded with ammonium nitrate and sulfur burned all day. Tugs tried in vain to tow her out of the ruined harbor. At 1:00 a. m., On April 17th, everyone was ordered away from the area, and ten minutes later the *High Flyer* went up in the most violent of all the blasts, taking with her a huge ship, the *Wilson B. Keene.* That explosion destroyed a concrete warehouse and a grain elevator and triggered more fires. Most of the firemen died, along with plant workers, dockworkers, school children, and other bystanders. Windows rattled in Baytown fifty miles away, and a fine mist of black oil rained on Galveston.

Each time disaster struck Texas City, it rose from the ruins, picked up the pieces, and moved on. Its resilience earned it the title *The City That Would Not Die.* Over the years the city built seawalls, levees, and flood pumps and instituted safeguards in ports and industries to protect others from Texas City's legacy. They called the smell of sulfur and pollution in the air the *smell of money*, and residents uncomplainingly got used to the stink: the pollution represented their bread and butter. Petrochemicals were the wave of the future. It was in this town of foul smells and pollution that Wanda and Henry began their family.

Texas City planned to celebrate the fiftieth anniversary of its incorporation on September 11th, 1961. On that day, Hurricane Carla swept through Texas City, sinking the town under the storm driven waters of Galveston Bay. That I was born in *The City That Would Not Die* is appropriate, because I am like my hometown in many ways. Low and unprotected, the city took its punishment each time disaster struck, then rebounded and recovered with renewed vitality. Today it is impossible to detect that the place has been the victim of raging floods, high winds, tidal waves, and explosions. Would Texas City be different today if it had not learned resilience through suffering again and again? Is it weaker or stronger as the result of its history?

I turned seven years old just when Hurricane Carla hit Texas City. I remember the anxiety of the days preceding the evacuation. Mama watched the meteorologist's map of the gulf on the small black and white television in the living room. She called the neighbors nervously to see if they would head for shelter or take their chances and ride the storm out at home. We had no place to flee. Our relatives all lived along the coast.

I sensed my sister Mary Jane's excitement when she told me to start packing my bags. I thought we must be in for an adventure, since packing our bags generally meant going on a rare vacation. Mary Jane was the eldest of four children, and we all looked up to her. We were close, and I relied upon her for the love and affection that I had never got from my parents. We both had blond hair, hers thin and wavy, mine thick, straight, and shiny. My hair looked like variegated silk fiber during the summer months when weeks of exposure bleached the strands into spun gold. It hung past my shoulders to frame my face; an olive tan on flawless skin illuminated my neon green eyes. I was a free spirit, skinny as a string bean, and very much a tomboy. Dad nicknamed me Stack-o-bones, because I was so tiny and thin. He called my younger brother, Billy, Tooter-cut. Dad called us those names when he was in a good mood.

Although Mary Jane was pretty, she was a bit of a sissy, overweight like my dad's mother, and had lighter skin and hazel eyes. She suffered frequent infections on her eyelids and lost some of her eyelashes. Her eyelids were always red and raw, and we teased her and called her Bald Eagle Eyes. I felt sorry for her because she reached puberty at an early age and didn't seem to have as much fun as my two brothers and me. Mary Jane stayed in the hot house all day. I never figured out what she did in the house. Perhaps she did some of the housework or talked to Mama or ate. My mother was partial to her, and that was fine with me; I wanted neither to be fat like my sister or chums with my mother. Mama encouraged my brothers and me to play outdoors all day. We hunted for two-cent Coke bottles. We jumped rope and picked on neighborhood kids. We played with frogs, balls, hula-hoops, tin cans, and rocks. We rolled in barrels, got wet in the sprinkler, or played hop-scotch. I felt safe outside the house.

Once Billy and I wrote a scary letter on a Big Chief tablet to the red-haired girl next door. We wrote that we had been watching her and planned to kidnap her when she went to sleep. We signed it with blood we squeezed from a slapped mosquito. I enlarged the hole in her bedroom window and pushed the note inside. By the time she found the note, we had long since forgotten about it, until Mama got a call from the girl's mother. They believed the note, and she was warning the families in the neighborhood that there was a madman on the loose. Mama heard us giggling after she hung up and figured out that we were the conspirators, but she was too embarrassed to call back and put them at ease. We had a good laugh over that one.

Mary wanted the storm to come our way. "I hope that storm comes, then we won't have to go to school," she giggled.

I had just started second grade and didn't want to miss school because I liked being there. The buildings, the teachers, and my friends provided a security I didn't have at home. The clouds were already rolling in even though Hurricane Carla wasn't expected to come ashore for a couple of days. As the winds picked up, Billy and I ran around the house pretending to be swept away by a tornado, like Dorothy in *The Wizard of OZ*. Our younger brother, Jessie was outside playing on an old worn out car tire when my dad called home from the plant.

Dad worked rotating shifts at the Refinery in Texas City, making a salary that would have made our family comfortable if my parents had managed their finances. They never seemed to have enough to make ends meet, however, and we always looked deprived. Dad worked so much he hardly had time to sleep. In addition to the full-time job at the Refinery, Dad owned a fence-building business. He probably put in another forty hours a week building fences and lost money on every fence he built. His nerves were always on edge when he was at home. We were too young to understand. His frequent callous treatment of us, when we had done nothing to deserve it bewildered us. I don't remember my father ever having friends who visited him; he and my mother never socialized with other couples. In fact, they didn't socialize with each other. They never went out for dinner or to see a movie. We knew they didn't enjoy each other's company.

The only person I can remember coming to our house, other than relatives, was a black man named Joe, who worked for Dad in his fence business. In those days, Dad was a bigot and used the word *nigger*. Although my brothers adopted his attitude, I did not. My father learned it from his father, and I am sure my grandfather learned it from his. When Joe came to our house my parents treated him kindly. Dad paid him more than other blacks could make anywhere else as posthole diggers. Even though Dad was prejudiced against blacks, he treated Joe well.

On the phone, Dad told my mother there was talk of evacuation, and he had been asked to stay at the refinery during the storm. That meant a lot of extra money. Reluctantly, my mother agreed that he could remain if we had to leave. "Stay tuned to the news and be ready to leave if you have to," he told her.

"I don't know where we will go if it comes this way. I'll just wait 'til morning to see. Maybe it will change direction by then," she said. That afternoon she loaded us into the car, and we drove to the Texas City dike to watch the gathering storm. The waves splashed up over the dike; men in slickers partitioned off part of the road.

As my mother approached the blockade, a man stepped forward, motioning her to roll down the window, "You'd best turn around, lady. The white caps are getting furious. It's getting dangerous."

Tiny sprinkles of rain spattered the windshield, so Mama turned the wipers on. We stopped at a bait camp to talk to some other people who were out looking for a thrill. I remember a seagull perched atop a telephone pole that anchored the fishing pier. The gull stuck its beak under its wing, protecting itself from the weather. I wanted to capture the bird and take it home with me to protect it. I didn't take my eyes off of the little bird on the wooden piling until it turned into a tiny, white spot as we drove away.

The next morning we awoke to discover that all of our neighbors left during the night. The storm had picked up speed and was gusting to over 150 miles per hour. Rain poured on our wood-framed home, and the streets were flooding. As the sky grew darker, an eerie feeling of apprehension descended over our family. We fell silent as gusts vibrated the house. Mama started throwing our clothes into a paper bag. A policeman in a black slicker knocked at the front door. "This is the final warning to residents. If you don't leave immediately, you won't get out. The water is rising." He convinced my mother that our lives were in danger. "There is no seawall, Mrs. Weaks. We expect this area to flood. Chances are your house will take a lot of water before this is all over."

We could not imagine that our house would soon become a pool of mud and snakes. We rushed to buckle our shoes, and Mama started to hurry. She packed us into the car and headed for a shelter in Huntsville, Texas. The police escorted us out of town to be sure we didn't get caught in the rising water. Rain pounded the windshield, ditches overflowed into streets, and our wheels created four-foot sprays as we drove through the flooded streets. Bushes driven down by the winds lay on their sides; abandoned, wild-eyed animals ran back and forth in panic, trying to escape. The police waved at us as we left the city in a cacophony of thunder and lightning. I thought of the little white seagull, all alone and unprotected.

In Huntsville, about a hundred miles from Texas City, we located the shelter at the high school. The rain persisted, but we knew Huntsville was safer than Texas City because it wasn't on the bay. We slept on the gymnasium floor, showered in the boys' locker room, and received the charity of good-hearted volunteers for several days while Hurricane Carla spawned tornados and caused havoc across Texas. I liked the temporary quarters, because there was an unending supply of sandwiches, fruit, and punch. All the children played together, running back and forth in the gymnasium, oblivious to our parents' concerns. We had no telephone contact with my father who was still in Texas City. Some folks had transistor radios and heard reports that Galveston County was under four feet of water.

"I might never see my Dad again," I whimpered. Later, I learned that he and the other operators not only survived the storm but also got special treatment. They ate baked ham and turkey dinners with delicious desserts and kept the refinery running. He was safe in the sturdy elevated control rooms built to withstand level five hurricanes.

When the water subsided, Dad went to our house but was not prepared for what he found there. Thick, oozing mud blocked the doors. Forcing the door ajar, he surveyed what was once his home. The storm surge forced water and mud inside covering the floors four feet deep in ooze. Our shoddy furniture was ruined, the ceiling caved in, the floors buckled, and the sheet rock was shredded like wet newspaper. Repairs seemed unlikely. Overwhelmed, a policeman told me my dad turned away, walked to the one surviving chinaberry tree in the front yard, dropped to his knees on the soggy ground, and wept. After a while, he pulled himself together and began making preparations for our return. He had the house cleaned and potable water restored. With no idea where he should start, help came to my father from a direction he least expected.

We left the Huntsville shelter while it was still raining. Before we were out of Huntsville, Mama had a car wreck. She was forever having accidents, always her fault. Mama liked to turn the radio up, take her hands off the wheel, and clap to the beat of the music. I was always happy to see her do this, because it meant she was in a good mood. She was doing one of her slaphappy, jingle-jangle dances when she rear-ended a parked car. Without seat belts, we bounced around like rag dolls, but nobody was injured. Although badly damaged, the car was still driveable, so after the police inquiry, we continued our journey to Texas City in our banged-up jalopy, only to find our home more appalling than the car. My parents must have thought the wrath of God was upon them.

I will never forget the vivid scenes of the storm's aftermath. Wild-eyed horses were frozen in running position against the barbed wire fences, where they had drowned. Houses forced from their foundations, splintered like matchsticks. Cars and trucks lay overturned and smashed in ditches along the highway. Chain-link fences intertwined with rubbish, clothes, and other personal debris. I was embarrassed to find a pair of my white cotton panties stuck in our fence. Water moccasins and other snakes were everywhere. For weeks we received distributions from charitable organizations and lived on food provided by the Red Cross. Very few of our possessions survived, although, some of our family pictures were lost, most of the large, professional photos of my siblings were safe. I never understood why there wasn't an eight-by-ten of me, since there was one of each of my siblings, but I never asked for an explanation.

My parents were humbled by the devastation of their home and were especially thankful for the kindness of church members who helped clean and rebuild it. Disappointment and trials soften hearts and change lives, and people meek and low in spirit become more teachable and often turn to a higher power for strength. The church-men swept mud, repaired sheet rock, cleaned out cabinets, and repainted walls. Although my mother came from generations of Latter-Day Saints, she had not been active in the Church for many years, so she was thankful that the congregation remembered us after the storm. The bishop of our ward worked countless hours cleaning our home. I am sure he saw the opportunity to reacquaint our family with the gospel. The storm marked a significant turning point in my life-our family became active in the Mormon Church. Although our enthusiasm for church lasted only twelve months, I learned principles that have been a strong influence in my life. Since I had no previous exposure to anything in my home life that resembled godliness, I absorbed spiritual truths and clung to them for comfort and peace, like a child to her favorite toy. Church became the one stabilizing force in my life.

Mormonism differs from other religions in that it is based on modern day revelations from God. The first came in the early 1800s, when Joseph Smith, a fourteen-year-old boy in Palmyra, New York, sought the Lord in prayer to discern which church he should join. While praying, he had a vision of God the Father and Jesus Christ dur-ing which he was told to join no church because the true gospel had been lost over the ages, due to wickedness and sin. The power of the priesthood, the authority to act in the name of God, was lost when those who held the priesthood during the time of Christ died. Eventually Joseph Smith, Jr. reestablished the Church and the priest-hood through a series of revelations from God. He uncovered The *Book of Mormon*, written on golden plates, and translated it into English. The plates were an ancient record of the inhabitants of America, encompassing a thousand years from 600 B.C. to approxi-mately 420 A.D. The record gives an account of Christ's visit to the people on the American continent after his crucifixion and resurrec-tion. The ancient prophet, Mormon, transcribed the record centuries earlier, and his son, Moroni, buried them in a hill in upstate New York around 420A.D. That is why Latter-Day Saints were nicknamed Mormons.

After Hurricane Carla, the National Guard patrolled the streets of the ravaged city. Many weeks went by before things seemed normal. Debris was cleared. Insurance claims were investigated. Schools reopened. People gradually repaired their homes and businesses.

CHAPTER III
Early Childhood

I was born during a decade of stability and progress in Texas City. The post-World War II decade rang in the era of baby boomers. Advances in birth control were just emerging, and the famous birth control pill was not yet discovered, so large families were common. During the 1950s, most mothers stayed home while fathers were the breadwinners. A woman's home was her career, and she was expected to enjoy housekeeping, meal planning, and child rearing. Advertisements portrayed mothers as pretty little homemakers with frilly, starched aprons, carrying beautifully baked turkeys to their perfectly happy families seated at the table. A daughter of the 1950s should remember birthday parties, merry-go-rounds, baby dolls, and pretty dresses. But my life was void of 1950s television images. To some of us, the word *mother* evoked more disturbing visions–mother as retaliator, mother as degrader, mother as critic, mother as withholder of refuge. Mother, the creator of painful and frightening experiences. Aggressive little girls can grow into mothers who punish their children harshly. My mother sought retribution for the mistreatment she knew in her own childhood. She proved false the myth that only boys are bullies.

As a child, I lived with a great deal of shame. My physical surroundings were abominable. I was never ashamed by the size of our home, but its deplorable condition embarrassed me. Our lawn was rarely mowed. The mower did not reach the weeds that grew three feet tall around the foundation of the house and fence. I liked to crawl through the tall grass and under the house where it was cool, peaceful, and dark. Sometimes, I fell asleep there in my dark, silent hideaway, the one place I found solace, where I could be alone. When my brothers discovered my hiding place, I lost my sanctuary. Privacy is rare when you are one of six people living in a two-bedroom house with only one bathroom.

Peeling paint on the exterior of our house exposed rotting wood. The bottom half of the garage doors rotted off, showing the junk heaps inside to the neighbors. I was ashamed of the broken windows, torn screens, rotting porch, and leaking roof. Inside, dirty dishes were piled high in the kitchen. Mounds of unfolded clothes occupied the threadbare living room sofa. The corroded tub was seldom scrubbed. Our beds had no spreads or decent pillows. When we had sheets, they went for weeks without washing. Mama's red douche bag hung boldly from the exposed hot water heater in our tiny bathroom. Doors had fallen off the kitchen cabinets; handles were missing from the cutlery drawers. The once pretty oak cupboards were covered with black grime. The washer and dryer next to the filthy refrigerator served as a breakfast bar, since the kitchen table was a pantry for cereal, staples, peanut butter, and paper plates. I thought eating together as a family was a luxury reserved only for affluent families whose dining chairs weren't reduced to rubble. Burned-out light bulbs made the interior dim and murky. Unattended, smelly garbage attracted roaches and mice by the dozens. The attic fan offered little relief from the Texas heat. I envied children who had cool homes and carpeted floors. Living in such a home humiliated me. I was ashamed to invite my friends over to see the appalling conditions in which I lived.

I loved to watch *Leave It to Beaver* and *Dennis the Menace.* I imagined that my family was like theirs with a mother who looked pretty and fresh, used lipstick, wore a starched dress with beads, and made after-school snacks. The possibility of such an existence was like something from a fairy-tale, and a father's look of affection was surreal. I was thrilled to know that some homes, even if they existed only on television, had desks for studying and reading. A household with organization and schedules intrigued me, and I wanted nothing more. The television homes had wall hangings, flower arrangements, end tables, pretty lamps, and dishes full of candies. Mary Jane and I invented a make-believe home where desserts were served after dinner and parents talked to one another civilly. We acted the parts of the women we saw on TV and imagined our lives would some day be like theirs.

"When I grow up I am going to marry a rich man," my sister proclaimed. "I don't care if I love him or not, as long as he is rich and can give me nice things. Then I will never have to live like this again."

"I don't care if I am rich," I told her. "As long as I love my husband, that is all I care about. I don't ever want to be like Mama and Dad. They don't love each other."

Our mother was very different from the role models I saw on television. She had a potbelly and small gray eyes, short brown hair, and a humped nose. Occasionally, she dyed her eyebrows and eyelashes, as was fashionable at the time. I always thought she looked scary after those dye jobs, but I guess she thought it made her glamorous. She lost her lower front teeth in a car accident and used a removable dental prosthesis to hide the gap. She never wore the bridge at home, but only when she went to the store. Billy and I thought she looked like a monster without her teeth. She chose bare feet over sandals or house slippers and hated wearing dresses, opting for a loose muumuu instead, since most of her clothes did not fit. She had one good feature, though; she had beautiful skin. She bragged that she was often complimented on her peaches and cream complexion. I inherited my mother's complexion, along with olive tones from my dad's American Indian roots.

My mother filled her days with long hours in bed, reading True Detective and tabloids about movie stars. She was uninterested in preparing meals regularly. If I asked for something to eat, she said, "If you are really hungry, get a glass of milk or bowl of corn flakes." Our choices were few, but we did not starve. We may have been malnourished, since we didn't eat a balanced diet. We had plenty of bread, milk, cereal, peanut butter, and bologna or pressed ham to make cold sandwiches. Maybe I should have been thankful for what we had, but I longed for a home-cooked meal. My stomach rarely felt filled; my taste buds were not satisfied. Unlike my brothers and sister, I did without rather than force myself to eat cold cereal day after day. Perhaps that is why I was so skinny. Occasionally, Mama cooked a pot of lima beans, rice, and cornbread. Since we ate a hot lunch at school every weekday she didn't think she had to cook an evening meal. Sometimes she would make teacakes from my grandmother's sugar cookie recipe or a pan of popcorn for us. She did this only during the summer, and I relished those moments.

Family outings were rare; vacations to Grandma's house were agonizing. Dad loaded the suitcase into the trunk of the car and packed an ice chest full of Golden Age canned soft drinks, cheese, and lunchmeat. Mama stuffed a sack of bread, mayonnaise, and vanilla wafers next to the ice chest. We looked forward to stopping at a park to have lunch in the outdoors. I loved going to Grandma's, because she always had a coconut cake, peanut butter candy, and a warm chicken stew waiting for us. My grandma told me many years later that she worried about our yellow skin, which she attributed to our being malnourished. When our family had to ride in the car together, Dad drove while my mother sat in the front passenger seat with Mary Jane between them. My brothers and I rode in the back. We listened to Elvis Presley on the radio and stuck our heads out the window to feel the breeze in our faces. My little body fit perfectly in the flat bed above the back seat under the rear window.

Once I was sitting in the back seat as usual with my thumb in my mouth. While leaning forward I touched my sister's hair, in a flash, my mother swung around and slapped my face with the full force of her hand. I slammed back into the seat, stunned and dazed. I could not cry out, because she knocked the wind out of me. My face stung from the handprint embossed across it. She was caught in the act. Dad barked at her like a mad dog for slapping me for no apparent reason, while my brothers laughed at the entertainment.

"Damn you, Wanda, what did you do that for?" Dad shouted. My mother usually did her dirty deeds when my father wasn't around. That time she forgot.

"I did it for her own good, to teach her not to suck her thumb," she chided back. "I have told her repeatedly to quit sucking her thumb, Henry, and she won't obey me." I was accustomed to her brutal treatment, but my dad didn't know it. I can't count the number of times she slapped my face because I sucked my thumb. She slapped me whenever she felt like it and rationalized by saying, "I told you not to suck your thumb!"

Unlike my mother, Dad gave us plenty of warning if we were in trouble. He wasn't exempt from overzealous punishment, but his was less frequent. Mama struck often and without warning; she enjoyed the element of surprise. She used physical force to ensure obedience, needing only the slightest provocation to respond. What might detonate her and propel her into action could seldom be predicted. We never knew if she would be civil or cruel. Her tactics included exploitation, shunning, degrading, and force. The smallest whiff of dissent upset her. Mothers like her justify the awful things they do saying their children deserve it. I don't believe Mama learned her behavior from example. Her parents were not physically cruel to their children, although they showed mental neglect and partiality. Still, their negligent behavior generated a combustible rage within my mother.

One evening before I started school, the other children were asleep. My mother locked me in the bedroom, though she knew that I was not asleep. With the door shut the bedroom was suffocating. I couldn't feel the draft from the attic fan in the hallway between the two bedrooms. My sister was snoring, and my brothers lay next to each other like sardines in the second twin bed. Mama didn't usually lock our bedroom door, but perhaps that was one of the few occasions she succumbed to my father, and she latched the door to prevent us from walking into their room. Being locked in the room didn't matter to the other children, because they were asleep. I started to cry.

Mother became very angry and hollered at me to shut-up. I kept crying. She eventually unlatched the door and stomped into our room; she never walked, she stomped. Since our house was built on pillars, instead of a slab, her footsteps vibrated like a bass drum. I loathed the sound. My crying must have interrupted their five-minute sex act. She scolded me furiously. She grabbed my arm and flung me from the bed. Through gritted teeth, she told my father that I was sick and she was going to give me an enema. I did not need an enema, but that was her way of punishing me.

"No, no, Mama, I'll be good. Please don't do it. I promise not to cry any more!" I begged.

"Leave her alone!" my dad yelled from their bedroom.

"I know what I'm doing, Henry. The girl is crying because she's constipated. She needs a bowel movement."

My dad withdrew and waited for it to be over. She laid a towel on the floor, yanked my panties off, and held me down on the floor with her foot while she filled that big, red douche bag with soapy water. I screamed when she rammed the nozzle into my rectum. When the bag was empty, she jerked me up onto the pot, and held me there to keep me from moving. Tears streaming down my face, I stayed there while the soapy water squirted from my buttocks. She acted like Florence Nightingale, taking credit for diagnosing my ills correctly and providing the healing therapy. Convincing my father that she was a healer left me defenseless. He probably did not want another argument with his grouchy wife, and after all, an enema wouldn't kill me. I retreated to the safety of my bed, she turned the light off, and I whimpered in the darkness.

The only time my mother touched me was when she was angry. If I fell and cried, she'd hit me and yell at me to shut-up. I got whippings so often they seemed ordinary. My fear of being slapped in the face was so constant that when she came near me, I jumped back, ducked, and threw my hand up to cover my face. My fear seemed to amuse her, until I unwittingly embarrassed her when I dodged her in public one day. While registering me for school, the principal noticed my cowering, defensive stance when she came near me. He recognized the response of an abused child. Her face turned red with guilt. She tried to act like the perfect mother in front of other people, especially if they intimidated her, and my reflex blew her cover. Although the principal knew there was a problem, he turned away and ignored it.

Since my mother touched me only in anger, I was confused when one day she offered to kiss my cheek. On my first day of elementary school, she took me to class and told me to sit in the back of the room. The teacher, Miss Cobb, assured all the mothers that we would be fine and encouraged them to give us a hug before leaving. All the mothers kissed their children, and my mother could not be the exception. As she approached, I froze in my seat. I felt she was invading my space when she stood next to my desk. She leaned down and gave me the only kiss I ever remember getting from her. I began to sob. I couldn't believe my mother had actually kissed my cheek. Miss Cobb thought that I was crying because I didn't want her to leave, but I cried because my mother had shown me affection.

Within days she found an opportunity to erase any positive effect that kiss might have had by humiliating me intentionally. The school nurse called and asked her to bring me a change of underwear, because I had wet my pants. She picked me up, shamed me all the way home, and told my family that evening that I peed my pants at school, which had greatly inconvenienced her. I hid in my room.

Perhaps my mother was teased unmercifully as a child. Perhaps she was shamed repeatedly for wetting her bed until she was a teen. She used her pain to commit many acts of motherly crime and got away with them, because she left no scars. On one occasion she did get sloppy and leave a scar, which she justified with a lie.

One evening I was standing in the living room with a glass of chocolate milk in my hand. I don't know why I dropped the glass, but it shattered on the floor and the milk splattered. My mother came running to see what happened. Fear gripped me, and I started to cry when I saw the snarl on her face. My brothers held their breaths.

"You little son-of-a-bitch!" she screamed with clenched fists. "You better clean that mess up right this minute!" Broken glass encircled my bare feet, so if I moved I was sure to be cut. The only thing that could have prevented bloodshed was if my mother lifted me to safety, but I knew instinctively that was not her plan.

"I'll clean it up, Mama. Please don't hurt me," I cried.

She grabbed my left arm and twisted it behind my back, forcing me to my knees. Methodically, in slow motion, she pushed my head down so she could put her foot on my shoulder and pushed my face into the chocolate milk and broken glass. Before my face reached the floor, I lost my balance and fell on my right forearm against a piece of glass, slicing my wrist. I screamed. With her vengeance satisfied by bloodshed, she relented. I was thankful for the red, velvety liquid dripping from the wound like falling rose petals, rescuing me from further piercing by the thorns.

The deep gash needed stitches, but I didn't get them. When she saw what she had done, she took me to the bathroom and washed me up before my father came home, stuck a band-aid on the wound, and cleaned up the bloody milk and glass. We all knew she caused the injury. Fully confident that my dad would believe her, she said I broke a glass, and when she tried to help me clean it up, I fell and cut myself. We never disputed her, and she never apologized. Sometimes I convinced myself that her lies were true. Maybe she was trying to help me, I thought. I wanted to believe she loved me. If I ever convinced myself, she jerked me back to reality with one of her episodes. I don't believe my mother ever actually meant to shed blood, though that sometimes happened. More important, I suffered great mental anguish and emotional torment because of her twisted need to control.

Although I did not have birthday parties, a nice home, a *Leave It To Beaver* mother, or hot meals, I did have something most kids did not: I had lice. We feared even the thought of having lice since Mama told stories about lice all the time. When she was a child, a friend of her sister's caught head lice and brought them to her family. They had to soak their heads, blankets, towels, and sheets in kerosene to get rid of them, and they never let that child spend the night again. I hate to think what would have happened to her family during that kerosene cure if someone lit a match too close to their heads. Just hearing my mother tell how those little critters made your head itch made me scratch myself from head to toe. Only nasty, disgraceful people got lice, and it was an embarrassment to admit you knew someone who had them. I don't remember in whose head my mother first noticed the lice, but I do remember we had been scratching our heads for about a week before she found them. By the time she realized that the itching wasn't just a scalp reaction to a new shampoo, we had lice coming out our ears.

I went to the drug store with Mama to buy the shampoo to get rid of the awful bugs. She bought the entire supply on the shelf. She could hardly carry all the bottles to the register. I had to carry a few. Since we were ashamed to have lice, we tried to be inconspicuous as we approached the checkout stand and prayed that nobody else would get in line and see what we were buying. I tried not to scratch my head while we waited for the old lady in front of us to get through the line. For a minute, we thought we were safe. There were no other customers around. The cashier looked alarmed at the amount of lice-kill my mother was buying, and she stared at me as if to say, "Oh, you must be the lice-head!" My mother told her she was buying it for a poor family who found out that they had lice but didn't have a car to get to the store. I looked at the lady and grinned—and scratched my head. Just as the cashier was sacking our hush-hush bug removal, a man in a pin-stripe suit stood in line behind us. Mama's face turned red when she saw him staring at her purchase. When the final bottle of lice remover was inside the sack, she paid the cashier and almost stumbled over her own feet getting out of the store. I stopped and asked for a penny for the gum machine. She obliged me but told me to be quick. Maybe the sack was too weak to hold the accumulated weight of all those bottles of D'LICE, but before we could get out of the pharmacy, it broke open and the bottles went everywhere. I saw the panic on her face as the man in the suit approached and offered to help pick them up. Before she could tell him no, he bent down and began to recover them one by one. She ran to the cashier and asked for another sack, while I stayed behind to help the man retrieve the containers. When Mama came back, he put the bottles in her sack, and she thanked him profusely, explaining once more that the medicine was for another family in a different neighborhood. He followed us to the car and opened the door for her. I jumped in the back seat and kept smiling at the man until he got in his truck. He waved as we drove away. I waved back with one hand and scratched my head with the other.

Sometime after we were rid of head-lice, my Aunt Paula came to visit. I loved her visits because we always made homemade ice cream, taking turns sitting on the ice-cream freezer while Dad turned the churn. One day when Dad was at work, Aunt Paula said, "Rose is so cute. She looks a lot like my children." Later Mama repeated that to my dad. It made her mad. Beside my relatives, I heard strangers, neighbors, and church people tell my mother I was a pretty little girl. I was almost ashamed of their comments. Mama didn't like anyone to tell me I was pretty and let people know that she didn't. For a long time, I thought pretty meant ugly, since Mama was offended. As I got older, she began to say, "Don't tell her that or she'll get the big-head!"

Shortly after Aunt Paula said I was cute, Mama lost her temper and took me to the bedroom and beat me so badly that Aunt Paula finally intervened. At the same time, a tornado appeared in the sky. I heard the commotion and excitement through the closed door, but all I could do was cry. I saw the funnel cloud out of my window and heard everyone go outside. Car doors slammed. They fled for their lives and drove off without me. The house was quiet. I was afraid to move. Although I was frightened, my chances were better with the tornado than with my mother. Aunt Paula saw that I was missing and made Mama go back to get me. By the time they returned, the tornado had passed. Mama told my father the commotion made her forget me. Once again, he excused her negligence. He let her get away with too much. He should have intervened, but instead he abandoned me.

My dad was about 5'9" with jet-black hair, a receding hairline, and black eyes, always bloodshot from lack of sleep. A back-street dentist was responsible for the gold-rimmed front tooth that matched his round, gold-framed glasses. He was a brilliant mathematician and a spelling champion. The plant manager once told him he was one of the smartest operators at the plant. I vaguely remember him cradling me in his arms when I was very young and thinking he might have a special place in his heart for me. My mother didn't suffer his affection for me gladly. She accused him of being partial to me, shamed him, and intimidated him so his attention to me ceased. My mother constantly browbeat and dominated him. If he spoke kindly to me, she made a vindictive remark.

Occasionally she commended the other children, my sister most often, but never me. Billy said Mama re-lived her childhood through Mary Jane and gave Mary Jane the things she wanted but never received as a child. I didn't begrudge my sister the things she had. Although she got much more than the rest of us, she had less than most girls her age.

Mama practiced conditional love: if you do what I say and what I want, I will give you approval; if you don't, I will withhold approval and favors. She used that technique to control the family, and we were all casualties of her conditional love. My sister was her loyal child, her favorite. I was the disloyal child who provoked her to special ruthlessness. If she said something positive about my sister, she finished with something negative about me. "Mary Jane has a beautiful voice, but Rose can't sing a lick." I wasn't jealous of my sister. She was four years older than me and gave me the comfort I received from nowhere else. I loved cuddling up to her for affection. I sensed she was sorry for the way my mother treated me, but she could not prevent it. My mother tried to drive a wedge between us but never succeeded.

Mary Jane was the oldest and worked at being Mama's good girl. She enjoyed being the oldest but was burdened with more responsibility. She tried to be available when Mama needed her. Mama would command, "Mary Jane, go to the refrigerator and bring me my 7-Up." She willingly obeyed. Mary Jane sometimes washed the dishes or tackled the enormous pile of clothes that needed to be folded. Mama rewarded her with favors. When my brothers and I were outside we often saw Mary Jane sneak off to Pelton's grocery store to buy Mama and herself a Sidewalk Sundae ice cream bar. Once we caught her on the way home and tore into her sack to discover two treats, one for her and one for Mama. We threatened to take them away, and she started to cry. We had seen Mama eat them, and we all wanted to taste the creamy mixture dipped deep in chocolate sauce. Mary Jane said she deserved the ice cream, because she swept and mopped the floors, while we had done no housework, only played. She was right! She deserved the ice cream. We let her go home to enjoy her reward. She thought she was winning Mama's love, but I thought she was being exploited. Mama loaded duties done by competent mothers in most households onto my sister. She held Mary Jane up as a yardstick against which we were measured. I didn't tell her about my frustration, because she made excuses for Mama. She shielded Mama from outside conflict and refused to admit Mama's cruelty. The lies Mama used to cover-up her meanness didn't convince Mary Jane, but she accepted them the same way my father did, giving Mama the benefit of the doubt.

My mother was purposely cruel to Mary Jane only once. Mary Jane was allowed to visit my dad's mother for two weeks one summer.

After Dad came back from the Army, his father quit drinking and became more stable. He became a plumber and bought Grandma a nice home, pretty furniture, and a fancy car. We all liked visiting them, but only Mary was ever invited to stay alone with them. We almost didn't recognize her when she came home. She gained a lot of weight during those two weeks. Grandma had to buy her new clothes for the trip home, because the ones she brought with her no longer fit. She told us how wonderful it was to stay with Grandma. "Grandma made me hot biscuits with honey and oatmeal for breakfast every morning. We went shopping during the day, and she bought me rollers for my hair and make up. Her house was always clean and tidy. I had my very own bed to sleep in with a pretty lace bedspread. She taught me how to make peanut-butter candy and let me eat all that I wanted of it." We listened in envy to her stories of being treated like a princess and secretly wished we too had a turn to visit that indulgent wonderland. She bragged and bragged, not realizing that every remark provoked Wanda to greater vengeance.

Mama hated her mother-in-law intensely and didn't like hearing anything positive about her. Mama thought Mary Jane was comparing her to Grandma, and her painful memories of inadequacy began to emerge. Feelings of jealousy, of falling short of expectations, of being compared, of being unable to compete, launched a vindictive retaliation upon my sister. She began to chide Mary Jane about her weight and made her march up and down the living room, back and forth, over and over, in front of the family. My father was at work. She said Mary Jane looked like an elephant and told us to call her Ellie for short. She led us in a chant–Ellie! Ellie! Ellie! We clapped our hands to the beat, over and over, louder and louder. The room seemed to spin like a merry-go-round. Mary Jane marched until, dizzy with disgrace, she broke into tears, put her hands over her face and ran screaming to the bathroom where she clawed her face from forehead to chin. Mama looked stunned when Mary Jane screamed but was secretly pleased. She wasn't trying to motivate Mary Jane to lose weight; she was punishing her for enjoying her visit to Grandma's house and for bringing her own shortcomings as a mother to the forefront. I felt guilty.

Billy and Jessie were occasional victims of Mama's impatience in a milder sense. They suffered more from neglect than from abuse, but we all have stories of shame, misery, and humiliation. Mama wasn't particularly kind to any of us, but I was clearly her whipping post. Although I didn't realize it then, she singled me out to take the brunt of her behavior, but my brothers often got similar treatment. She amused herself by taking us by the hand to cross a street, and when we couldn't keep up, she dragged us, one in each hand, our knees and shins scraping against the hot pavement.

Less than eleven months apart, Billy and Jessie were treated like twins. For years, we called them "the babies." Dad favored Billy over Jessie, because as a newborn, Billy was deathly ill from dehydration for several days. Dad sat dutifully next to the incubator and refused to leave. The experience created a bond between them that made him forever partial to Billy. Billy was a smart, tow-headed, feisty little tyke, with snake-green eyes and a mischievous grin. Regrettably, he inherited my mother's speech impediment and was teased about it, just as she had been. In my father's eyes, Billy could do no wrong. If he did, he was rarely corrected, and correction never involved consequences. As a result, Billy had a hard time distinguishing right from wrong. In fact, my father often rewarded his misbehavior with laughter and commendation instead of punishment. My mother sometimes admonished my father for showing Billy such favoritism, but she tolerated his affection for Billy—not for me. Billy could get away with anything. He became increasingly demanding, disrespectful, belligerent, and disobedient. He learned to stand up to my parents at a very young age, and they consistently gave in to him.

Jessie was the youngest of the four children and was his twin-like brother's punching bag. The only memory that I have of him prior to Hurricane Carla is that Billy beat him up daily. He always had big purple knots on his head. Jessie had thin, white hair like Mary Jane, and he was clumsy and uncoordinated. Dad had no affinity for Jessie. My parents thought it was funny to watch the boys fight. Perhaps that reminded my mother of her childhood battles with Crumley. When they were not fighting each other they teamed up to badger other children in the neighborhood. They were the neighborhood bullies, and some children would not walk down the street for fear my brothers would beat them up.

Dad always laughed when Billy dominated Jessie. If they split a candy bar, Billy gave Jessie the smaller piece; if they split a soda, Jessie got less; if Dad held out a nickel and dime, Billy grabbed the dime and left the nickel for Jessie. He told Jessie the nickel was better because it was bigger. Billy could convince Jessie that he was letting him have an equal or better portion although everyone else saw he was cheating Jessie. Jessie conceded Billy absolute chief status and was the follower. The soft side of Jessie's personality was absent in Billy. He adored animals and was fascinated by birds. He spent hours with pigeons, horses, cows, goats, and chickens, giving them all the love and attention missing from his own life.

One day my mother made Billy and Jessie fight to exhaustion. She was the only spectator when she put them in an invisible ring in the front yard and ordered them to fight. When Jessie was beaten to a pulp she told Billy to go on hitting him. She said that if he didn't, she would beat him. Billy wanted to stop, but my mother made him keep it up. His heart began to break. Through tears, he begged her to let him stop. Jessie didn't say a word. Finally she relented. The experience haunted Billy into adulthood, and if he tries to retell it almost forty years later, his voice breaks. Perhaps my mother accomplished what she intended. She wanted them to get the fighting out of their systems, but the method was malicious. Billy got the better of Jessie then, but when they became teenagers Jessie grew to twice Billy's size and was as strong as a bull.

CHAPTER IV
The Gold Watch

John F. Kennedy was inaugurated President of the United States the same year Hurricane Carla struck the Texas coast. The craze for Elvis the King was starting to fade, and the Beach Boys' music was popular with the younger generation. Many American women emulated the style and dress of Jackie Kennedy. The Kennedy's were young, rich, handsome, keenly political, and the closest thing America had to royalty. Women everywhere wore suits with short coats, pillbox hats, and gloves, to achieve the Jackie look. They teased their hair into French twists and lacquered it with Aqua Net.

After we recovered from the storm, we started attending church, and I enjoyed seeing the pretty women dressed-up at sacrament meetings. Vera, our bishop's wife, was especially attractive, but Mama said she was a flirt and didn't sit with her legs together. Every time my dad shook Vera's hand at church, he grinned and blushed.

My experience in the Mormon Church provided the only happy memories of my childhood. Our family never took part before that year. We had no social interaction with other families until we started attending church. At the tiny chapel in LaMarque, about seven miles from our home, we went to celebrations, parties, missionary activities, dances, weddings, and spiritual meetings. The building only held about a hundred people, but it looked enormous to me. The chapel's green tile floor was waxed to a shine, and cold, metal chairs substituted for cushioned pews. Everyone was thankful for the two window air conditioner units that kept the building cool. The church library was a tiny closet that housed a few books, pictures, construction paper, and crayons. The kitchen was about sixty feet square, the foyer the same size. The sanctuary provided special seating for the bishopric on a narrow stage with a pulpit and microphone for speakers. Members took turns speaking on assigned subjects at sacrament meetings.

An oft-quoted Latter-Day Saint (LDS) aphorism is, "No other success in life can compensate for failure in the home." My mother repeated it often, trying to convince herself of the importance of her home. Mormonism stresses family togetherness and sees the family unit and home as a sacred institution. Our family went to church together, dressed in our only decent clothes and pretended to be exemplary. We whitewashed our image around members and tried to fit-in. I knew we didn't. My mother attended meetings of the Relief Society, an LDS organization that teaches women to be better wives and mothers. They were taught and learned basic meal planning, quilt making, family games for children, spiritual development, to show acts of charity, missionary work, sewing, and other skills necessary for a Christian life. Mama's new church friends were good examples for her. The Church's teachings had a positive effect on her willingness to improve her conduct. Despite her aberrant behavior, she was truly converted. To her credit, she introduced me to the truths I hold sacred to this day.

I learned many valuable lessons at church that helped me in my life and later, in my career. Children learn public speaking by giving simple speeches on gospel topics in front of large audiences in Mormon chapels. I learned not to be afraid onstage, but I enjoyed the attention, since that was the only place that I got it. I cherished the time in class with my Sunday school teacher. Her voice sounded like a melodious chime contrasted to my mother's. I figured my teacher never yelled at her children or slapped their faces. I visited her home once and noticed a marked difference from mine in the atmosphere-peaceful, cool, clean, and orderly. The fragrance of baked sweet bread came from the kitchen. She spoke softly, and her demeanor was mild. She smiled at me and patted my back when we talked, as if she knew I needed the comfort of her touch. I wanted to stay with her forever. She told my mother I was very good in class and she thought that I was pretty. Mama wouldn't let that comment pass without shaming me.

"Well, I wish she was good at home! Pretty is as pretty does. Pretty is what's inside, not what's on the outside." Her negative attitude toward me surprised my teacher. She didn't know what to say. Mama ignored me and walked away. I hung my head.

Although my dad was baptized, I wonder if he really had a testimony. He acted righteous at church and donated his time and materials to build a fence along the drainage ditch behind the church. His behavior at home, however, wasn't always so charitable. His fury was at times just as bad as my mother's. Both my parents were guilty of cursing and calling us names that lowered our self-esteem. Filthy language spewed from their mouths like venom from a snake's. Dad belittled us and made us feel stupid if we tried to talk to him, so we kept quiet around him. If we spilled something on the floor, he said, "Damn you! Get down on the floor and lick it up!" Although he never actually made us lick anything up, we believed he would. The statement alone was enough to make us cry. Another threat he used was, "I'm going to knock your teeth down your throat." When he said that, we knew he was really angry!

Once Billy and I infuriated my father by pouring too much cereal into a bowl. "You wasteful little bastards," he shouted, "you are going to sit and eat every bite of that cereal before you get up from the table!" He didn't call us Stack-o-bones or Tooter-cut that day. We ate as much as we could hold. Half way through the cereal, we began to cry and told him we couldn't eat any more. "You stay the hell at the table until every bit of it is finished." I knew he would let us go outside when we were about to throw up. We learned never to take more than we could eat. After that we hated the sight of cereal, to our detriment since cereal was often the only thing in the house to eat.

When the redheaded girl next door had a party and didn't invite us, we hung around their back yard during the festivities to get a glimpse of the cake. She saw us and shut the door. When the party was over, her entire family got into their car to go somewhere. Most people didn't bother to lock their doors back then, so Billy and I decided to sneak in their back door and see if any cake was left. I put him up to making the first move. We opened the screen door and tiptoed into their kitchen where we saw dirty plates and an empty punch bowl next to the sink.

"There ain't no cake left, Rose," Billy whispered.

"There has to be. Those fat pigs couldn't have eaten all that cake so fast, could they?"

Just then we spotted half a chocolate cake with white marshmallow icing on the kitchen table. "There it is!" he whispered with delight.

"Let's get some." We each dug out a piece with our hands and stuffed it into our mouths so quickly I hardly tasted it.

"We better leave before they catch us, Rose. We're going to get in trouble."

"Wait," I said. "We can't leave the cake in this awful mess. They will know someone snuck into their house. Get a knife out of that drawer and hand it to me."

I took the knife and cut the cake cleanly, and we ate the remnants. Just as I finished, a car door slammed. They were back. I threw the knife into the kitchen sink, and we darted out of the back door and slammed it behind us. Hidden in our playhouse, we saw her father step onto the back porch and look around. His daughter claimed she saw us run from the house. Our phone rang, and Dad came outside calling our names, but we didn't answer. After a while, we went inside and he asked if we had broken into the neighbors' house. We said we had not been out of the yard all day, but when he spotted white icing on Billy's cheeks he couldn't help laughing. We admitted what we had done. "We wouldn't have done it if she had invited us to the party, Dad. We just wanted some cake!" He told us not to do anything like that again and asked Mama to bake a cake-and she did, a yellow cake with thick, hard fudge frosting. We loved it.

When Dad was nice, he was very nice but when he was mad we knew it. Still, while my parents were supposed to be practicing good Mormon behavior, he gave me the most savage beating of my life. He was home from work only about an hour when he saw his gold watch around the handlebar of Billy's bicycle. He had very few personal possessions, and that watch was his prize. He kept it in the top dresser drawer, forbidden territory to all the children, and we knew it. Dad saw me riding the bike. I did not notice the watch on the handlebar, since I was enjoying the wind in my hair as I flew down the center of the road in front of our house. Billy had removed the training wheels from his bike, and I was glad to have a turn on it. My brothers and sister got at least one new bicycle during our childhood, but I never did. I had to borrow theirs. Anyway, the bikes around our house were almost always broken down or had flat tires.

I heard my father calling me angrily. I was afraid, because I didn't know what I had done wrong. His bloodshot eyes bulged, his lips were tight, and his face looked mean. My mother crouched next to him with an accusing grin on her face. "You're in big trouble now!" she said.

"You were the last one riding Billy's bike weren't you?" Dad asked.

"I don't know."

"Yes, she was," my mother confirmed. "I saw her on that bike not ten minutes ago."

With Mama's support, he said he found his watch on the handlebars of Billy's bike. When my brothers and Mary Jane heard the commotion, they came to watch while things blew out of proportion.

"Well, I didn't put your watch there," I said, my voice quivering.

"She's lying," my mother interrupted, pointing an accusing finger at me.

"You better tell the truth or I am going to beat you with my belt buckle," my dad responded.

"I am telling the truth. I didn't get the watch. I promise, Dad!"

Hearing the yelling, neighbor children approached our driveway to get a closer look. I begged him to listen to me while my mother repeated her accusation. She said I was a little liar and needed to be broken from lying. He yanked me into the living room.

My siblings were directed to observe the lesson their pitiful sister was about to get so they could avoid the same fate. I was barefoot, wearing thin shorts, probably without underwear, and my favorite shirt with a blue sailor collar and matching bow. I rarely had new clothes, and the shirt was a treasure Grandma gave me. I usually wore clothes from the second-hand store or hand-me-downs from Mary Jane. I awaited my fate, crying, sweating, and trembling.

After what seemed like hours, my dad reappeared with a black leather strap. Mama's smirk face expressed her anticipation at witnessing instead of executing the beating. I swore I didn't do it, she swore I did, and my father believed her. He lifted me from the floor, twisting my shirt and hair. The leather strap stung my bony legs, arms, buttocks, back, and hands.

"I am not going to stop until you admit that you took my watch, you little liar!" He tortured me in cycles, and between outbursts, he demanded I confess my guilt.

To admit I took the watch might have ended the rampage, but I would not admit to something I had not done. Why did he want me to lie? My Sunday school teacher told us never to lie. He could beat me, humiliate me, strip me of dignity, but he could not make me lie. My parents took almost everything else from me, but I would not let them take my honor. My spirit was too strong, my will indestructible, which is what my mother hated most about me. He ripped my shirt once, twice, three times, finally into shreds. Horrified, my siblings uttered not a sound, but I knew that they hated seeing me tortured and were helpless to intervene. If I had seen any of them getting such a beating, I would have yelled at my mother for allowing it and at my father for doing it. The strap raised blood-marks on my thighs. My dad lost control once he started beating us. He went too far. After a while my mother quit adding fuel to the fire. Maybe she thought I'd had enough. Although she was getting nervous about the intensity of the beating, she never told him to stop.

Billy screamed, "Stop! Stop! Please, stop, Dad! I did it. I took the watch from the drawer." At once his face showed he wanted to retract his confession.

When my father heard his favorite child confess, he made him repeat his admission. Billy did so through tears of fear and shame. My dad didn't want to believe Billy had taken the watch.

"Yes, I took the watch, but I promise not to do it again," he said. Shamed, Dad looked down at his hands, still warm from slapping me. He knew that he had lost control. For a minute, he said nothing.

Still lying on the floor, I moaned painfully, feeling too forsaken to look at my family. Finally my mother broke the silence. "Well, enough punishment for one day. We won't·beat anyone else, but let this be a lesson to all of you to stay out of your dad's drawer!" Dad could not bring himself to punish Billy, nor did I want him to.

I wasn't mad at Billy for confessing too late. I was thankful that he did, because it stopped the beating. How could I blame him for not wanting to be tortured?

No one mentioned the episode again until forty years later. When we were grown, I asked Billy if he remembered that day. He said he did, vividly. "I have always believed you knew I took the watch. I thought that you meant to protect me." He gave me more credit than I deserved. I really didn't know who took the watch from my dad's drawer. Had I known, I would have said so. My siblings were never beaten so ruthlessly, and any of them would have suffered far less for the same mistakes. My family walked away from the beating with their heads down. I was left to comfort myself, and nobody ever apologized to me.

The general definition of going too far in our family meant punishment that ended in a hospital visit. My parents knew enough to stop short of that, but that beating left bloody belt marks on my legs, and my dress didn't hide them. Mama didn't want me to go to school, but she let me and warned me to keep my dress down. I didn't want my teacher to see the marks, lest she think I had done something to deserve them. Soon after I arrived at school, though, she noticed the marks and asked if I had gotten a beating with a belt. I nodded. A look of compassion came over her beautiful face as she pulled me to her. Oh, how I loved her caresses! She smelled so good, and her touch was gentle.

She combed my hair with her fingernails and said, "I'm sorry, Rose." I didn't want her to let go. She asked me to give my mother a message.

"Tell your mother that if I ever see marks like that on you again, I will notify the Child Welfare Department." I didn't know what that meant, but I was glad she hugged me.

When I went home that day, I forgot about Miss Gillespie's message until Mama asked if anyone noticed the marks on my legs. I said my teacher did.

"What did she say?"

"She said I should tell you she will report you if she ever sees it again."

"Report me to whom?"

"I don't know. I can't remember the name."

Later that evening, she told my dad Miss Gillespie saw the welts on my legs. She shamed him as if she had nothing to do with it.

"Henry, you better be a little more careful, or you might get into trouble with the law."

Their personalities were made of hazardous substances. Each had a mixture of ignorance, violence, and temper. That recipe combined with their own tormented childhoods created not one but two vengeful parents, one controlled by the other. Perhaps my mother's desire to avoid an investigation by the Child Welfare Department and her newly found Christian motives caused her to curtail the abuse to some extent after that. The change was subtle and gradual. The mistreatment was by no means over, but it seemed to have peaked that day. I tried to be perfect to avoid being targeted again.

Our family's dichotomy of splintered motives fluctuated between good and evil. Righteous pretense could fool the congregation for a while, but in due course real personalities emerged, secrets were exposed, and the truth was revealed.

CHAPTER V
The Narcissist

Mama loved to go to the tiny Moore Memorial Public Library and look for information about the Church or genealogy. Because Mormons are encouraged to do genealogical research, she tried to find books about her ancestors. While browsing one afternoon, she met a sweet lady named Mildred Patton. Mama told Mildred about the Church and gave her the *Book of Mormon.* Mildred invited Mama to her home to visit. We finally went to see Mildred and her family and found that her husband, Lamar, had already read the *Book of Mormon.* He wanted to be baptized, but he knew he would have trouble keeping the Word of Wisdom; the commitment LDS members make to refrain from alcohol, tea, coffee, and tobacco. The rule was revealed to Joseph Smith and is documented in his writings, *The Doctrine and Covenants.* Lamar smoked, drank coffee, and had an occasional glass of wine, but he promised to give them up so he could be baptized. He struggled with abstinence for many years, pretending to be free of those habits. Before long, Mildred, Lamar, and all their family joined the church. Shortly after his baptism, Lamar received the priesthood by the laying on of hands, as do most men. The priesthood gives men the power to perform ordinances and blessings in the Lord's name.

I became best friends with two of the Patton children, Matt and Addie, the only children I knew with hair blonder than mine. Addie and Matt were both a little older than me. Her real name was Alice, but Matt couldn't pronounce it when he was a baby and called her Addie.

Mildred added *Blue* to her nickname because she had big, blue eyes. Addie Blue's two front teeth were split apart and twisted sideways as if she had pushed a button between them. Her parents wanted to give her braces, but they couldn't afford them. Addie's beautiful eyes, platinum hair, and perfect skin didn't add up to femininity; she was a tomboy and Matt was a sissy. Sometimes he played with my brothers or other boys, but he preferred to play with Addie and me. When he wasn't with us, he was drawing, or painting, or coloring. Forever a comedian, Matt entertained us with his infectious laugh and quick wit, which made church much more enjoyable.

When my brothers and I were seated next to Matt and Addie in the back row at church during sacrament meeting, Matt created a hilarious scene. At sacrament meeting, the most sacred of Sunday meetings, the entire congregation partakes of bread and water in remembrance of the Savior. We pray, sing, and listen to talks or testimonies of the gospel. Once Matt got our attention and pointed to the baldhead of the man seated in front of us. Grinning with delight, he extended his finger about one inch away from the big mole protruding from the man's scalp. Billy thought it was funny and told Matt to do it again. When he did, Billy pushed his finger against the man's mole and made his head bounce forward awaking him from his peaceful sleep. Baldy turned around abruptly to identify the mole-masher. We cackled out loud and disturbed the entire congregation. Our parents turned around and gave us the evil eye. Suddenly we saw liquid dripping from Matt's chair and realized he had peed in his black dress pants. Judging from the quantity of pee pouring off the chair and running down the aisle, we figured Matt had been holding it in for some time. We laughed harder and tried not to pee in our own pants. Matt was purple with embarrassment, doubled over like a sack of potatoes, unable to move until the meeting ended. When it did, he wrapped his suit coat around his legs and darted out the double doors faster than a fox, dripping all the way. Every time we were with the Patton kids, we got into trouble. We developed a reputation for mischief and gave the Church leaders a challenge at every opportunity. They finally gave up on our salvation.

My mother sought and got her brother William's approval for her missionary zeal and church work. Uncle William and most of my mother's family lived in Jasper, a small town with a racist reputation. Jasper was about a two-hour drive from Texas City. William had become the father figure in Mama's family after my grandpa abandoned them, at least for the three younger children–Crumley, my mother, and Pearl. They revered him, but Sarah resented him. She was independent and didn't need his approval or guidance. Unlike Crumley, William never mistreated Mama. He was compassionate to her, and she felt indebted for his kindness, since few people showed her consideration as a child. Uncle William held a high position in the Mormon Church, and she knew he would be proud of her for studying the scriptures and getting her family active in the Church.

William's wife, Aunt Beverly, exaggerated and fantasized about her daughter's unlimited success, power, brilliance, beauty, and ideal loves. I don't know if Sue Ellen knew how lucky she was to have a charming home with loving parents. William and Beverly didn't belittle her, slap her face, or humiliate her. Aunt Beverly cooked hot meals, set the table, and made sure they ate together as a family. Unlike my mother who put me down at every turn, Beverly bragged about her only child continuously.

While she praised Sue Ellen, she ignored other children's abilities, especially if they competed with her daughter's talent. Aunt Beverly reared Sue Ellen to think that she was a princess, a perfect angel, beautiful, sweet, and righteous. Sue Ellen had a beautiful singing voice, and Aunt Beverly saw that she performed at every public gathering. She spent weeks fashioning her formal gowns or costumes with sequins and spangles. She fed Sue Ellen's ego. Sue Ellen acted as if only special or upper-class people understood her. Sue Ellen required constant admiration and developed a sense of entitlement to favorable treatment. She depended entirely on her mother and let her mother control her. Sue Ellen's home life was the antithesis of mine.

She was three years older than Mary Jane, who also had a heavenly voice. When we visited, Mary Jane and Sue Ellen sang together for us. Aunt Beverly always followed the performance with something like, "Everyone says Sue Ellen has the best voice in Texas." If my sister sang a solo, Aunt Beverly and Sue Ellen said, "That is such a beautiful song!" That was their way to seem polite without paying a compliment. They thought we were too dumb to see the obvious.

When Mary Jane and Sue Ellen went to a teen-age church dance together, Beverly told my mother that everyone said Sue Ellen was the prettiest girl at the dance. I resented Mama's failure to rebut her. Beverly constantly trumped Sue Ellen over my sister, and my mother nodded in agreement with the put-down. It hurt Mary Jane's feelings. Not only did my mother not defend us, she constantly bragged about Sue Ellen to us, making us feel inferior to her. She held her in higher esteem than she did her own, since she held her brother in higher esteem than she did herself. But, I refused to be intimidated.

Our other cousins told us that Sue Ellen ignored them completely and was known around school as a snob. As Sue Ellen grew older, she became more arrogant and haughty. She and her mother never approached others first. The other person had to acknowledge them first, or they remained aloof. She acted as if she was too good to speak. Sue Ellen eventually became a major complication in my life. I never liked her as a child, and I learned to like her even less as an adult.

I was happy when I turned eight in August of 1962, because that meant I could be baptized. I wanted a cake or maybe a birthday party, but I knew better. Since my father held the priesthood, he was allowed to baptize me. Uncle William baptized Mary Jane. On the day of my baptism, Mama borrowed a white dress for me from a little girl at church, and I was very proud wearing it. My father was more nervous than me, so we rehearsed the ceremony several times. I enjoyed the attention. That evening, my father immersed me in the baptismal font, and I was confirmed a member of the Church.

Shortly before my baptism, my father embarked upon a project to add a master bedroom and bath to our two-bedroom house. His brother helped him with the construction. It got as far as the framing stage–no sheet rock, tile, doors, bathroom fixtures, or heat–and stayed that way for many years. Until then, all four children slept in one bedroom on two twin beds. Mary Jane and I shared a bed, and the babies slept together in the other, but the ten-by-twelve room had become too small to share. We looked forward to having our own room together away from the boys, but an unfortunate series of events interrupted construction, and my father never finished the project.

CHAPTER VI

The Bishop's Wife

A few weeks after my baptism, Billy and Jessie found a sex magazine under the seat of Dad's car and showed it to my mother. She was
incensed that my dad, claiming to be a righteous Latter-Day Saint,
would buy pornography. She told us he was a sex maniac and accused
him of every disgraceful act imaginable. To this day I don't know if the
accusations were true. She said he had venereal diseases, used prosti-
tutes, made obscene phone calls to women, and was sexually obsessed.
Her jealousy made her drunk with suspicion. She said he feigned conversion to the Church, so she asked the bishop if she should have me
re-baptized since my father wasn't worthy of the priesthood. The bishop said that was not necessary. She told him that his wife, Vera, was a
flirt and my father was secretly in love with her.

"When Vera sits on the stage she never holds her legs together and
the men get an eyeful." He must have known she was losing it.

To our dismay, my dad admitted that he found Vera attractive, and
my mother told everyone. It was the gossip of the congregation. Mama
thought he fantasized about Vera. To her, the fact that he found Vera
attractive was the same as taking her to bed. She could not see that
Dad was not the only one affected by her exaggerations. The horrible
tales she spread about him also cast shame on our entire family. Even
as a child, I was embarrassed to show my face at church.

Mama convinced Dad he needed psychiatric help. He worked so
many hours at the plant and building fences, not to mention dealing

with her that he was indeed on the verge of a nervous breakdown. He went to a psychiatrist named Dr. Hackbarth who admitted him to the hospital for some badly needed rest from his miserable circumstances. Dr. Hackbarth treated him with sodium pentathlon and said Dad cried like a baby when he asked him to describe his childhood. I don't know what my dad said, but Dr. Hackbarth decided to give him shock therapy. While my dad was in the hospital, my mother continued to take us to church. I don't believe she ever apologized to the bishop, and she quit speaking to Vera.

In the 1960s doctors used shock treatments much more than they do today. Dad underwent thirty-six treatments during his three-month hospital stay, more than is considered safe today. Dr. Hackbarth diagnosed him as schizophrenic, but, more likely, he was bipolar. In the last forty years, medicine has learned a lot about the distinctions between those two disorders. My mother couldn't pronounce schizophrenia, but since she knew it was a terrible psychological ailment, she was happy to add it to the calumny she heaped on my father. Seeking sympathy for having to live with such a creature, she told everyone Dad was schizoid.

When we went with Mama to visit Dad at John Sealy Hospital, in Galveston, we waited in the car for what seemed like hours. Once when she finally reappeared, she had one Po-Boy sandwich. She offered each child one bite. She knew we were hungry and that one sandwich wouldn't feed us all. Getting only one bite of the sandwich when we were so hungry was torture. We hated waiting in the car, but we entertained ourselves by yelling bad words at passers-by. Sometimes strangers stopped and talked to us. Billy and Jessie asked the black people why they were chocolate-colored. It's a wonder we didn't get into real trouble.

On one hospital visit, my mother came back to the car in a frenzy. She found out that the psychiatric rehabilitation program included letting the patients dance together. She threw a jealous tantrum and caused a horrible scene. She upset my father so badly that the doctors banned her from visiting for some time. Dr. Hackbarth told my parents he was not sure he was treating the right person. He suggested that my mother needed psychiatric help even more than my father, but he couldn't have both parents in the hospital at once since they had four children. I often wondered which one was sicker. My mother was impervious to the doctor's comment and said the only thing wrong with her was that she had to live with my father. She seemed to hate my dad and wanted to see him ruined.

I was in the third grade then and decided to tell my teacher of my family's plight. I guess I wanted sympathy. I told her Dr. Hackbarth said both of my parents needed shock therapy, but my dad was taking his turn first. The teacher looked at me in disbelief; she wasn't buying it. This teacher was different from Miss Gillespie. She was partial to the rich, smart kids, and I was neither.

After a while, Dad came home on weekend leaves giving Mama an opportunity to degrade and lambaste him and remind him how horrible he was. She tried to make him remember all the things the shock therapy was supposed to make him forget. He couldn't drive during treatment, so he was her house-prisoner. She made him so miserable he often asked her to take him back to the hospital early, and one weekend he refused to come home at all. In addition to shock treatments, the doctors experimented on Dad with drugs, so he was very nervous. Once he mistook a bottle of catsup for a soda pop and drank it without flinching. He couldn't play dominoes or cards or read the newspaper. He sat in a rocking chair hour after hour and stared out the front screen door while Mama took every advantage of his fragile condition.

Since Dad's medical records are sealed, the dates of certain events are uncertain, but around the time of the Cuban missile crisis something happened that affected my family dramatically. Not only was our own family's life in an uproar but also the whole country was in pandemonium over the attempted Soviet missile installation in Cuba. At school, we learned to get under our desks if we heard certain bells indicating danger. President Kennedy appeared on worldwide radio and TV to demand that Premier Khrushchev withdraw the missiles. He imposed a naval blockade around Cuba, and for days the world feared nuclear war. In the end, the Soviets withdrew the missiles in exchange for America's pledge not to invade Cuba. The tension subsided, and President Kennedy was a hero.

During the crisis my dad came home for a weekend visit, and Mama decided to take him to a baptismal event at church. He could not remember anyone's name and everyone knew he was on leave from a psychiatric hospital. In those days, being under psychiatric care was shameful. People sick enough for shock treatment were crazed maniacs. Most people kept it a secret if someone in the family was in mental therapy, but my mother made it public.

After the baptism, Mama got a call from Mildred Patton who told her that just after we left, Vera, the bishop's wife, thinking my father was in love with her and knowing he was in a mental hospital, felt extremely threatened when she saw him at the baptism. She fainted after he left the chapel, and screamed hysterically that my father was staring at her. She begged the Church to protect her from the madman. Needless to say, after shock treatment my father didn't even know her, but who could blame poor Vera? Her reactions were understandable in light of my mother's accusations and the terrible things she heard about my father. Mama was furious and took it out on my dad, humiliating him with every detail and shaming him for looking at Vera. That was the last time our family ever attended church together. Dad never went back, and twelve years passed before my mother returned. In the meantime, we lost the only positive reinforcement in our lives.

Dr. Hackbarth–who I now believe was a quack–continued to use my dad as a test lab monkey. He ordered four more series of shock therapy over the years, rendering him 100% disabled. My dad became a slave to medication and was never normal again. While he was still in the hospital, Mama drove to Jasper to share her plight with her relatives, consult with Uncle William, and collect whatever advice, goodwill, or empathy they had.

I loved visiting my Aunt Pearl in Jasper, because she had daughters my age. Her home was not fancy, but it was always clean; and she made the best bread in the world. Once I was in the back seat of the car, and Mama was driving a little too fast as usual. As we pulled into Aunt Pearl's driveway, I started to open the door before the car came to a complete stop. Angry, Mama reached in the back seat to grab me, calling me a little son-of-a-bitch as she dug her fingernails into my right thigh. When she stopped the car, I held back my tears as she examined another telltale sign of her abuse. She told me to stand up to see if my shorts were long enough to hide the bloody gashes. She was out of luck. There was no hope of hiding the imprints of her nails from her sister. I entered the house prepared to hear a tale fabricated to make me look foolish and make a hero out of her. My aunt and cousins, gathered in the kitchen around fresh cookies and lemonade, gasped at the bloody fingernail marks. "Oh, my gosh, Rose! What on earth did you do to your leg?" asked Aunt Pearl.

My mother answered for me. "She opened the door when I was turning into your driveway. I was afraid that she would fall out of the car, so I reached around to the back seat to try to hold her in and my fingernails left a mark. At least she didn't fall out of the car!"

They were obviously taken in by the lie. Embarrassed and trying not to look foolish, I shrugged it off by saying, "It doesn't hurt." Aunt Pearl looked down at the floor determined not to interfere. She knew of my mother's capacity for cruelty from her own childhood.

When I was alone with Aunt Pearl, I asked her if my mother was always mean. She laughingly responded, "Yes, she was sort of mean, but she's not mean now, is she?"

"Oh, yes, she is mean!"

"Well, she doesn't intend to be. She has a good heart, Rose," she said glancing again at the fingernail gouges on my thigh. Aunt Pearl never spoke ill of anyone.

We waited for the addition to our house to be completed, but it didn't happen. In desperation, Mary Jane and I moved into the unfinished room. Although it was supposed to be my parents' master bedroom, it became our incomplete sleeping quarters. With plywood floors and exposed two-by-four studs for walls, it was nothing to be proud of, but at least the room gave us privacy from our brothers, which we desperately wanted. In time, my parents paneled over the studs, Mama doing most of the work. Little did I know that the bedroom would not be finished for forty years, and I would be the one who finished it.

CHAPTER VII
Drums, Cymbals, and Crescendos

President and Mrs. Kennedy were in Dallas, trying to win support in a state he barely carried in 1960. They were on their way to a luncheon in downtown Dallas in an open convertible. At the head of a motorcade approaching an underpass, two shots were fired in rapid succession. One bullet passed through the president's neck and struck Governor Connally in the back. The other struck the president in the head. He fell forward, and the car sped away to Parkland Hospital. He was the fourth President of the United States to be assassinated and the first president of our country that I remember.

Just before the Thanksgiving holiday in 1963, I was in the fourth grade classroom when an announcement of his death came over the loud speaker. The sky outside the classroom window looked ominous, and I thought it was a sign from heaven that God was angry. Many students and teachers cried unashamedly.

Before I got home from school the nation had a new president. Aboard the president's plane at the Dallas airport, Lyndon B. Johnson, the vice president from Texas, was sworn in as the 36th President of the United States. We spent the entire Thanksgiving holiday watching television news. Thousands filed past the slain president's coffin. I remember the horse-drawn carriage passing from the White House to the Capitol Rotunda the President's casket shrouded in the nation's flag. A million people lined the streets of Washington as the funeral procession made its way slowly to Arlington National Cemetery. I will always remember the sight of little John-John saluting the flag that draped his father's casket. The whole nation mourned his loss. My parents were very sad. My mother wrote a heartfelt note to Mrs. Kennedy and received a kind note from the White House in return.

This event catapulted the country into a decade of rebellion, assassinations, protests, and demonstrations. Everything started to change—music, behavior, human rights messages, style, dance, thinking, and rules. A younger, stronger, smarter generation was emerging in the United States, and it wouldn't be quiet. They stood up to the system, challenged it, and refused to be part of it. The counterculture decried materialism, mocked convention, spurned authority, and celebrated love and peace. They questioned the moral and spiritual health of the nation. Like the new generation emerging in America, I was reaching a critical turning point of my own. I was younger, stronger, and smarter than the system that bound me, and I was about to become an activist.

I needed a mechanism to deal with the emotional abuse and neglect I lived with everyday. Something had to change. I knew I didn't deserve the treatment I got, and I concluded that my parents' own emotional baggage caused the trouble. I knew it was not my fault, yet I cowered, retreated, sobbed, feared, begged, and suffered humiliation. My humiliation seemed to motivate them. I decided that since my behavior did not cause the abuse, changing it was useless. I had to change my response to the abuse. I had to stop cowering, sobbing, begging. I had to stop the tears and ignore their insults, but I needed a catalyst to give me strength. I didn't have that—yet.

That year my teacher asked the class to write and illustrate a book of poems. I loved poetry and I liked to draw, so the assignment excited me. The only place to do homework at our house was at the kitchen table, no substitute for a desk in a quiet room, but my only option. Pushing aside cereal boxes, dirty dishes, and paper plates, I stayed up late one night, illustrating the poems I had collected. I was proud of my poetry book and the pictures I sketched to illustrate them. I could look at a picture and replicate it almost exactly. I was adding color with map pencils to a drawing of the Pied Piper with curly tipped shoes and striped tights. I was proud of it and took it to show my dad, since we were the only ones awake. He was rocking in a chair in the living room. He had been back at work for about a year since his release from the hospital, but still had abnormal mood fluctuations. I walked into the living room, my masterpiece in hand, and asked, "Dad, do you think I did a good job of drawing this?" I handed it to him.

He looked at it and said hatefully, "You didn't draw that! Do you expect me to believe you? How could you draw something like that? Don't you come in here again lying to me or I'll knock your teeth down your throat!" I stepped back.

"But I did draw it, Dad," holding the map colors out to show him. "I just finished it at the table."

"Go to bed, right now, little liar!"

My eyes were filled with tears as I retrieved my Pied Piper, returned to the table, and dropped the map colors back into the cigar box. I tried to get a compliment for a job well done, but I got neither compliment nor credit. I didn't bother to show it to my mother. What was the use? Would either of them ever praise me for anything I did? How much more could I take? I was hurt. I needed to transform the hurt into anger and stand up to them. Nobody else was going to protect me. I had to protect myself. But I was becoming resilient to pain. I was changing the effect that their abuse had on me. Slowly but surely, I grew emotionally frozen, unable to cry.

When I wasn't coping with abuse, I was enduring my parents' abuse of each other. They got into terrible battles, calling each other every atrocious name imaginable. Neighbors sat outside in their cars to listen to the entertainment. We kids considered selling popcorn and peanuts to make a little money. Even more remarkable was their insistence that we had to witness the fights. When a squabble started, we tried to escape to our bedrooms, but they forced us to sit still and listen to them curse each other. Our house was a combat zone, and we were caught in the crossfire, taking lots of emotional shrapnel.

During one argument, I tried to sneak out the back door, but I wasn't quick enough. Dad caught me and forced me back inside.

"I don't want to hear it, Dad!" I pled.

"By God, you are going to hear it! Sit down or I'll beat you myself."

I broke into a cold sweat when their personal riots began. I closed my eyes and tuned out the bass drums, cymbals, and crescendos. The arguments usually escalated into violence, and one of us became the referee until the police appeared. The emotional abuse was sadistic. Just living with them was punishment.

Once Dad chased Mama who was wearing only a bra and slip, outside with a clothes-iron in his hand. He chased her around the house, around the garage and the car, out the fence, and into the neighbors' yard. She grabbed a crowbar and hit him on the forearm so hard it swelled to a green goose egg. I thought it was broken and felt sorry for him, but if she hadn't hit him, he might have crushed her skull. The violence was so frequent we knew the police department phone number by heart, and they knew our voices so well they never asked for an address when we called them in hysterics. A police car in front of our home never surprised the neighbors. Once, the police had to take Mama to the hospital, because Dad had thrown a knife and hit her just under the eye. She got stitches, and her eye was black for two weeks. Another time he threw a jar of dill pickles at her. It missed her and went through the sheet rock of the dining room wall and into my bedroom. They hung a picture over the hole instead of repairing it.

The most horrific memory is of Mama, who, after fighting to the point of exhaustion, fell unconscious to the floor. Dad had her by the hair and told me to get the butcher knife so he could cut her head off. I backed up to the silverware drawer and covered it.

"I will not get a knife, and I will not let you get it!" I declared. The other children fled, and I was alone to protect her from my temporarily insane father. He finally retreated, and the battle ended until the next time. I had nightmares of my father holding my mother's head in one hand and a butcher knife in the other. In the dream, I gave him the knife and blamed myself for her death.

Maimed by emotional neglect and abuse, I saw the world as essentially inhospitable. Rather than deny my anger, I began to draw upon it. I learned how not to be vulnerable. I hardened and developed an extraordinary ability to cope. Somehow, I had to stay sane until I could escape. I insulated myself from the chaos and became more spiritual, believing there was a higher purpose in my misery from which faith would eventually rescue me. I subconsciously began to graph my defection and fantasized about living on my own. Even though I was a child, I knew I would be better off without my parents. Flight would be the ultimate means of coping, and it came sooner than I expected.

CHAPTER VIII

Pinky, Addie, and the Vampire Bite

In the fourth grade I met Patti Kaye Deluca, a new girl in the neighborhood my same age. The Deluca's lived directly in front of the small, white brick Baptist Church. Before we became active Mormons, we attended summer Vacation Bible School there. Patti Kaye was born with a strawberry birthmark on the top of her head, so her father nicknamed her Pinky. Her dad was a tall, handsome, Italian man who spoke broken English.

Billy and Jessie bet Pinky's brother I could beat her in a fight. I did not want to fight her, but I had no choice. A legion of neighborhood kids quickly formed a circle to watch the duel. Pinky was six months older than I was and three inches taller; I could tell she was stronger by the size of her feet. I dismissed my disadvantage by rationalizing that my toughness would compensate for her larger size. Her starched, polka dot blouse was tidy and tucked into her shorts; her clean, white tennis shoes were securely tied. Pinky's fingernails were freshly painted, and her brown hair neatly rolled. I hoped she was a sissy and wouldn't know how to fight.

My unbrushed, knotted strands looked like I had just rolled out of bed. Barefoot, I wore large, hand-me-down blue jean shorts that hung awkwardly on my narrow hips. My sleeveless shirt exposed my midriff and revealed my belly button. I was embarrassed by my appearance. I gave her a dirty look. I resented her triumphant demeanor before the fight had even begun. I tried to look confident and unafraid as I stepped forward. The ring of on-lookers grew tighter, and we circled one another like two young roosters. Then I felt a blow to the left side of my face and a push on my chest. I went down in an instant but immediately latched onto her legs and pulled her down with me. We rolled on the ground for about three minutes, scratching, pulling, slapping, and kicking, before someone in the crowd broke us apart. Her pretty white tennis shoes were untied. Grass clung to her chestnut hair, and her clothes were wrinkled and stained. The tussle hadn't changed my appearance at all. I looked the same way after the fight as before. We were both breathing hard, and I was thankful it was over. I don't know how long it took for us to become friends after that, but by and by we did.

Pinky and I called each other on the phone and met half way down the block to play after school. She was the only one in the neighborhood who lived in an air-conditioned house with carpeted floors. Her mother worked at a local department store, and her father was a plant worker like mine. She had one brother. We were never allowed inside their house, because her parents were very strict. I sometimes knocked on the door, but her mother turned me away and said Pinky couldn't play with me. She made me feel like a peasant, unworthy of her daughter's company. Pinky wanted to play with me but couldn't if her mother was home. Pinky was afraid of her parents. She could never please her mother, no matter how hard she tried. Her father beat her and her brother unmercifully at times, especially when he had too much to drink.

Pinky and I bonded because we both had mothers who disapproved of us, however, we never spoke about our experiences in detail. Pinky's mother criticized and degraded her constantly. I didn't know it at the time, but Pinky's father molested her more than once. She didn't tell anyone for years, but I believed her when she finally admitted it. We were adults when she told me that if she wanted a new dress or to go to a party, she had to submit to her father's fondling. On Saturdays, when he was home drunk and her mother was at the beauty parlor, he used her as his sexual toy. She asked her mom to change her hair appointment to another day, so she would be home on Saturdays. Poor Pinky thought that if her mother had her hair done on Thursdays, she would escape the weekend fondling. The molestation had long-term effects on her. Sexual abuse must be the worst of all forms of child abuse. Although I suffered from childhood mistreatment, I was never molested sexually. Perhaps Pinky's mother sensed her husband's perverted attraction to their daughter and was envious. She treated Pinky like the other woman, punished her for no reason, blamed her, compared her, challenged her, and grounded her.

Once Pinky asked to borrow a cousin's dresses to wear to school. Her mother got angry and made Pinky wear the same dress to school for a week. Pinky was eager to please her mother, but the more she tried the more her mother put her down. After a while, she began to rebel, quietly and subtly at first. Realizing that a loving bond with her mother was unattainable, she quit trying to please her. She started making bad grades and became a habitual liar. She pulled her eyelashes out until they were completely gone. Addie said Pinky ate her eyelashes, though I never witnessed that. The hair pulling may have been her way of dealing with unresolved anger. She looked awful without lashes, but the habit was compulsive and made her plain-eyed for years. When I asked her why she did it, she said her eyelashes bothered her. I couldn't imagine pulling out even one of mine intentionally, much less all of them.

The kids at school thought she was strange since she had no eyelashes. She developed a reputation as a liar and a weirdo, but she was one of the funniest girls around. I loved her company, regardless of her peculiarity. She enjoyed playing tricks on unsuspecting people. Once I saw her sitting near her mailbox in a lawn chair with a bicycle tire placed against each side of it. Her legs were covered with a blanket, and she had a tin can labeled, "Help for the cripple, please!" She sat there all day and shook the tin can at every car that passed.

"Pinky, what are you doing?" I asked.

"I'm making money!" she replied. "Go get that old crutch out of the garage and come back here and stand with me."

I got the crutch, poured ketchup on an old diaper, and bandaged my foot, then joined her by the curb with a sign around my neck that read, "Injured, every penny helps." By the end of the day we had collected ten quarters. We bought matching shorts from the local thrift store with the money and modeled them for everyone in the neighborhood.

Pinky loved to sing for anyone who would listen to her pretty, country-western twang. She started a lie at school, telling everyone she was going to be on the Grand Ol' Oprey, so the kids started asking for her autograph. Her parents should have taken her to a psychologist to see what caused her self-inflicted torture and constant lies, but they didn't want anyone to know the truth. They had secrets to hide. Consequently, Pinky never got the help she needed. Every time Pinky failed, her mother claimed a victory, but her victories required her daughter's defeat.

I was happy when the Patton family moved into our neighborhood, just a few houses down from Pinky. Addie, Matt, and I became so close we needed no other friendships and excluded everyone else. We gave each other companionship, happiness, closeness, everything. We were inseparable. We roamed the streets, three on a bike–Addie on the seat, Matt on the handlebars, me on the back fender. We earned money collecting Coke bottles, mowing lawns, cleaning houses, and raking leaves, but mostly we just played–climbed trees, built forts, ran races, told scary stories, and investigated vacant houses.

While my family became totally inactive in the church, the Patton family's commitment grew stronger. At least their father Lamar's did. The children complained about going to church, but he made them go anyway. He never quite broke his addiction to coffee and cigarettes, and his children said he claimed to be something he was not. Addie hated her dad's counterfeit ways and subconsciously blamed the Church for making him a hypocrite. If he was what church people were like, she wanted nothing to do with it. To her it was all a farce.

Addie's mother, Mildred, was a cashier at a local Mexican restaurant, and Lamar owned a carpet store. Their children went without adult supervision for hours at a time, so they learned to fend for themselves. Matt and Addie had about as little to eat as we did. Mildred was kind but heartbreakingly weak and dependent. She could never muster the strength to take control. She impressed me as a victim of life's inequalities, a prey for her mean-spirited husband, always powerless, stuck in her childhood, unable to grow up. Addie compensated by accepting responsibilities before she was ready. For that she became the favorite child, the chosen one.

Addie rescued her mother from her domineering father. Nothing Mildred or the children did was good enough for Lamar. He didn't want his children to become better or stronger or more successful than he was, so he never encouraged them to achieve. They succeeded in spite of him, not because of him. Lamar and Mildred never got along well. Although they didn't fight like my parents, they complained about one another constantly and put each other down. Addie and I were surprised to learn from Mildred that they had a wonderful sex life, even though they bickered constantly. Always the liaison between them, Addie vacillated between confused loyalties and unsorted feelings.

Addie was only two years older than me, but she became the mother I never had. She adored me–molded me, taught me, and loved me–and I loved her. What would I have become without her? Addie never let anyone hurt me and fought for me unhesitatingly. I began to draw from her strength and learned to protect myself. The Lord must have known I needed a friend, and he sent me a mentor. She was so strong, so brave, so athletic, so liberated, so beautiful–and such a tomboy. She not only mothered me, she also mothered Matt. She even had to mother her own mother, so she was never a child. The self-reliant Addie was there for us all. The irony of life plays unexpected tricks: young Addie, always the mother, grew old without ever giving birth.

Our trio had no social status so we learned to maneuver without prestige. We didn't care if others looked down on us because we dressed pitifully or came from unkempt homes and dysfunctional families. In time, we began thinking alike. With Addie in my life, I developed determination, inner-strength, will power, and an unconquerable spirit. My heart took hold. She taught me to give no one power over me. I finally found the catalyst I needed. Under her influence I stopped giving my parents the pleasure of watching me squirm with fear or cower under their blows.

We cultivated synergy as a survival tool. We were stronger together than alone. Surprisingly, we developed moral fiber without role models at home. We had the strength to endure hardships, overcome them, and rise above the hand dealt to us. We must have received our strength of character during pre-existence. Our faith teaches that our spirits exist before we are born, that we live with our Heavenly Father before birth and have personalities before we come to earth. Much of who we are in this life is a reflection of who we were in that life. Surely, Addie, Matt, and I knew each other there.

On my tenth birthday Addie gave me the only birthday party I ever had. She baked a small cake, covered it with white icing, and put a big candle right in the center. She decorated their garage with twisted toilet paper streamers and invited a few kids in the neighborhood, including Pinky. We didn't often include Pinky, because Addie thought she was weird. There were no presents, which was fine with me. At least I had a birthday party! We played games and devoured the little white cake.

Mama liked the Patton children because she considered them her missionary success story. She put on her good Mormon behavior around their family. Mama said Addie looked like Goldie Hawn. Addie always questioned and probed situations she didn't understand. I should have guessed she would grow up to be a psychologist, since she analyzed everyone's behavior. She asked me why my mother preferred Mary Jane to me.

"Rose, what's the deal? Your mother acts like Mary Jane is a queen and treats you like a dog. She ignores you, Rose!" Addie was outraged by what she called parental favoritism.

"She doesn't like me, Addie. That's why she treats me like a dog. I hate her too, so we're even."

Addie's philosophy of women's rights was ahead of her time. No boy was about to outdo her. She could beat any boy in the neighborhood in a foot race, and she put them in their place if they smart-mouthed her. She said she hated the word woman, because it connoted weakness, and she didn't want to be labeled powerless or feeble in any way.

Addie gave me the strength to stand up and challenge the system. I first learned to protect myself, then to safeguard my brother. One afternoon my mother was lying in bed watching a TV drama. Dad was due home from work at any minute. We were outside playing, and Billy hit Jessie and made him cry. That interrupted Mama's movie, so she ordered us into the house. I went in. Right then I decided it was time to change the effect. I would not back down, cry, or be her punching bag any longer. We approached her bedside, reluctantly.

Looking at me, she demanded, "What did you do to Jessie?"

I said I had done nothing with a look on my face that dared her to disagree. She noticed the change and looked surprised. She next accused Billy of hitting Jessie and told him to come to her. He braced himself for a slap in the face. I didn't leave the room. Billy was seven years old, and I didn't want her to hurt him the way she always hurt me. She made him sit next to her, grabbed his hand, and pulled it toward her. He struggled to get loose. Her eyes glazed over; she looked crazy. She pulled Billy's fingers into her mouth. I couldn't believe she would actually do it. Billy screamed in agony as she bit into his flesh. I ran to Billy and raised my hand to slap her face, yelling, "Stop it! Stop it, you crazy woman! Stop it or I'll kill you myself! I hate you, I hate you, and I wish you were dead!"

It worked! She let go. "I am going to tell Dad what you did," I said. The three of us darted out the door as Dad drove up in his truck.

I ran to him and described what had happened through tears. "Dad, Mama bit Billy's finger until it bled! I hate her, Dad. Do something!"

He gritted his teeth in anger, and Billy lunged to him for protection. Dad saw the bloody tooth marks, picked up a baseball bat from the ground, and headed to the back door. Mama realized she was in trouble. She jumped up and commanded him to put the bat down. I don't remember her explanation, but like a coward, Dad retreated. They both knew she was out of line, but hitting her with the bat wouldn't make the bite disappear. As usual, she got by with it. But something changed that day. I knew it and she knew it.

CHAPTER IX

Integration vs. Separatism

The Beatles emerged on the American music scene in 1964, and took the world by surprise. They appeared on the *Ed Sullivan Show* in February, and teens all over America went crazy over them. Mama invited Mildred and her kids over to our house the night they appeared on the Ed Sullivan Show. She shook the big pot on the gas stove over and over as the corn popped. Laced with butter and salt, its aroma filled the house. We didn't have enough seats in the living room, so the children sat contentedly on the floor and munched the white, crunchy morsels. When Mr. Sullivan announced the group, my sister started screaming that she was in love with Paul McCartney. Addie and I laughed. Before long Mama and Mary Jane were both crazy for The Beatles.

Our bedroom was covered with Beatles pictures. Mama bought their posters, records, postcards, and magazines to decorate the walls. She cut tiny pictures of them out of magazines and pasted them on Mary Jane's fingernails. She made Mary Jane a cake on her thirteenth birthday with a picture of the Beatles drawn into the icing. I wanted to taste that cake so badly, but Mary Jane took it to a friend's house and invited a few girls over to eat it.

Mama wanted Mary Jane to be popular and attractive, so she took her to a doctor in Galveston who specialized in weight loss. He prescribed some strong diet pills that made her nervous and sleepless, but they worked. She lost a lot of weight and looked very cute. She cut her hair in a sassy, short British style that complimented her looks. I liked playing with her lipstick and watching her tease her hair. One day, my mother decided it was time to teach Mary Jane to dance. They practiced in the living room, Mama leading while Mary Jane followed to the beat of music on the radio. The rest of us sat around and watched. I wanted to dance too, but Mama taught only Mary Jane. Since she didn't know the current dances like the Twist or the Swim, she taught Mary Jane to waltz and swing. Addie and Matt came over to watch them dance, and Addie cracked up. "Your mother is weird, Rose." She pointed out everything my mother did for Mary Jane and asked why she paid no attention to me.

At Addie's prompting, I asked Mama, "Why do you do everything for Mary Jane and nothing for me?"

Knowing she could not deny her partiality, she responded defensively, "When you become a teen I will do the same things for you." I knew she wouldn't, and I didn't intend to stay around long enough to find out. Before I could get away I had to endure my mother throwing a screwdriver at my face. When I caught the pointed end in the palm of my hand, I gritted my teeth to prevent tears. She stared at me defiantly as if to say, "You deserved it!" That same evening, she brought Billy and Jessie into the bathroom while I was bathing to wash their dirty feet in my bathwater. I was twelve. She would have never done that to my sister. I couldn't understand why my sister did not stand up for me. She was bigger than I was. I wanted her to help me, but she never did. How could I expect her to put herself in harms way for my sake? After all, she had it much better than I did, and she knew it. She wasn't going to jeopardize herself for me. My sister said, "You know how Mama is, Rose. Just don't do anything to make her mad." Mama never apologized for anything she did to me.

Under the influence of Malcolm X and the Black Panthers, the demands for black power changed the tone of Martin Luther King's movement from its commitment to non-violence and integration to an emphasis on black separatism and self-sufficiency by any means possible. Like Malcolm X, I became committed to an equal rights movement of my own. I lost interest in peaceful resolution and family integration. I turned to separatism and self-sufficiency by any means possible. But on a cold day early in 1965, when I was in the hospital for an appendectomy, Malcolm X was assassinated. TV reports predicted riots across America, and police protection was stepped up everywhere. Mama warned us against talking to black people. She said they hated white people and carried razors in their socks.

"How do they keep the razor blades in their socks from cutting their feet?" I asked. She ignored me.

Not long after I came home from the hospital, Dad returned to the hospital for more electric shocks. He no longer built fences and hated working at the plant because he thought people talked about him. He told Mama he heard voices behind his back when no one was there. He shook when it was time to go to work, so Mama took him back to the psychiatrist. When that series of shock treatments was over, he was permanently impotent. I heard Mama tell someone on the phone she would rather have him that way, than the way he was before. I wasn't sure what that meant, but she seemed relieved! They were only in their thirties, but they could never have sex again. She never complained about it. I thought they hated each other too much anyway. As I grew older, I came to realize it was really very sad.

The day Addie moved away was a sad one. She left the summer before I entered junior high school, and although she was only moving fifteen miles away, I felt like she was moving to another state. I told her she was lucky to be moving into a pretty, air-conditioned house with nice carpeted floors. We stood looking through the fence at one another until it started to drizzle.

"Get in the car, Addie Blue!" her father said. I retreated under the porch of her vacant house, waving goodbye as their station wagon drove away and stayed there until I could no longer see the car. I slowly walked home in the warm rain. I felt empty. When Addie first moved to the neighborhood she ran barefoot in shorts and a T-shirt with the look of an innocent young child, but puberty caught up with her during those two years. She had a beautiful, athletic figure, full hips, and rounded breasts. At first, she refused to wear a bra but eventually succumbed when the bouncing pain under her shirt began to affect her running. She came to me at a time when I needed her, and she stayed until I had the strength to be without her. I think God must have sent her to me. Those few years together endeared us to each other for life.

PART II, CHAPTER X

Excommunication

I came out of the trance as if I had taken a trip in a time machine and remembered I was in the bishop's office with four men absorbed in my confession. I paused as if awaking from a daydream and looked at the eight eyes staring at me. Hoping someone would rescue me from my confession, I tacitly pled with the bishop to erase it all and tell me he understood. Instead he handed me a tissue and asked if that was all that I had to say. I told him I could say no more.

"Rose, do you plan to ever see this man again?" He asked.

"I would be lying if I said no, Bishop. I know that is not what I should say, but I believe in my heart that I will see him again some day."

"If you think you will see him again, it is hard for us to believe you are sorry for your sin."

I couldn't answer. He asked me to leave the room for a few minutes while they consulted and prayed about a decision. There was no question in my mind that I would be excommunicated. When the office door opened thirty minutes later, the bishop confirmed that their decision was made with prayerful consideration and with deep regret informed me that I was excommunicated. I wasn't surprised. He said the reason for my excommunication would be kept confidential, but the excommunication would be announced to the priesthood on Sunday. The Church later abandoned the practice of sharing such information with the priesthood quorum, and no longer shares the judgments of church courts.

The bishop explained that the desired result was that I would make the changes necessary to return to the Church. I had to earn the right to receive the Church's blessings again. When I reached that point the current bishop would convene a new disciplinary council and consider re-baptism. Until then, I could not pray openly in church meetings, attend the temple, receive the sacrament, or participate in Sunday school discussions. I knew the gift of the Holy Ghost would not return until I was baptized again.

Before closing the meeting, the bishop took a pamphlet from his desk drawer and read a statement from the president of the Church:

I would not have anyone believe that there is no hope if there are some who have made such a grievous mistake as to require excommunication, because repentance and forgiveness are also a part of the Gospel. But it must be real repentance. Such repentance is a deep, heartfelt sorrow for sin that produces a reformation of life. Only then may the God of Heaven in His mercy and His goodness see fit to forgive us. He, not the priesthood on Earth, is the judge. Forgiveness comes from above. "Behold, he who has repented of his sins, the same is forgiven, and I, the Lord, remember them no more." The priesthood must act as mediator.

I left the room without bitterness, after shaking each person's hand. I didn't question what had been done or the penalty. I didn't want to bring further shame upon the Lord by being a member of his Church. Not every adulterer is excommunicated, but I was not willing to say that I would not see the man again, and that determined the severity of my penalty. Guilt burned crimson upon my chest. I expected to feel a great sense of remorse or a great sense of relief. I felt neither.

When I got home, everyone was asleep, and I didn't bother to wake Bud. I wanted to be alone with my thoughts and absorb the evening's events. Quietly I kicked my shoes off in the living room and curled up on the sofa and enjoyed the stillness in the room. My life was forever changed. I took a deep breath and tried to imagine what tomorrow would bring. Whatever the answer, I didn't care. My numbness protected me, like shock protects the wounded. In the softness of the midnight hour, I inscribed these verses on the back of a paper plate.

> *There is no check by my name when the roll is passed around*
> *To signify my presence for my name cannot be found.*
> *There was a time, long ago, when my name was in His book,*
> *Until I turned my back and His commandments I forsook.*
>
> *Soon I became unworthy to even bear His name*
> *And wanted not to do so, for He would suffer shame.*
> *Boldly, I attest to all, the price is very great,*
> *All privileges and blessings were removed from my estate.*
>
> *I do not stand in meetings to give a talk or pray.*
> *I take not of the sacrament when it is passed my way.*
> *My hand is never raised when church leaders are sustained.*
> *The testimony that I have must now be kept contained.*
>
> *In this flesh, the Holy Ghost no longer can abide.*
> *As for his sacred temples, I cannot go inside.*
> *Oh my Lord, my Father, it is piercing to my heart,*
> *The gospel and the gifts therein, I am no more a part.*
>
> *Must I endure this severance for all eternity?*
> *I hear a small voice whisper He bled and died for me.*
> *Through His atoning sacrifice I am able to repent*
> *And be forgiven wholly, for this purpose He was sent.*

The words flowed easily from my pen. I couldn't think of a title, so I left it unnamed until the title came to me as effortlessly as the words. Asleep on the sofa that night, I dreamed the title, *Severed Soldier.*

Bud and I were proud of our little brick home on a Texas City cul-de-sac. It could have won a garden club award for any category–most manicured yard, freshest paint, or cleanest garage. I was a perfection-ist housekeeper and never left home without making every bed. There was always a bowl of fruit or newly picked flowers on the table. Clothes were folded and put away still hot from the dryer. Floors were swept clean and never a dirty dish left in the sink. The duties of mothering my three children, aged three to ten, occupied me. My children enjoyed hot meals, fresh baked cookies, and homemade bread in an orderly home. I commonly awoke before dawn, hurried to the grocery store, returned home, put up the groceries, cooked a pot of chicken and dumplings, and packed Bud's lunchbox–all before the children awoke.

Rarely a semester went by when I didn't take at least one college course to keep my mind invigorated. In my childhood, college was never mentioned, and nobody expected me to get a college education. I won a $200.00 scholarship in my senior year and made a commitment to education that lasted twenty years. I loved learning. When I was excommunicated, I worked part-time as an engineering aide at the Johnson Space Center (JSC). Although I only worked three days a week for Federal Flight Services (FFS), an affiliate of the airlines I received free flight privileges as a benefit. When my drafting instructor asked if I were interested in interviewing, I jumped at the chance.

When I was offered the job, I wondered if I could handle another commitment. What would I give up? I already had to manage my life with military discipline to meet my obligations. How could I take on more? How could I turn it down? I knew I couldn't count on Bud's help. He worked in shifts at the plant, like his father and mine, and could not handle more. Besides his job, he was active in the church, watched television, and went fishing occasionally. I did everything else. I hired a gardener, because Bud put off mowing until the yard became an embarrassment. For a while, I mowed it myself. When I was seven months pregnant, the neighbors asked why Bud wasn't mowing the grass, but I always made excuses for him. He didn't help with the children, the housework, or the finances. I never let go of any of my responsibility when I took on more. He was content to let me do more, which enabled him to do less.

I was more responsible, more accessible, more dependable, more reliable, and more mature than Bud, although I didn't know it. I did what Bud should have done for himself and our family. I had to be a person-and-a-half to make up for Bud being barely half. Doing virtually everything with little help from him wore me down to the point where I was ready to break. When I stopped long enough to recognize the imbalance, I saw that I was clearly on the downside of the tilt. In an advanced psychology course I learned about co-dependency. I thought the author of the text had come to my home, observed my relationship with Bud, and documented what she saw. I recognized myself as a co-dependent personality. I submerged my life into his without any inkling of the injury to us both. Without knowing it, I had been taken for a long, painful, destructive ride. Our co-dependency involved an unhealthy fusing of our lives and the loss of our boundaries, identities, and proper responsibilities. Unable to separate our individual selves, I had no sense of where my being stopped and Bud's began. I wondered who was at fault. I wanted to blame Bud for being so lazy, but at the same time I wondered if my domineering ways were at fault.

Bud and I started liking each other in junior high school. For a long time, he didn't know that I existed. I thought he would never notice me. Starting junior high was a thorny rose for me. It was one step closer to independence, yet I wasn't ready to mingle with teenagers. I started the seventh grade with three cheap dresses, one pair of black dress shoes, and a pair of tennis shoes for gym. My hair was long and straight. I weighed about seventy pounds and had no shape, no pretty clothes, and no boyfriend. Most of the other girls were more developed. They wore make up, teased and colored their hair, and shaved their legs. I yearned to be accepted, but most of the girls made fun of me. They wore mini skirts, paisley tent dresses, clunky shoes, and fishnet hose. Neon green, pink, orange, and yellow patent leather purses and shoes with daisy designs were the rage, and I owned none of those.

Pinky and I were excited about going to junior high school, because it meant we were growing up. I am sure her father continued to molest her, but we never discussed it. We became closer after Addie moved away, but since Pinky had problems of her own, she could not give me the strength Addie did. We were equally plagued with heartbreak from jealous mothers. We dreamed and fantasized together. Pinky was allowed to wear a light shade of lipstick, and she even had a compact with powder and a mirror. We both wore training bras that we stuffed with powder puffs. While her mother was at work, I sneaked into her house. We romanticized about boys and looked forward to our first kiss. We practiced kissing the mirror. Pinky stuck her tongue out the side of her mouth and pressed her face against the mirror, flashing her bald eyes at me to be sure I laughed. Slobber ran all the way down her mother's full-length mirror.

The girls in junior high school were much richer and more grown up than I. They made fun of me for not shaving my legs, for wearing garage sale clothes, and for being built like a third-grader. I remember praying to overcome the rejection. I wondered if God heard me.

To my surprise, the most popular girl in school soon began to like me. Her name was Jolyn, and she was beautiful. Every boy liked Jolyn, and the girls all flocked around her. She was well developed, never wore the same dress twice, and was an award-winning gymnast. She was elected Most Beautiful all three years in junior high school. That she liked me was a miracle, because she paid no attention to me before, unless to laugh at my hairy legs. Maybe she felt sorry for me. She invited me to a slumber party, and we made snacks, swam in her pool, and imitated our teachers. I had a talent as a mimic, and before long I had everyone in stitches. That night marked a new beginning for me. Jolyn took me under her wings, and because of her, I became popular at school. The Lord answered my prayer through her, and the rejection soon stopped. She never knew she was the Lord's instrument to answer a faithful child's plea.

I had a secret crush on Bud. The kids at school liked him, and he played every sport. He wasn't pretty-boy handsome, but he was good looking enough–tall, with short brown hair and freckles. He wasn't particularly smart or romantic or interesting, but he was known as a "good boy."

One day on the way to lunch, Jolyn said she and Bud kissed at a party. At that instant I had a vision that Bud and I would some day be married. At that point, I hadn't talked with him and knew him only by name. That was my first vision but not the last. I was given the gift of premonition. I didn't always know what the premonitions meant, but in time the meanings were revealed. I could also hear a story or read a book and become a character in a story–feel the environment, smell the aromas, taste the fruit, and experience the pain. These two gifts often served me well, but were occasionally difficult to handle. If I read a newspaper article about a murder or heard of a horrible crime, I entered the scene and couldn't shake it from my mind.

After I started junior high school, my mother got an evening shift job as a convenience store cashier in a nearby town. By the time we came home from school she was gone, so most of the time we fended for ourselves. Since my dad worked rotating shifts, he was hardly ever home either. At least their fights were less frequent when she went to work. Mama's income hardly justified her absence from the family, but it got her away from the house. She came home about one or two in the morning, bringing donuts and pastries home from the store for our breakfast.

Parental absence hurt Billy and Jessie most. Billy started Little League baseball but never had a ride to practice. My parents never attended his games, and he quit. In our family we grew up basically unaware of each other, too busy putting one foot in front of the other, surviving one day at a time. I wish I had helped my brothers with their needs, but I was too busy trying to help myself. Billy and Jessie spent almost every summer day at the Texas City swimming pool. They had a quarter each for the entrance fee and only a dime to buy a snack during the eight-hour stay.

Billy became an excellent diver. I remember watching him in an unofficial diving competition with two boys who were pretty good amateur divers, since they had pools and diving boards at home. The three lifeguards agreed to score their five best dives. Billy had no training, but he had raw courage. The other boys executed crisp swan dives, back dives, and jackknives with perfectly arched backs and pointed toes. Billy attempted a back flip, a cut-a-way, a one-and-a-half, and a double but was a little sloppy; he seldom kept his feet together, never pointed his toes, and usually missed the vertical entry. He consistently scored lower than the other boys who did safe, simple dives. They congratulated themselves for being more elegant. One of them said, "He's all heart and no finesse. We keep our feet together and our toes pointed."

When the winner was announced, Billy beat them all. I kept track of the scores in my head and knew the math didn't add up. The other boys consistently outscored him. One boy stormed the lifeguard table and demanded an explanation. "Degree of difficulty!" the scorers replied matter-of-factly. "Sure, you had better form, but he did harder dives. When you factor in the degree of difficulty, he beat you hands down, kids." Billy was elated. Until then I didn't know you got extra credit for greater difficulty.

Billy stopped going to the pool when it became racially integrated. My dad told him to get out of the water the minute the first nigger jumped in, and he did. He could have been on a diving team, played baseball, or become a Boy Scout, but he had no encouragement or guidance.

At times we had no toilet paper, soap, deodorant, toothpaste, or feminine pads. Instead of keeping a supply of toiletries, my mother generally waited until we were out and someone was in an awkward position before she bought more. We were in effect abandoned children without supervision, adequate nutrition, medical or dental care, proper clothing, proper hygiene, or proper shelter. Every day was a challenge, and shame became my constant companion.

That year, Aunt Beverly arranged for Cousin Sue Ellen to marry a young man with a bright future. He was six years older, handsome, smart, and considered a good catch. Being a returned missionary and law student, he seemed the perfect match for her daughter. Sue Ellen probably did not love him, but her mother encouraged the match and she did what was expected of her. Mary Jane was one of her bridesmaids and wore a long, blue velvet dress to the reception. With Sue Ellen marrying and leaving home, Uncle William and Aunt Beverly became empty nesters.

Mary Jane's voice won her the lead part in the high school play. Mama bragged to everyone about the honor and commissioned a seamstress to make costumes for every scene in the play. Mama felt foolish when the teacher said Mary Jane could not wear the costumes because they did not represent the time period. Mary Jane wore costumes furnished by the school, so those clothes were never worn.

Shortly after the play, Mary Jane started dating Dean Ray, a surfer whose bleached hair, silly personality, and lack of class turned Mama off. I thought my mother had gall to judge another person's class, considering she had none herself. To get her away from Dean Ray, she made Mary Jane move to Jasper and live with Aunt Beverly and Uncle William. They must have been lonely, because they were happy to have her. Aunt Beverly put Mary Jane on a diet–dry toast for breakfast, green beans and tomatoes for supper. Mary Jane thought she was starving and bought candy bars from the vending machines at school.

Once Dean Ray came to visit Mary Jane in Jasper, and Uncle William and Aunt Beverly told Mary Jane that if she knew what was good for her, she would stay away from him. They didn't like Dean Ray any more than Mama did. Mary Jane lived with them the first semester of her senior year, but she missed Dean Ray so badly she came home. Mama was disgusted with her choice in boys and ridiculed her constantly for dating him. She slapped Mary Jane a couple of times when she came home late from dates with Dean Ray. She called her "wild thing," and said she was wicked.

Just as my sister was ready to graduate, I was elected cheerleader. It was the end of the eighth grade and I would be on the ninth grade team the next fall. My mother barely acknowledged the honor. She just dismissed the news with, "Don't let it go to your head!" I babysat all summer into the wee hours of the mornings to get enough money to pay for cheerleading uniforms and camp. I had become almost completely self sufficient, so I didn't ask my parents for basic necessities.

That year Martin Luther King was assassinated and two months later Robert Kennedy was killed. Free love and peace were the slogans of the day. For the first time, our schools began to teach sex education as part of the curriculum, and it became socially acceptable to live with a lover before marriage. Boys, including my brothers, let their hair grow long and wore bell-bottomed pants, hippie beads with peace symbols, and tie-dyed shirts, like Sonny and Cher. Nothing in America seemed safe, stable, or sacred. With my sister and Addie gone, I was ready to latch onto anything that gave me a semblance of security, even a mismatched boyfriend.

I was thrilled when Bud sent a messenger to ask me to go steady with him. He went to a carnival and won a big, pink stuffed animal and gave it to me at the baseball park one evening, the first stuffed animal I ever had, and I loved it. A gift from him meant so much to me. No one had ever bought me anything like that. Bud bought me heart-shaped boxes of chocolates for Valentine's. He knew about my home life, and he understood. He was always polite and respectful. We should have remained close friends instead of marrying. We may have been able to be good friends.

That summer my picture was in the paper as a cheerleader. A picture of Billy and Jessie was right next to mine. They and Matt Patton were going to a Salvation Army camp for underprivileged boys. Mama convinced Mildred to let Matt go to the camp too to get rid of them for a week. The picture of my "underprivileged" brothers next to my cheerleader picture in the paper embarrassed me. They went to the underprivileged boys camp the same week that I went to cheerleading camp.

Addie phoned to joke with me about the pictures. "Hey, Rose, I see that our brothers went to camp the same week you did. I read about it in the newspaper, right next to the big side-by-side pictures." She was embarrassed for me but we both laughed.

"Addie, why did our mothers let them go to an underprivileged boys camp?" I asked.

"Well, I don't know why Wanda did, but my mother wanted to get rid of Matt for a week, and it was free so she encouraged him. I am sure she didn't know he would make headlines and have our name plastered across the front page as being *underprivileged!*"

"I am so embarrassed, Addie. The only thing I can do is laugh, or I'll feel worse. It doesn't seem to matter to anyone but me."

Addie had adjusted to her new surroundings and had no problems making new friends. She made an impression wherever she went. She complained of having to go to church and told me I was lucky my parents no longer attended, but I didn't feel lucky. Plenty of boys made their way to her door as she developed a knockout figure. I wanted a little of her voluptuous shape and some of the attention it drew. Addie didn't use her figure to attract boys, however; if a boy flirted with her, she put him in his place. Later, she accepted her femininity more, but it took a long time for her to warm up to the idea. Matt, on the other hand, matured in his love for the arts and began to show real promise as an artist. Puberty made Matt aware that he was not just a sissy. He was beginning to recognize that he might be homosexual.

Pinky let her eyelashes grow back, but that didn't mean things were going better for her at home. She started hanging out with a bad crowd and began to flunk, so we grew apart. She had very low self-esteem, and her mother made her feel awful about failing. As an adult, Pinky said her brother began molesting her too. He threatened to tell their dad when Pinky left the house after being grounded if she didn't masturbate him to orgasm. Pinky was willing to do anything to avoid a whipping with her father's belt, so she obliged him a few times. That changed when she caught him breaking the rules when he took the family car to his girlfriend's house while her dad was out of town. The next time he wanted her to pleasure him, Pinky said, "Go ahead and tell on me. If you do, I'll tell Dad you took the car without permission." Pinky never had to do that dirty deed again, but she was growing promiscuous. The rumor at school was that Pinky kept a jar of Vaseline next to her bed. Boys came to her window at night, and she opened the window and masturbated them. I don't believe Pinky really did, but she got a bad reputation. We no longer spent time together, but we were always kind to each other when our paths crossed–and she could still make me laugh.

Only a few days after she graduated from high school, Mary Jane left home. She was eighteen and no one could stop her. She and Dean Ray were in love, and she was tired of defending him to my parents. She left when Mama was at work, so she wouldn't have to face her. I didn't blame her for leaving, but she didn't even say goodbye to me. She took her suitcases into the living room and told Dad she was moving out. Dad was angry with her and told her never to come back. She moved in with Dean Ray's grandmother. We all felt abandoned and no one talked to her for months. My mother was crushed, since her loyal daughter was no longer under her control. I don't remember Mama even trying to care for the rest of us after Mary Jane left. She must have felt like a failure since the only child she had invested any effort in had betrayed her. She just left us to decide our own paths and never bothered to encourage us one way or the other. The only advice she ever gave me was that if I gave my virginity to a boy before marriage, no other boy would want me. I believed her.

Fortunately, I had strong bonds with my girlfriends and that made life easier. I now survived comfortably without my sister or Addie. I found sanctuary in my friends' homes, which were pretty and clean. Their mothers made dinner in the evenings and always invited me to eat with them. My parents never gave me a ride to parties or football games, but those wonderful mothers and fathers picked me up and dropped me off daily. When I was too embarrassed to ask for a ride home from a party, I walked miles across town late at night, alone. Observing those good parents, I learned what a functional home was about, what mothers and fathers roles were, and how normal families interacted. I wanted to pattern my life after what I saw in their homes. Even today, I thank those parents for helping me.

My ninth grade year turned out to be the happiest of my life. It was fun to be a cheerleader and everyone at school knew I was a good little Mormon girl. I didn't smoke or drink Coke, tea, coffee, or alcohol, since it was against my religion. They also figured out my family life was miserable. I was nominated for football sweetheart which meant I would be escorted onto the field for homecoming. I saved my babysitting money and bought a cheap dress for nine dollars, so I wouldn't have to ask Mama for money. I didn't win, but I was happy to be nominated. Mama never said anything about my nomination.

Bud Murphy's family was just like the one in *Leave It to Beaver*, and Bud was every bit the "Beav." His mother was a wonderful cook, kept a clean house, and went to all Bud's baseball and football games. They had big dreams for their athletic son. They hoped he might get a baseball or football scholarship to college, but they overlooked one thing: Bud had no interest in attending college. He hated school! Bud was very temperamental, and his mother did everything to keep him from becoming frustrated and breaking into an angry outburst. Bud erupted any time he was criticized, intimidated, or made to feel inadequate. He was always one degree below the boiling point. For years I blamed his temper and lack of confidence on his older brother, Reily.

Reily contributed to Bud's lack of self-esteem, but he was not entirely to blame. Four years older than Bud, Reily could out-talk, out-perform, out-noise, and out-shine his younger brother. He was smart, loud, emphatic, and bold. Bud's parents gloried in Reily's skills and opinions. If Bud tried to interject an opinion or comment, his brother corrected or belittled him. Bud couldn't do anything right. He did not learn to talk until he was three years old. He was prone to mishaps and misfortune, even as a child. Every undertaking was a huge challenge for him, and he usually made stupid mistakes. Bud seemed jinxed! Even without someone like Reily in the house, life was hard enough for Bud.

Reily treated Bud like a hopeless case, made fun of him, and laughed at his failures. Bud's parents never corrected his ridicule or overbearing behavior. Bud developed low self-esteem, and became angry. Unable to express his resentment of his brother verbally and too young to conquer him physically, he became a seething cauldron of hostility. Once in the fourth grade a teacher made him feel foolish in front of the class. Hearing the roar of his schoolmates' laughter, he became infuriated, lifted his desk over his head, and took aim at the teacher. The laughter stopped and the teacher froze. Bud put the desk down. The principal reprimanded him and notified his parents. Bud was the talk of the school. Reily had another reason to criticize him. Unfortunately, anger and temper were not the only negative aspects in Bud's personality that resulted from his childhood conditioning. Convinced that Bud was less capable than Reily, his parents compensated by doing things for him to appease him.

My sister called in the fall and told us she was marrying Dean Ray. Mama accepted the news and helped her plan the small wedding. They married in October, and before long a baby was on the way. We were all happy. Dean Ray joined the Army so he could support his new wife and baby, and they moved to Okinawa.

Dad's nerves were fragile, and he didn't want to go back to the plants to work. He couldn't quit his job, so his only choice was to go back into the clutches of Dr. Hackbarth who administered a third set of shock treatments Dad grew more feeble after each set. He could no longer do math in his head or spell like a champion. The medications Dr. Hackbarth prescribed never seemed to be correct. Dad was always on edge and should have taken medical leave, but Dr. Hackbarth was too inept to suggest it. Mama continued to work and seemed caught up in her convenience store world. I steered my own course, surviving in the world I found away from home. Children left alone must plant their own field. The company they keep determines the seed they scatter and the fruits they harvest.

CHAPTER XI

The Secret

I awoke on the sofa just before daybreak the next morning and heard the sound of running water coming from the bedroom. Bud was up. I grabbed the paper plate from the floor, and remembered the poem I wrote the night before, still without a title. I recalled I had dreamed the name of the poem. *Severed Soldier.* To be severed is to be detached. A soldier marches forward to overcome the enemy. The title defined my life–a battlefield of choices and detachments, strengths and weakness with enemy concealed. I walked into the bedroom and saw Bud putting on his shirt.

"I slept on the couch last night. I didn't want to wake you when I came home."

"How was it?" he asked.

"Not too good actually. I was ex-ed." I began to make the bed.

"Well, isn't that what you expected?"

"Yes, of course." He knew I had had an affair. We discussed it several days earlier, so it was no surprise to him. I lied to Bud about the other man's identity. I told him it was over, the man no longer worked with me, and had moved away. We didn't know if we could repair our very damaged marriage. We discussed whether we should stay together or split-up again. We had three beautiful children, two boys and a girl, and had to stay together for them–or so I thought. I thought Bud could forgive me. After all, I was sure he cheated on me when we were first married. My friends reported the rumors of his hidden acts, but I defended Bud and refused to believe them.

"I should never have let you get that boob job, Rose. It's all because of those fake boobs you got that this happened. You started acting different when you got them. I should have known you'd be showing them off!"

"I didn't show them off, Bud. But what if I did? You like men to want what you have and they can't get. It turns you on, remember?"

Bud looked down with guilty recollection. "Well, I didn't think you would go that far." Bud had his own sins to confess, but his admission timetable differed from mine. I have to confess promptly to feel better, but he could live a lie for years to delay the penalty.

I left the room and went to the kitchen to make the children's breakfast. Ben was ten years old; little Molly and Seth hadn't started school. They gathered around the table for their cereal, laughing and giggling. My children were fortunate. I decided long ago not to perpetuate my parents' mistreatment. I didn't humiliate or degrade them. I did not crush their innate qualities or punish their intrinsic goodness. However, I became frustrated at times and hit them when I shouldn't, or I lost my temper and yelled at them, but the behavior was not pervasive. My children were never afraid of me; they loved to be with me. Once, they told Addie they loved me because I was so much fun.

They were oblivious to my situation, and I tried to hide my unhappiness from them, though they knew Bud and I quarreled and fought. My children were the joys of my life and I joked and teased with them, but I found no joy in my mismatched marriage. I dreamed of what life would have been like if I hadn't married so young. Part of me wanted to recapture those youthful years. I never had the chance to date or be on my own. I missed all the things other young women do before they marry. I wished I had not married Bud. I didn't love him and never had. I married him at age fifteen to escape my home. I thought anything would be better than living with my parents, but to marry Bud while I was still in high school was a mistake. We missed so much. How could I have done such a thing? I wasn't pregnant. I wish we had annulled the marriage. Though I finally rectified things by divorcing him five years later, I remarried him. Why did I go back to him? I looked out the window at the sunrise and recalled my high school days, the time of life that is suppose to be fun for teens, those terribly confusing years.

Bud and I didn't see each other during the summer of 1969. We both wanted to be free before we started high school. I sometimes hitched a ride to church with other members to visit Addie and Matt. The little church was growing, and a new building was under construction. That summer we went to the youth events, attended church camp, roasted hot dogs, and enjoyed teen dances. We were energetic, good looking, popular, and incorrigible. The three of us often went to Galveston beach. We seemed to get into mischief every time we were together. We snuck into the Jack Tar Hotel and swam in the beautiful outdoor pool, pretending to be guests. Addie's figure attracted sharks from every direction. We both wore bikinis, but she looked a lot better in hers. I had developed a cute figure, but I was no competition for Addie. NASA put a man on the moon and captured the country's imagination. For a minute the nation forgot about assassins, hippies, bra burnings, and draft dodgers; and paused to revel in glory.

After Mary Jane left, Mama and I entered into an unspoken truce and an attitude of mutual indifference. Age mellowed her somewhat; her job was her outlet. She no longer abused me, although she still withheld kind words or encouragement. Perhaps she sensed that I, like my brothers, would turn on her. She and Dad both had seen enough of Billy and Jessie's physical wrath to fear it. She left me alone. I never resorted to physical violence toward her, but I am not surprised that Billy and Jessie did. They stopped the abuse by counterattacking. They learned violence, intimidation, and ruthlessness from my parents and used it to defend themselves, often making my parents their victims.

While I was busy with my friends at the beach, Billy and Jessie worked all summer for an old man who should have been jailed for breaking child labor laws. My brothers worked ten hours a day building fences in the hot sun. They got two old horses for their toil. I told Mama the man was abusing them, but she said that she was glad for them to work and stay busy, even if for nothing. Otherwise they would have wandered around and gotten into trouble. I was horrified when, instead of leaving the horses in a pasture, they brought them into our fenced yard. Our deplorable home with four broken-down cars in the driveway now had a horse pasture for a front yard. Horse manure piled up all over the sidewalk. Mama and Dad didn't care or were too afraid of "the babies" to say anything. When they entered junior high the next fall, they refused to cut their hippie hair for school and wore wigs instead. Mama was out of touch with what her children did and paid no attention to the boys' needs. They often went to school dirty. The day of the class picture, Billy wore a coat to school without a shirt, because he couldn't find a clean one. When the teacher asked him to remove the coat for the picture he refused, since he was naked underneath. The principal made Billy come to school an hour early so he could bathe in the boys' locker room. The teachers complained about his hygiene.

Jessie used to stuff his bed with pillows, crawl out the window, and head for the Trade Wind Theater, an abandoned outdoor theater about three miles from our house where hundreds of pigeons lived behind the screen. He crawled high into the rafters at night without a flashlight to catch pigeons. One slip and he would have fallen forty feet to his death. Jessie often fell asleep in school, and the teachers didn't bother to wake him. They knew he wasn't properly cared for at home and assumed he needed sleep.

Billy and Jessie didn't have the same type of role models I did. Their models were other neglected children living in dysfunctional families. They began to smoke cigarettes when they were ten-years-old. Soon they smoked weed. They did everything with Ricky, their best friend. His father was Caucasian and his mother Hispanic, so my brothers told him he was only half-good. Ricky thought that was funny. If he became upset, they teased him more. They loved to tease and dare each other. Anybody who picked a fight with one had to fight all three. Without guidance, Billy and Jessie became rough and tough. They got caught up in aggressive criminal activity, drug and alcohol abuse, and juvenile delinquency. Billy, Jessie, and Ricky smoked, drank, robbed, fought, and got into trouble with the law before they were out of junior high school. They were fast becoming the town renegades.

I started high school as a tenth grader at a time when the nation's upheaval paralleled that of my home. Charles Manson's hideous face, with his black, devilish eyes, glared from every television screen in America. There were many hippies at our school–potheads, we called them. They set the fashion trends, and we followed. We wore short skirts, faded jeans, hot pants, and boots. It was cool to be counter to the culture and rebellious.

Bud and I had been apart for the summer, but when school started we got back together. He was on the football team that year, and we were the sweetheart couple that would never break up. Had we been sensible we would have dated other people; instead we did something that we would live to regret. At the end of my sophomore year, we engaged in heavy petting one afternoon after a swim party. I thought I lost my virginity but by definition I probably had not. Mama always told me that if I lost my virginity no boy would have me, and I believed her. I thought that if I broke up with Bud, I would be a spinster all my life. Although Bud assured me that we would marry some day, I was distraught. Bud read an article in the paper about legal common-law marriages for boys and girls under eighteen; we thought we had the solution for our guilt. The law, which was repealed the following year, stipulated that a man and woman could marry if they swore they lived together as man and wife. No blood tests were required. We decided it was our chance, and on a muggy July day, shortly after Bud received his license, we drove to Houston and got married. The marriage license was sent to Bud's house where he intercepted it before his parents saw it and hid it behind a picture of me on his dresser. We didn't use birth control. We just went on with our lives as if we were still dating and told no one.

CHAPTER XII

Where Have all the Flowers Gone?

Bud would sneak to my house at night after his parents were in bed and crawl through my window. Once he was half in and half out when my mother came home from work. We continued living in our separate houses. But for some reason I told my mother we were married. She didn't get angry, or somber, or shocked, or upset. She seemed glad. She had no reservations about my being married at that early age. Perhaps she thought it was a good way to get rid of me. I thought she would keep our secret, but she didn't. She called my grandma and told her. Grandma insisted we tell Bud's parents, so Mama picked me up from school and took me to Bud's house. She made me go inside and tell Mrs. Murphy she had a new daughter-in-law. Mrs. Murphy broke into tears and asked me to come back that evening so we could tell Mr. Murphy.

Mama took me back to school, and during lunch I told Bud what had happened.

"You actually went to my house and told my mother?"

"Yes, my mother made me."

He was nervous about telling his dad, but now that his mother knew, we had to move forward. That evening at Bud's house we were both scared to death. His dad reacted with sorrow and anger. He said Bud had done a stupid thing, and the only consolation was that I was not pregnant. They asked us to have the marriage annulled. We might have done that, but within a few days I was throwing up in the mornings. There we were, sixteen, married, in high school, and about to become parents. We weren't prepared for the responsibility. We both wanted to undo the foolish mistake, but it was too late.

We decided I would move into Bud's room, since his brother was away at college. Bud's house had only two bedrooms and one bath, but it was clean and nicely furnished. We pushed the twin beds together and we continued to go to school. Bud quit the football team and got a job after school, delivering pizza. I babysat a six-year-old boy for extra money. Mrs. Murphy treated me fairly well until my mother called her and lectured her on the way I should be treated. I heard her talking to Mama on the phone, and I couldn't believe what I overheard. Mama told her to make me work around the house and not to compliment me, because I would get the bighead. She said I was a smart aleck and that she shouldn't let me talk back to her. I had no chance to develop a relationship with my mother-in-law before she sabotaged it.

After that call, Mrs. Murphy became intimidating and rude. I was uncomfortable in her house. I thought their family was boring. They sat watching sports on television and hardly spoke to each other. They never talked about anything meaningful. Only after we were married did I notice that Bud had difficulty in communicating. At first, I thought he was afraid to expose his feelings because he was afraid of criticism. To reveal his feeling or values, he had to know himself, but he never really knew who he was. He adopted the behavior of his friends or associates at work. My chameleon husband changed based on the personality of the buddy he was with at the time. If they smoked marijuana, he smoked marijuana; if they liked sports, he liked sports; if they looked at pornography, he looked at pornography; if they were deeply religious, he was too; if they were jokesters, so was he. He and I couldn't have been greater opposites. Although I had not established my identity either, I didn't morph to the expectations of others to be accepted.

After living with Bud's parents for three months, we moved into a furnished efficiency home, a cute little gingerbread house. The couch that let out into a bed, the tiny kitchen and dining table, were all in the same room. Mrs. Murphy cried when she saw it the first time. She was having difficulty with her son's transition to husband and father. Many times I had to roll pennies for milk and bread, because we were too proud to ask our parents for money. Our friends at school were nice to us and invited us to parties. But we didn't fit in with the crowd any more. We were different. The other young, married couples in the area were ten years older than we were, so we didn't fit in with them either. We were unlike anybody else we knew. Since we didn't have a car, my mother and Mrs. Murphy picked us up and took us wherever we needed to go. In June, just before I turned seventeen, I gave birth to a beautiful baby boy. We named him Benjamin and called him Ben. He had big, blue eyes and tiny curls. We were proud of him and loved playing with him, but we also missed living as teenagers. We tried to fit a world where we no longer belonged.

Although my mother was a terrible mother, she was a wonderful grandmother. I had no compunction about leaving Ben in her care. She adored him. My brothers loved him, too. I think she tried to compensate for having been a bad mother by being a good grandmother. Since my sister had two daughters, little Ben was the first grandson. She never treated her grandchildren the way she treated me. How could such a mean mother become such a wonderful grandmother? She complimented them, cooked for them, bought them presents, and told them stories. Nothing was too good for her grandchildren.

Dad had a fourth set of shock treatments while I was in high school. Why Dr. Hackbarth decided to give him another set is hard to understand. His brain cells were so burned up after the shocks that he could hardly manage his job at the plant any more. He looked twenty years older than his age. His gray hair was now shaved close to his scalp, his face was drawn, and he didn't have all his teeth. He could hardly walk to the mailbox without getting completely out of breath, and he took candy-coated meds three times a day. By then, I no longer felt contempt for the regrettable figure before me, only sorrow for a wasted life, void of satisfaction.

Mama and Dad didn't fight any more; they just argued and called each other names. They had to unite to ward off my brothers' drug-driven rages. Those boys ran all over them. The babies had no reservations about getting physical if my parents refused them something.

Once Billy was having a bad trip on some drug and threw a huge glass planter at my mother and cut her leg badly. The turning point came when Billy was thirteen. My dad took his belt off to whip Billy for cursing at him. Jessie said Billy reversed the attack, jerked the belt away from Dad, and started hitting him with it. After that, Dad never took his belt to either of them again.

The summer before my senior year, when Billy was fourteen, he ran away from home and was gone for three days before Mama noticed. He hitchhiked all the way to Florida with only a few dollars in his pocket. She was surprised to get a call from the police informing her they had her son in custody for vagrancy. Mary Jane was living in Florida at the time, so Mama asked Dean Ray to get him a bus ticket home. Those boys were always in trouble. They were notorious at school for beating up black people. Billy fought a teacher once when the teacher tried to break up a fight. They were kicked out of every middle school in Texas City, leaving them with no school to attend. My parents were afraid to go before the school board and ask for readmission. They didn't blame the schools. The boys were impossible to handle. Billy and Jessie were left without basic education in a world that required it for success.

Jessie and Ricky played chicken with their friends. They put lit cigarettes between their arms to see who would pull away first. Naturally their arms got burned. One day Mama noticed a third-degree burn about the size of a slice of bread on Jessie's forearm. He had put a cigarette between his forearm and a wall to prove his bravery and didn't pull away until the cigarette burned out. My mother could not convince him to go to the doctor, but when I saw the wound, I was flabbergasted and took him to the doctor at the clinic where Mrs. Murphy worked. He was admitted immediately and had surgery the next morning. The doctor cut the entire burn out of his arm, leaving an eight-inch scar. I thought he must have been on drugs to endure the pain, but later he said he did it completely sober and had used a cigar instead of a cigarette!

I don't remember how I learned that Addie's parents were getting a divorce. Lamar rediscovered his high school sweetheart and rekindled the flame. He sent Mildred and the children away to Florida to live with Mildred's relatives, penniless. Addie graduated from high school in Florida, and Matt accepted that he was gay but kept it secret. When he was little, we sometimes called him queer. Perhaps that became a self-fulfilling prophecy for him. Matt was very handsome, with beautiful green eyes and pretty skin. Although smaller than his three brothers, with his hairy chest and full beard he looked masculine enough, but his demeanor made people think he was gay. I don't think that he ever dated a girl, but all the girls loved him. After Matt and Addie graduated, they eventually left their mother in Florida and moved back to Texas.

I began to hear more dramatic stories about Pinky. She had become archenemies with Rita Mobley, a popular girl at school. Her mother worked with Pinky's mother at the department store. Mrs. Mobley bragged about her popular daughter and made snide remarks to Mrs. Deluca about Pinky's reputation. Soon Pinky decided she had heard enough of the woman's gossip. One evening, Pinky went to the store to confront Mrs. Mobley. Before the woman could get away, Pinky lit into her like a bolt of lightning and wouldn't stop. She pulled her hair, threw her on the gravel in the parking lot, and kicked and slapped her repeatedly. Pinky did to Rita's mother everything she really wanted to enact upon her own mother. The store management called the police, and Pinky went to the police station. Since she was a juvenile, no charges were filed. Pinky treated it like a day of glory, but her mother was ashamed. Rita told everybody at school, but Pinky didn't care. She started getting into fights at school and was expelled a couple of times. As her mother became increasingly critical of her, her delinquency increased.

At a parade to celebrate Texas City's incorporation, I spotted Pinky across the street. With Ben in my arms, I made my way over to talk to her. Her appearance reflected what I had heard about her. Her tight silky skirt clung to her hips and revealed the top of her thighs. A form-fitted stretch blouse was unzipped down to the start of her cleavage. When she saw me she smiled from ear to ear.

"Hi Rose! Haven't seen you in so long. Let me see the baby. Oh, he's so cute! I can't believe you are actually married and have a baby. You don't look like you have had a baby."

"Thanks. You look pretty sexy yourself!" I said looking conspicuously at her as the noisy band passed in front of us. "Pinky, remember the last time they had this celebration, ten years ago for the fifty year jubilee?"

"Oh, yeah, I remember. That was September 11, 1961 when hurricane Carla hit and we all evacuated. It ruined everything in our house. Do you know that I slept in a baby bed in my parents' room until then? I didn't get my own room and a regular bed until after the storm."

"You mean you were seven years old and still sleeping in a baby bed?"

"Yes. I ate all the paint off the edges of that baby bed before it was thrown away."

"You probably got lead poisoning, Pinky! It's hard to believe ten years have passed since that storm."

Pinky was eager to get back to a discussion of my marriage. "Do you like being married?"

"No, not really, but I love my little boy. I miss doing teenage things. I can't just take off to the beach with friends now that I have a baby," I replied. "Besides, Bud and I don't really seem suited for each other. We're growing farther and farther apart."

"I don't blame you. I would hate to be tied down with a baby and husband now."

"Who are you dating?" I asked.

"Do you promise not to tell?"

"Sure, I promise, but what's the big secret?"

"He's sort of dating someone else, and I don't want her to find out."

"Oh, you are seeing him behind her back?"

"Yeah, and she's my best friend."

"Well, Pinky, that's no way to treat a friend."

"I know, Rose. I feel awful about it but I'm in love with him."

"Darn, now I'm really curious. Who in the world is he?" I asked.

"J.D. Diego. He's dating Barbara Ann, you know."

"Yeah, I know. Are you guys doing it?"

"You better believe it. Every time we have the chance."

I laughed. "Aren't you afraid Barbara is going to find out you're getting it on with J.D.?"

"Maybe she will, but I hope not. I can't resist him, Rose. He's hung like a horse, and I love sex with him." She rolled her eyes back in her head, and panted as if she were having an orgasm. She then gave me a graphic demonstration of the size of his penis. I laughed and said that was more information than I needed. She always made me laugh.

"Well, you better be careful, Pinky. It sounds like you're playing with fire." I had heard that Pinky's promiscuity was an attraction at parties. She used sex to get attention. After a date with Pinky, the boys bragged to each other in the locker room. A story went around that she was the only girl at an all-boy party. She performed with one boy while the others looked on. I felt sorry for her. Because of her reputation, J.D. would not date her openly, but he enjoyed her behind his prim and proper girlfriend's back.

By Thanksgiving Pinky was pregnant. Desperate, she blamed the pregnancy on a boy who had joined the military and was stationed in Hawaii. She quit school and convinced her parents to pay her way to Hawaii to confront him. He didn't know she was pregnant. When she got off the plane, he took one look at her protruding belly and put her on the next plane home. Needless to say, none of her suitors came forward to claim the prize. Pinky came home, awaited the birth of her baby and faced the humiliation with her parents. The pregnancy curtailed her promiscuity for a while.

CHAPTER XIII

Changing Colors

Ben was a year old when Bud and I graduated from high school. My mother brought him to the ceremony. That day I won a $200 Rotary Scholarship that probably changed the course of my life. I never thought about continuing my education until one teacher encouraged me to apply for the scholarship. A new community college had just been built in Texas City and was a convenient place for me to use the small stipend, so I started the next fall. Bud had no interest in going to college. His parents offered to pay for his tuition and books, but he declined. Nothing could stop me from going. My mother agreed to keep Ben for me while I was at school.

Pinky gave birth to a baby boy. She adored her little Jobe, and so did her parents. When I visited her, we held each other's babies and compared them. She said she didn't want to hang around Texas City much longer and would leave as soon as she could find a way out. I thought it would be good for her to leave and start a new life.

"Pinky, who is his father?" I asked, hoping she would be honest.

"I can't say."

"Is it J.D.?" I prodded.

She paused for a minute. "Yes, but he won't admit it because he's still dating Barbara."

I wasn't sure I believed her.

"Pinky, does your dad still molest you?"

"No, not any more."

"When did he stop?"

Looking up to the ceiling, reluctant to reveal more than she wanted, she responded, "Oh, a long time ago."

"Did he ever penetrate you, Pinky?"

She looked down. "No, he just played with me."

Because she didn't look me in the eye, I suspected she was lying.

Pinky loved and adored little Jobe, but she wasn't ready to be tied down. She wanted to get away from Texas City, from responsibility, from her mother, her father, her life. She felt like a prisoner. She wanted to run-anywhere with anyone to anyplace. She wanted to see neon lights, drive fancy cars, and travel to exotic places. Pinky lived in a dream world, hoping some rich man would sweep her off her feet and give her all the things she wanted. She fantasized and lied constantly. Sometimes she convinced herself her fantasies were true. She would rather tell a lie than the truth, but I could tell when she was lying. She was confused about men, sex, lust, love, money, and responsibility. Before little Jobe was a year old, Pinky got her wish. She ran away with a man she met at a party in Houston.

She told no one she was leaving. She left a note for her parents asking them to take care of Jobe. They were so angry they disowned her and filed suit to take away her maternal rights. They sued for guardianship, because they knew Pinky was unstable. Pinky's lover paid a lawyer to defend her, and she retained her rights as a mother; but her parents became Jobe's legal guardians. In an argument outside the courtroom she blurted out her secret.

"It is high time you knew that Dad molested me all of my life, Mother! How does that make you feel?"

Her mother slapped her face and called her a liar.

"You can slap me if you want, but that doesn't take away the fact that it happened. Maybe if you had taken care of him in the bedroom he wouldn't have turned to me!" •

After that her mother quit speaking to her. Her father had to mediate visits between Jobe and Pinky. After some time, Pinky began to miss her mother and tried to get close to her again, she sent letters, presents, and flowers–but they all went into the trash unopened.

Her father adamantly denied her claim insisting, she was out of her mind. Everyone knew Pinky lied a lot, so it was not hard to call her a liar. Even when she told the truth, most people didn't believe her. Her father taught her to lie. Pinky told me about the courthouse brawl with her mother and we talked more about her sexual abuse. When her father first started molesting her, he told her that all fathers did those things with their little girls.

"This is what fathers are supposed to do to teach their daughters about their body parts," he said. "You can't tell anyone our secret or you will get into big trouble. These things are not to be discussed with anyone, not even your mother." She didn't want to betray him, so she kept the secret. Only when she asked her cousins if their fathers played similar games with them and they responded with abhorrence did she realize her father had lied to her.

After Jobe was born, Mr. and Mrs. Deluca quit drinking and became deeply religious. They turned their lives around and attended the Baptist Church across the street from their house. Like my parents, they were excellent grandparents. Jobe grew up in a very good environment and had the best of care. Pinky told everyone in town that J.D. was Jobe's father, but he denied it. I saw J.D. at the gas station one day and asked him if he was the father.

"Look, Rose, if he was my baby, I would claim him. But he's not my baby. I went away to college that fall, and Pinky got pregnant in October. I was never home from college, so I didn't see Pinky during the entire semester, not until the Christmas break, and by that time she was already pregnant." He seemed frustrated that she blamed him, but Pinky loved J.D. and wanted to believe the baby belonged to the man she loved.

Pinky was young and beautiful and she did whatever it took to get what she needed. She moved to Dallas and became a model–living life in the fast lane, snorting cocaine, participating in orgies, dancing nude at parties, and experimenting with lesbianism. At a wild party in Dallas where the guests had their choice of drugs served on hors d'oeuvres platters she was introduced to same-sex lovemaking. While she lay drunk on a sofa, a man kissed her and blocked her view from onlookers. Her dress was pushed up, and someone began giving her oral sex. Only when she burst into orgasm did she realize a woman had pleasured her. She sat up, pushed the man kissing her aside, and looked the woman right in the face. The woman smiled at her, and Pinky's only response was, "Hello, Lady!" Pinky toyed with bi-sexual behavior for many years after that first experience.

Even though I deeply regretted my marriage, I did not want to give up on it or fail as mother and wife. Though many times I felt like running away like Pinky. Young and inexperienced, I continued to hope. Bud had a new job at a chemical plant thirty miles from our home. Since he would not attend college, his parents gave us the money they had saved for his education. That, together with his new salary, gave us enough for a down payment on a new car. When the fall semester began, I drove Bud to and from work, took the baby to my mother, went to school, did all the housework, took care of the family, did homework, and maintained a high grade point average. Bud worked an eight-hour shift and did absolutely nothing else. He expected me to take care of him as well as the house. He was content to sit back and let me handle it all. The more capable I grew, the more incapable he became.

I made the honor roll and was elected to the student council. I loved opening my mind to new subjects and philosophies. While my horizons broadened, Bud grew increasingly narrow-minded. Where I was assertive, he was passive. I enjoyed the opportunities that change brought, but he was content to stagnate. I was ambitious; he was unmotivated. I wanted to learn, and he was satisfied in ignorance. He enjoyed hunting, fishing, and watching sports on television. Bud's immaturity and inadequacies embarrassed me. He looked helpless, dependent, almost crippled. Ironically, his helplessness attracted others to him. He failed at everything he tried. I became stronger to compensate for his weakness. I hated my role.

As my disrespect for him increased I started to suspect it was all an act. 'Nobody can be this helpless,' I thought. Was he acting like a crippled male to gain power over me and force me to organize my life around his inadequacies and insufficiencies? Somehow I felt needed, but the need wasn't healthy or constructive; it was destructive. Bud was pathologically needy. He assessed friendships by how well others met his all-encompassing needs. We had no flexibility or variety, and my life was totally dedicated to his care. I was nurse, social worker, housemaid, and business manager. His weakness controlled me, and I enabled it. Deep down we resented each other.

As time went on, our behavior toward each other grew worse. He tried to improve his self-image by degrading me, and I reciprocated. As my progress threatened him, he began displaying his temper more frequently. Most people didn't know about Bud's temper. A few saw it, his parents knew it, and I took the brunt of it. Once in action, it was almost uncontrollable. Although life was hard and our marriage was a mess, I didn't shroud myself in depression and despair. Instead, I saw misfortunes as challenges to be met and overcome.

Our mindset toward each other didn't progress after we married. Although our interactions and behavior with others developed and matured, we were teenagers so we acted like the children that we were and frequently argued. I resented taking care of him. We had absolutely no intimacy. We couldn't talk openly or let each other think, feel, or believe differently without trying to change or fix each other. I missed the intimacy more than I missed love. He quit exercising and got fat, which turned me off. We had no romance, and sex was uninteresting. We fantasized about others. I felt strongly that Bud had been unfaithful which prompted his mistreatment of me.

I did everything to please Bud, but to no avail. I chopped off my hair when he showed me a magazine cover with a pretty young blonde with very short hair he thought was gorgeous. I thought if I wore my hair like hers, he might find me attractive. He still howled over other girls and never said a kind word to me. I turned him off as much as he turned me off. Our mutual frustration turned into verbal abuse, sometimes physical abuse. Once we were in the car with our baby, and Bud saw a pretty girl. He hung his head out the window and howled like a wolf.

"Hey, Baby, you're looking good!" He blew her a kiss. I couldn't believe it! The girl looked at him with disgust. I wanted to die of embarrassment. Could I have expected anything else from a boy his age—young, ignorant, and foolish? Even I knew better than to act like a fool. I wanted to hide. When I chided him, he got angry and called me names.

To get even I told him I found other guys attractive. I knew men thought I was pretty, even if he didn't. He put me down all the time. He acted jealous because of my ambition. He spoke positively about others but never about me. I had seen that before. Although, statistically our marriage was doomed, I wanted desperately to prove we could make it. Ours would be the exception among young marriages. 'This one must work,' I told myself. 'We will prove statistics wrong.'

CHAPTER XIV

The Dentist

During the second semester at college, I drove to my mother's house after school to pick up Ben and found forty plain-clothes officers and police surrounding the house with guns drawn. I wanted to get my son out of that house.

"What in the world is happening?" I asked one of the officers.

"Do you live here, ma'am?" he asked.

"No. Not any more. But I have to go inside. This is my mother's house, and she is babysitting for me." I wondered if Ben was all right. My mother saw me drive up and came to the door with Ben to assure me that he was okay. She motioned me to come in. I told the policemen I was going inside. They didn't try to stop me. As I grabbed little Ben from her arms I asked, "What in the heck is going on?"

"Jessie and Matt robbed Gibson's department store and made off with about 200 guns," Mama said frantically. They broke into the store late at night and hid the guns in Jessie's pigeon coop, our former playhouse. All the guns were recovered peacefully, and the boys were hauled off in police cars. Because they were juveniles, no criminal charges were filed, although they were put on probation. To my surprise, Billy wasn't involved. Lamar tried to have Matt put in a reformatory, but Addie fought him in court. She asked the judge to let Matt go back to live with their mother in Florida. He granted her plea. Lamar was livid that his daughter had defied him, but that was Addie. She wasn't afraid to stand up to anyone, not even to her father.

Although the boys were often in trouble with the police, both learned trades that could have sustained them had they been more responsible. Lamar Patton employed Billy at his carpet shop and taught him carpet installation. He was good, but Lamar knew that he was not dependable; his addictions controlled him. Jessie traded horses while he learned how to repair heat exchangers. He was the best heat exchanger repairman in the area. He worked full-time at a Texas City refinery for several years, earning a good income. But, Billy and Jessie lived with my parents and depended on them for years.

Billy sported a huge Bandito tattoo on his right shoulder. Ricky and Billy were at a bar one evening having a beer when a rival motorcycle gang came in. Suddenly a pocketknife slid down the bar and stopped in front of Billy, compliments of one of the gang members. Billy looked over to see who tossed the knife his way. A man in sunglasses with a bandana wrapped around his long greasy hair spoke up.

"Cut that tattoo off your arm, brother," he demanded.

Knowing they were outnumbered, Billy looked at Ricky as if to ask, "Are you ready for this?" Ricky took a final swig of beer, wiped his mouth, and stood up. Billy looked back at the eight gangsters.

"Why don't you try to cut it off for me?" Billy said, reaching for the stool beneath him. Ricky grabbed a pool stick. The gang pulled their knives and started swinging while the bartender called the police. Ricky and Billy got in several good hits but were about to be overpowered. They ran outside, through fields and over fences, to escape with their lives.

As they ran Ricky yelled to Billy, "By God I think they broke my arm!"

"Well, I know they broke my jaw!"

Ricky gesticulated. "Hell, we would have been better off if you had just cut that damn tattoo off your arm!"

"I'll remember that when we meet someone who orders you to cut your tattoo off your chest!" Billy responded trying to hold his jaw in place while hightailing it.

They never looked back until they were sure they were safe and out of the sight of that gang. Both recognized they could have been killed. They were clearly outnumbered but would not back down.

Even at their most macho moments, they admitted they were scared that night. Ricky didn't have a broken arm, but Billy had to have his jaw wired for six weeks and almost starved to death during that time.

At the end of my first college year, Bud and I bought a little doll-house. I took a year off from school to work and help pay for the house, an older home, totally remodeled with shag carpet, vinyl floors, new cabinets, and a screened patio. The cedar shake siding was painted yellow, and the roof was brand new.

Dean Ray and my sister had come home when he completed his military service. They sold us their colonial furniture to furnish our little house. Buying a house was quite an accomplishment for two people our age. Left to Bud, we would never have moved from his parents' house. Soon after moving into our new home, Bud and I had a fight during which he admitted that many of the rumors my girlfriends had told to me about him doing things behind my back were true. I fell on the floor crying. I was so hysterical. In anger, he kicked me with his steel-toed boots. Something went out of me that night. Whatever glimmer of hope I had of our marriage surviving, whatever semblance of affection remained between us, was blotted out in that instant. I knew I could never love Bud, I never had. I no longer wanted to prove that we would defy predictions by staying together at all cost. I didn't really know what love was, but I had finally figured out what it was not. Bud was despicable; I no longer wanted to be married to him. Subconsciously, I began to plot my escape.

That summer brought an energy crisis to America. A year earlier gasoline was forty cents a gallon. Now it was twice that. Motorists waited in long lines at gas stations. The country was in recession and I would be lucky to find a job.

I saw a "Help Wanted" ad for a dental assistant position in Galveston newspaper with the line, "no experience necessary." The dentist, Dr. Jamison, said that since nobody he interviewed had any experience, he would hire the prettiest applicant. He chose me. Our son was two years old and stayed with our neighbor when I went to work.

I was forewarned about Dr. Jamison's womanizing and his jealous wife. He was thirty-eight-years old and very handsome, and I was nervous around him. Naive about workplace behavior, I fumbled and fouled in the professional environment. I thought for a while he would fire me, but eventually I became more comfortable.

After about six months, Dr. Jamison closed the office for a day to let the office staff attend a dental convention in Houston. On the second day of the convention, he asked me to meet him for breakfast and told me to tell the others I had a doctor's appointment. I suspected he was making a pass at me, but he had shown no previous romantic inclination toward me. I thought he might give me a performance review and a salary increase. It didn't take me long to figure out he wasn't interested in my performance in the office. He wanted to evaluate my performance in bed. I felt a little flattered that a man of his maturity would be interested in me, even though we were both married. 'Why should anyone be interested in me?'

Dr. Jamison had broad shoulders and narrow hips and was the best-dressed man on the island. I was attracted to him though he was twice my age. That morning at breakfast, after some flirtatious conversation, he asked if we could get a room at the hotel. I said no. I told him I had never even seen any man undressed other than Bud, not even in a picture. We drove back to Galveston together, and he held my hand. Then he made an unexpected turn down a dirt road. When I asked where he was going, he said he wanted to kiss me. My heart started to beat faster. I wanted to tell him we should go back, but I did not know how. He was my boss, and I was afraid of losing my job.

Things were happening so quickly I could not think of anything to say. He kept driving. I froze when he stopped the car and turned off the engine. He looked at me and pulled me close to him. I loved the way he kissed me, but the next thing I knew he was pulling and tugging on my belt and trying to get my pants off. Struggling to keep them on, I told him that he was scaring me and that I had never done anything like that before. He unzipped his trousers, looking desperate to touch me. He pulled my pants down enough to expose my tan line. Suddenly, he had a strange look on his face. He pulled a handkerchief from his pocket and wiped his hand. I didn't know what had happened. We learned about premature ejaculation in sex education class, but I had never seen it before. We were both embarrassed. He apologized, and I tried to convince myself it hadn't happened.

The next day at work he asked me how I felt. I said, "I felt bad—and I felt good." I felt bad for moral reasons, and I felt good to know someone desired me. I justified my action as repayment for Bud's dishonesty.

When Addie learned I was working for a dentist, she phoned for an appointment to have her front teeth straightened. Instead of getting braces, she had crowns applied to her front teeth. I was delighted to see her. We talked in the waiting room for a while about my parents and my brothers. She told me I looked like a nurse in my white uniform. Even when I had not seen her for years, Addie and I could pick up right where we left off as if we had never been apart. She rejected the church when her father and mother divorced and never went back. I was inactive, but I didn't feel badly toward the Church. She couldn't believe I was a mother.

"How is your dad doing with his new bride?" I asked.

"Oh, I don't suppose he is any happier than he was before. He complains about everything. He certainly never does anything to help my mother or his kids. But I have to admit I do like his new wife. She is a nice lady. Mother says she feels sorry for her for having to put up with Dad!"

"What about Matt? Where is he?" I asked.

"He moved to San Francisco to pursue his interest in art," she responded.

"It's sad to see how everything changes so fast, isn't it, Addie?"

"Yes, especially for you, Rose. I still can't believe you got married so young. Is it working out?"

"I don't know, Addie. Not really."

"Well, I'm sorry. You know what they say about young marriages. I want to see your little boy. I bet he's darling."

"He is, Addie. He is."

"Rose, I've been thinking about why you married so young. I think you got married just to get away from your house."

"Oh, I'm sure you're right. It wasn't much fun there."

"Do you remember when we were little and I tried to make you hug your dad one day and you just couldn't do it?" She asked.

"Yeah, I remember."

"Have you ever hugged him or your mom since then?"

"No. Our family just isn't like that. I know that you always hugged your parents even after they made you mad, but I never could."

"I am not sure it matters," she replied, "your parents are still together and mine aren't."

I led her to the dental chair and hung a napkin on a chain around her neck. Dr. Jamison came in and explained that she needed braces.

"Oh, no. That takes too long, and I'm too old for braces."

"Well, we will just have to cap them then."

I think Addie sensed my attraction to Dr. Jamison. When he left the operatory, she grinned sheepishly and asked, "Rose, has Dr. Jamison ever tried to seduce you?" She knew me too well for me to try to hide anything from her.

"Shhhh! Addie, be quiet. He might walk back in."

"No, he won't. He has tried, hasn't he?"

I didn't answer at first. "Yes, he has tried, Addie, but he has a problem in that department."

"What do you mean, Rose? Do you mean he's impotent?"

"Almost. I mean . . . he might just as well be impotent. The poor sucker can't get it out of his pants before he comes!"

"Gross! Rose, you mean he goes off prematurely?"

"Yeah, something like that."

"Gross! Isn't he twice your age anyway?"

"Yes, he's thirty-eight, and I'm only nineteen. I guess that is what happens to men when they get old, Addie."

"Yeah, maybe so. He's a dirty, old man, but he's a good looking, dirty, old man!" she added.

We cracked up. She never judged me, so I felt that I could be honest with her. Dr. Jamison came back and found us giggling.

"What's so funny, girls?"

I answered his question before Addie had the chance. "We were just talking about Pinky, our friend from the old neighborhood."

"We were?" Addie asked with surprise.

"Yes. We were!"

"Who is Pinky?" he asked.

"She's a real funny girl from our old neighborhood. We grew up together, but she moved away to find the lifestyle of the rich and famous. Now *there's* a character for you, Dr. Jamison," I told him.

"Oh, really! Where does she live now?" he asked.

"I haven't heard from her for a while. The last I heard she was in Dallas."

"What's she doing in Dallas?" Addie asked.

I shrugged and said, "I guess she's doing Dallas. You know how she is–she's a wild and crazy girl."

"She picked out all her eyelashes when she was little!" Addie told Dr. Jamison.

"But she let them grow back as soon as she moved away from home," I added.

"Is she good looking?" he asked in a sexy voice.

Addie interjected, "Yeah, she's pretty. She's young, pretty, funny, and a wild and crazy thing. You would probably like her, Dr. Jamison."

"It sounds like I would," he said laughing, "but why would you assume I like pretty, young, wild things?"

"Just instinct, I suppose," she replied just as he told her to open her mouth wide. I stuffed a tongue protector, two cotton rolls, and a saliva suction syringe into her mouth to keep her from saying another word. Addie was very outspoken and said whatever she felt like saying, and I was afraid she might ask if he liked to seduce young women. While he drilled her teeth she kept her big, blue eyes open, looking him directly in the face. I could almost hear what she was thinking, humming, singing, as she stared at him, *You dirty, old man, you dirty, old man, you good-looking, dirty, old man, you good-looking, dirty, old, premature ejaculating man!*

Later, I told Bud about the encounter with my boss because I wanted to hurt him as he had hurt me. I hoped my confession would make him want a divorce, but he wasn't hurt. His reaction was totally different from what I expected. As I told him the sordid details he smiled and became aroused. I couldn't believe it. He was delighted I had been with another man. I thought he was perverted to get a hard-on over my confession. His reaction substantiated what I found out years later; he had already had other flings. He never suggested discussing it with Dr. Jamison, nor did he ask me to quit my job or demand an apology. He just giggled like the child he was. I felt bad for Dr. Jamison's wife, because she knew that he was a run-around.

The doctor made a second advance, and then a third. In time, I accepted his advances, by allowing a kiss or a pinch, but we never did anything serious. He was simply incapable. I knew I was doing wrong, and I regretted lowering my standards. Some people in the office were suspicious of us, and I was growing tired of the hypocrisy. I vacillated between right and wrong until my work began to suffer. I knew I couldn't work with him much longer.

When Addie came back to get her permanent crowns, I told her about Bud's reaction to my confession. "I'm disgusted with him, and I'm planning to leave both my job and Bud. I've decided to go back to school, but I'm not sure how I'm going to make it."

Addie was sympathetic, but she didn't encourage me to stay or leave. "It's hard for me to believe that Bud didn't want to put a knot on Dr. Jamison's head after you told him that stuff."

"I know, Addie. I wished I had never married him."

I received a Joiner Scholarship that paid for books, tuition, and living expenses for two years. Having a way to support myself, I told Bud I wanted to separate and maybe divorce. He did not object, since he wanted his freedom too. We sold our house, and he took an apartment in Houston near his job.

Our parents were devastated, and my mother blamed me for the separation. "You should stay with your husband because no other man will ever love your child the way he does."

I never missed Bud for a second. I felt nothing but relief to be away from him. I told Dr. Jamison I was leaving to go back to school. He was sorry to see me go, but we both knew it was for the best. After my experience with Dr. Jamison, older men always attracted me. I felt ten years older than I was anyway, probably because the circumstances of my life propelled me forward in experience.

My three-year-old son and I moved into an old house in the bad part of town, because that was all that I could afford even with the scholarship money. It was wonderful to be free of my parents and Bud. For the first time, there was no negative control in my life. When I returned to school, I felt like a bird released from a cage. I wanted to find out who I really was. I knew myself only as my parents' daughter or Bud's wife or Ben's mother.

As a product of conditional love, disrespect, intolerance, ridicule, chaos, and dysfunction, I had neither identity nor goals. Although I had never analyzed the levels of dysfunction in my life and didn't know how I was affected emotionally, I was smart enough to figure out that the choices I made as a teen were caused by earlier events. I wanted to understand my choices and myself. Perhaps I secretly wanted to blame someone other than myself for my life, but regardless of whom I blamed, I suffered the consequences. Furthermore, I was accountable for my choices, despite who or what drove them.

Mama called me evil because I was separated from Bud and dated other men. She didn't care if Bud had treated me badly and beat me. She didn't care if I didn't love him, because she didn't love my dad and managed to stay with him through worse circumstances. She considered it my duty to stay with my husband, no matter how hopeless my life. Perhaps she was jealous that I had the opportunity to get out when she didn't. At that time, women stayed in bad marriages out of necessity since they didn't have the same job or educational opportunities as my generation. Perhaps she thought that if she could endure a marriage worse than mine, then I should be able to endure my own. My mother always said that she stayed with Dad for us. I think she always wondered if she could have found happiness by leaving him. She sacrificed her happiness and stayed with him, because she thought it was best for us.

She called to tell me Dr. Hackbarth had admitted my dad for his fifth and what would be final set of shock treatments. I was no longer prepared to accept that he had to have those treatments. None of us liked to see Dad become increasingly feeble with every set, and I wanted to talk to the man responsible for his vegetative state. Dr. Hackbarth knew my mother was too ignorant to defend my dad, but their children had reached adulthood, and I was about to get involved in his treatment. I made a call to his office.

"Dr. Hackbarth, this is Rose Murphy. I am the daughter of Henry Weaks, and I'm calling to ask if you have been educated in any form of mental therapy other than shock treatments?"

Taken aback by my directness, he told me my dad was a sick man.

I interrupted, "Yes, he's a sick man, and you're largely responsible for making him that way. Tons of shock treatments aren't good for anyone, sir! I don't have to be a doctor to figure that out. Are you by any chance collecting fees from some other source for using my father as a human guinea pig? Those shock treatments have turned him into a freaking vegetable!"

He had to be somewhat sympathetic. He knew too much about my parents to think that they could have provided anything but a miserable home life for their children. He ended our conversation by saying he would be happy to meet with me, but when I phoned a few weeks later to make the appointment, I learned he was no longer in practice. Some thing or someone caught up with him, and he was in trouble. Maybe he had a nervous breakdown himself. I never had the opportunity to meet the man who fried my father's brain. Dad was assigned a new doctor, Dr. Goodman, who never gave Dad another electric shock but treated him with medication. He also gave my dad a total mental disability discharge from his job since he was too pathetic to work. His retirement plan provided enough for him and my mother to live on for the rest of their lives.

Since my parents said they never loved each other, I asked my grandmother before she died if Mama loved Dad when they were young. She looked astonished and replied, "Yes, she did love him. Of course, she did. Don't let her fool you. He used to come courting, and she would run out to the fence to meet him before he could get to the porch. I encouraged her to marry Henry because I knew he would be a good provider."

"Well, it's hard to believe they ever loved one another, Grandma," I said.

"But they did. Believe me they did. Maybe things seem different now because they have been through so much. But there was a time when they loved each other. And they love you kids, too. I have seen your dad jump every few minutes trying to keep an eye on you kids so you wouldn't get hurt. He stayed day and night in the hospital with Billy when he was born. You may not realize it, or believe it, but they both love you kids more than anything." That was the last conversation I had with Grandma before she died.

I closed my eyes and tried to imagine a time when they dated and were happy and in love, a time when my mother was pretty, young, and alive. I imagined her at home, running to the white picket fence, her long hair blowing in the wind, to meet the dark-haired soldier returning from war. Walking side-by-side, holding hands, laughing. Roasting peanuts over coals. I imagined them slim and attractive in the swimsuits they wore in the river while tubing the rapids. Spreading a quilt and eating may-haw jelly on homemade bread from Grandma's kitchen. If they could have seen their future they wouldn't have believed their lives could turn out so pitifully. Henry visited the restaurant where she worked every day and teased her when she waited on him. She flirted. Wanda wanted children, lots of them, and Henry did not mind. He was smart, strong, and ambitious, and she knew he would be a good provider. Although his mother didn't encourage the courtship, he couldn't imagine marrying anyone else. One day, Dad came to the restaurant, sat at the bar, ordered a cup of coffee and a doughnut, and told her he was buying a car and moving to Texas City. Her face fell. She thought he was leaving her again.

"I have a job there working for an oil refinery, making pretty good money, so I have to go. There are no jobs here."

She tried to hide her disappointment. "Well, when do you leave?"

"In a week," he answered.

"I guess we won't be seeing each other much any more," she said.

"No, not unless you want to come with me," he offered.

"What do you mean, Henry?"

"I don't suppose you would want to get married, would you?"

Her face lit up. She didn't hesitate to accept his proposal and gave notice that evening that she would be leaving in a few days. They must have been excited about starting life together in a new place away from their families. But she soon regretted the decision.

CHAPTER XV
The Philanthropist

My scholarship came from The Joiner Scholarship Foundation, set up by a wealthy old Houstonian family known throughout Texas for their philanthropy. I drove to Houston to turn in the required paperwork for the scholarship. I wore periwinkle blue corduroy jeans with a tight sweater to match and boots. My hair was frosted and had grown into the shag style of the time. I did not pay much attention to the crowd of older men in three-piece suits gathered outside the door, but I learned later that Mr. Leo Joiner was one of them.

Al, Mr. Joiner's attorney, saw me in the waiting room. He thought I was pretty, so he interrupted Mr. Joiner from a very important meeting. "You have to get over here to see this beautiful girl, Leo."

"Are you insane? I am in the middle of negotiating a major contract. How good looking is she?"

"She is worth bringing the guys you're meeting with to see her," he replied.

Mr. Joiner had a thing for pretty women. He and his entourage came downstairs to the scholarship office to check out the merchandise. That evening I received a call from Al asking if I would be interested in a part-time job working for Leo Joiner while I attended college. I thought the call was strange, but I agreed to talk more about it, and we set a lunch appointment for the following day.

We met at a coffee shop. Like everyone else in Texas, I had heard of Leo Joiner, but I was not going to act impressed by his wealth or status. Leo and Al were waiting for me when I entered the shop. Leo was probably in his late forties, graying at the temples, with a stiff, left part in his barbershop haircut. He was dressed conservatively in a brown suit with a striped tie. He was surprisingly unpretentious and not at all intimidating. On the other hand, Al was fat and out of shape and looked like he enjoyed a little too much liberty at restaurants on the Joiner expense account. He wore a navy sports coat accented by a ridiculous owl-covered necktie. He proudly explained that he was a Rice University graduate, and the school mascot was the owl. He followed the Rice football team and was active in the Rice Alumni Association. Al had big eyes, and I remember thinking he looked like an owl himself. 'Al the Owl,' I giggled to myself. He did most of the talking, and I soon figured out that there was no job. They told me why they were gathered around the door when I was checking on my scholarship. Mr. Joiner seemed very interested in me and asked for a lunch date the following week. Before accepting I asked if he was married, he said that he was divorced. During lunch, models came to our table, and he offered to buy me the clothes they wore. He took me to a jewelry store and bought me a diamond ring. We shopped most of the day for window dressing befitting a woman he might date. I had never before been treated like a queen, and he knew it. I realized he was trying to buy my affection, and I told him not to expect me to repay him. He told everyone he could fall in love with me, but I was so poor and ignorant I didn't know how to respond. He probably had done this sort of thing with dozens of girls. I did not feel comfortable accepting the gifts, and before long I returned them all.

He soon invited me to join him and his business partners on a weekend trip to New Orleans. Having never flown before, I was excited. When he agreed to give me a separate room, I accepted. We traveled with Al and a man named Paul Little. Leslie, Paul's girlfriend, met us at the hotel in New Orleans. Leslie was my age, brunette, and had a great figure. Before we checked into the hotel we all had dinner. During dinner, I realized that Leslie wasn't Paul's girlfriend; she was his whore. At the hotel, I discovered I didn't have the room of my own that Mr. Joiner promised; I was booked in a room with him. Since no other rooms were available, I told him I would sleep in the chair. He begged me at least to lie next to him in the bed and promised not to touch me, but I refused. That evening, Leo answered a knock to find Leslie dressed in underwear she had just bought on Bourbon Street. When she saw I was nestled in a chair to sleep she offered to sleep with Leo, but he turned her down. We spent the night in the same room, he in the bed, I was in the chair. He realized I was not attracted to him and seemed hurt. I was thankful he didn't force himself on me.

The next morning the men attended a meeting, and Leslie came over to have breakfast with me. She told me she was bi-sexual. I was not certain what it meant, so she explained. I was afraid she was trying to encourage me, but I told her I couldn't fathom it in my wildest dreams. When Leo returned, he asked, "Well, did Leslie try to make it with you while we were gone?"

"Why didn't you tell me that she was like that, Leo? I never met a bi-sexual before."

"Well, you have now."

Leo's friends told me I could have anything that I wanted if I would be his lover, that he was crazy about me. I could travel the world or have a furnished home and a regular allowance. He liked the fact that I was not a whore and wanted a relationship with me. I still had not figured out that Leo was married, but I wasn't interested in being a kept woman. Still, we continued to date after we returned from New Orleans.

One evening we went to a Jet Set, International, swinging club with several of his friends. Though the club seemed normal, I soon realized it was a place where couples met to swap mates for an evening of casual sex. No one explained that to me, and I was oblivious to what was happening when three other couples in their mid-thirties came to our table. They were friendly, and I thought it was nice when one of the men invited everyone to his Houston pent house apartment.

Within minutes after arriving, everyone was smoking cigars, dancing, and drinking. About an hour later, I noticed that several people were no longer in the room. Before long, I was alone, sitting on the couch. On my way to the bathroom, I looked into the bedroom. Naked people were crawling all over each other like a bunch of snakes. I was at an orgy! I didn't know what to do. I walked back to the living room and looked down twenty-five floors at the city lights below. My haunting Mormon morals engulfed me. 'What are you doing here?' I asked myself. With no money for a cab, I hid behind an overstuffed chair.

Eventually the host came out with a towel around his waist and sat in the chair. He was surprised when I peered at him from behind the chair. He laughed. "What are you doing behind my chair?"

"I am not going in that snake pit. Is Leo in that room, too?"

"Yes, I think so."

Before long Leo emerged from the room, naked with his appendage dangling between his legs. "Where's Rose?" he asked.

"Put a towel around your waist so I can talk to you, Leo." I spouted.

"I don't have one," he replied.

"Well, then I won't talk to you."

"What if I put my pants on? Will that work?" he asked, stuffing his legs into his pants.

"Yes, but why didn't you tell me you were bringing me to an orgy?"

"How was I to know the party was going to get a little wild?"

"You knew it, Leo. I'm beginning to think you have lied to me about other stuff, too."

After a while the men came out of the bedroom and left the women to play. Leo knew I was uncomfortable.

"Rose, why don't you just relax and let yourself go. You know what your problem is? You're frigid!"

"I am?"

"Yes, I'm certain of it. You probably have never had an orgasm in your life, have you?"

"I don't know."

"Believe me, Rose, if you don't know, then the answer is no!"

I didn't know it then, but he was right. Many years would pass before I knew the true joy of lovemaking.

One of the women came out of the room, approached me, and began rubbing my arm. "Why weren't you in the bedroom with the rest of us? I would have noticed you if you'd been there."

"She's not into this scene," Leo told her. She gave me a dirty look and walked away. I knew men liked easy women only for a casual toss, and I knew from my experience with Dr. Jamison that I didn't like being second. My refusal to participate seemed to enchant the men, since that set me apart from the others. Before long two women, a red head and a brunette, sat together on the couch and began kissing and caressing each other. I couldn't believe my eyes. I had never seen such open sexual behavior. Leo watched enthusiastically, and I tried to act like I wasn't there. Everyone in the room but me was accustomed to such things. I was glad when the evening was over.

After learning that Mr. Joiner was truly married, I confronted him. "Why did you lie to me, Leo?"

"I didn't lie. I said that I was divorced, and I was divorced. I have just remarried since my divorce."

"You're clever, but a lie is a lie, and I don't like liars. I don't want to see you again." I never did anything sexual with him. I suppose I could have had an easier life as a rich man's whore, but I couldn't do it. I had tinkered with infidelity with Dr. Jamison, so why not with one of the richest men in Texas? Young girls judge almost everything in relationships in physical terms. They rarely look beyond the flesh to discover the hidden qualities in a man. With all his flaws, Leo had a better heart than the dentist. When I entertained sexual advances, I felt guilty, so I avoided them . . . but not always. At times I defied my conscience, and was not always circumspect.

That Christmas, I filed for divorce, and it was granted in February. I spent the college year in a reverie. I was tired, very tired. I felt guilty for not spending more time with my son. I dated a lot of different guys, had parties and went to parties; smoked marijuana once, hated it; went to class, learned new philosophies, played racquetball, and took gymnastics. I thought I should date every man who asked me out rather than risk hurting his feelings. My priorities were all screwed up. I didn't know how to be selective in dating, because I had no criteria to base my decisions. I wandered and drifted without direction, going nowhere.

Living a very busy life as a single woman, I gave motherhood a low priority. I met Ben's baby needs, and he had a very good babysitter. Still, I wasn't there for him the way I should have been. 'I am no different from my mother,' I thought. I was spinning out of control.

Trying to discover who I was, I learned only who I wasn't. I tried to find what I wanted from life, but I found what I did not want. I didn't know how to act or where to turn. My parents certainly weren't a resource. Every encounter with men taught me that love was not real and life was not meant to be happy. Discouraged and impatient, I thought every man I dated wanted only to use me. I thought I would find happiness if I got out of my marriage. I thought I would find happiness if I didn't live at home with my parents. I didn't give myself enough time to steady my course or discover who I was and what I wanted out of life. I had no confidence. I needed a plan, a guide, something or someone to balance me, to lead me in the right direction—but I had nothing and no one. I lived from one day to the next, going nowhere. I felt like I was drowning, dying, slowly. I needed a rope.

CHAPTER XVI
Shot Three Times

My divorce was final only a few weeks when I received a call from Billy's girlfriend, Nancy, late at night. Nancy calmly told me my mother had just been robbed at the convenience store where she worked.

"Well, is everything okay?" I asked.

"No, Rose. I am sorry to tell you that your mother was shot."

"Shot? Oh, no!"

"Rose, the robber shot her three times. She's in critical condition."

I hung up and left for the hospital immediately. When I got there, I learned that a teenage boy, who had worked at the store and was fired two weeks earlier for stealing, shot her, once in the chest and twice in the back. He came in, head covered in pantyhose, while Mama was on duty. He wanted to steal money from the cash register. She gave him the money, but when he started to leave she followed him, yelling that she recognized him and was going to call the police. The boy turned and shot her. She fell to the ground, and he put two more bullets into her back and left her for dead. I thought I should cry or be upset, but I felt numb. I put my face in my hands and tried to act the way I was supposed to, but I felt nothing. How could I be so callous?

As soon as she regained consciousness, she asked for a blessing by Mormon elders. She believed the power of the priesthood could heal her. She was still in intensive care when Bishop Smith arrived and gave his blessing. No bullet struck her heart, but her lungs, spleen, and liver were damaged. When she came out of surgery and we were allowed to visit, I could not bring myself to touch her. I just looked at her. She was asleep from the anesthesia and did not see my lack of emotion. Although I was sorry she underwent such trauma, I just couldn't hug her. I had never hugged her before and felt awkward even in the face of death.

She spent six weeks in the hospital, three of them in intensive care, and I visited her once a week. She told my sister that all of her children hugged her, except me. I felt guilty, so on my next visit I forced myself to kiss her cheek. I wondered if my siblings cringed when they touched her. Hadn't we all been raised in the same household and had the same treatment? Hadn't we all witnessed the same mutual spousal abuse? Had their conduct not shamed us all? How could they forget the atrocities?' I wanted to be more like them but I couldn't. They must have had more forgiving hearts in them than I had in me.

I took Ben to church while Mama was in the hospital. The bishop noticed me and called me into his office to inquire about my mother's progress. He also asked about my life. I told him about my divorce and dating. I explained that I had struggled to find hope, and now I felt lost. Bishop Smith realized I was in trouble, and he helped me. Gradually, he led me back to the Church. He was my counselor, my friend, my father, and my Good Samaritan. He was the rope and life vest that I needed, and I longed for his help and guidance. He promised that if I lived by the commandments I would find a worthy man with whom I could marry in the temple for time and eternity. Mormons believe that marriages can be forever, not only until death. All Latter-Day Saints hope for a temple marriage. He visited my mother, and also my father, my brothers, and Mary Jane. He was an excellent representative of Jesus Christ.

Although born into a Mormon household, I knew nothing about the Church. I knew nothing about the *Book of Mormon*, modern revelation, or Joseph Smith, but I wanted to learn so I read the *Book of Mormon*. I loved the book and appreciated the gospel teachings that I derive from it. I cherished the serenity, the peace, the spirit, and comfort I gained while reading and pondering its message. I believed that Christ visited the American continent after his resurrection and that a record of his visit had been preserved and translated into English by

Joseph Smith. The priesthood, the authority to act in God's name, had been restored, after being lost when the apostles died. The gospel answered many questions for me: Where did I come from? Why am I here on Earth? What will happen to me when I die? I wanted Christ in my life and in my son's life. The Church's perfect organization and its wonderful programs for women and men, families, youth, and children amazed me. The Church was a stabilizing force and gave purpose to my life. I repented and became meek, forgiving, and loving toward everyone. I yearned for a family life like my bishop's.

When my mother was released from the hospital she began attending church again. It took a bullet through her heart to make her stop attending church, and three bullets to bring her back. Saved from almost certain death, she felt the Lord had preserved her for a purpose. She promised she would serve him the rest of her life. My mother and I began treating each other differently. We both had been humbled and began relating to one another with the Church as our common bond. Having experienced my own difficulties in marriage and motherhood, I was less judgmental than I was previously. She watched as I gained a testimony of the gospel, became spiritual, and accepted leadership positions in the Church. She glowed with approval, but something was missing. I wanted a husband to complete our family circle. Mama said no other man could love my son the way Bud did and encouraged me to go back to him. She said Bud would join the Church, and with the Church in our lives we could succeed in marriage. I was convinced that if I lived the gospel, all would be well. The gospel could solve anything, so I considered taking Bud back into my life.

I told Bud about the Church. He could see the changes in my spirit and attitude, and he wanted the same satisfaction in his life. He took the missionary lessons and was converted. I told the bishop I was considering giving my marriage to Bud another chance. He knew I didn't love Bud and I could tell he thought it would be a mistake but he said nothing against it. My mother convinced me we would succeed and be happy if we lived the commandments and raised our family in the Church. I soon learned, however, that spiritual conversion and the desire for a worthy life do not compensate for the absence of love in marriage.

I found Bud's tender side again, that part of him that originally attracted me to him. I saw him mature in the Church and hold callings of responsibility. Unfortunately, I confused compassion and love. I thought that with God's help Bud would cultivate his good aspects and suppress his negative side. If he did, my feelings about him would improve, and we could make it. We deserved a second chance, and this time would be different. The Lord would be with us. Now at only twenty-years-old, we remarried.

That summer, Bud and I attended a family reunion with my mother's family at a farm in Jasper, Texas. The last time I saw that part of the family I was twelve years old. Picnic tables bore ham, baked beans, potato salad, watermelon, homemade pickles, bread, jams, and sweet cakes. Old men entertained us with fiddles, harmonicas, and banjos, while children threw horseshoes or played croquet. Everyone was glad to see my mother, because they heard she had been shot.

I walked across the grounds where my mother was seated with great aunts, uncles, and distant cousins. Nearby were Aunt Beverly and my cousin, Sue Ellen, in a red checked dress; her little girls were dressed in matching dresses. Sue Ellen had curly, jet-black hair, ivory skin, black eyes and ruby red lips. When she smiled her gums showed just a little. She always maintained a slim figure and seemed to stand in pose as if awaiting a photographer to take her picture. As I approached, a man addressed me boisterously, "Who are you?"

My mother answered, "Oh, she's my younger daughter, Rose."

"Well, she is absolutely beautiful! She is absolutely beautiful!"

His enthusiasm embarrassed me, and I braced myself for my mother's usual objection. Surprisingly, she showed pride instead of anger. I was astonished. Later she asked if I had noticed Aunt Beverly and Sue Ellen's jealous expressions. I lied when I said, "No." I don't remember if Sue Ellen and I spoke that day, but I remember that she and Aunt Beverly looked at me a lot. She competed with my sister's voice in the past; now she conceived a new rivalry with my looks. I asked Bud if he thought Sue Ellen was pretty, and he said, "No." I told him that all our lives Mama told us she was the prettiest girl ever, so we all accepted it. He looked at me unbelievingly and said, "Well, she's not my type!" Those words would come back to haunt him.

Sue Ellen's husband was now a successful lawyer, and they were a wealthy family. On the other hand, Bud and I barely made ends meet. Although Sue Ellen did not disclose her marital problems to me, I later discovered she was as miserable in her marriage as I was in mine. Religious commitment can enhance a healthy, loving marriage with a solid foundation, but religion is no substitute for love. In time both our houses would fall from the lack of human intimacy.

Although our experiences in the Church matured us and filled our lives with wholesome practices, the Church was never enough. We read scriptures together, went to church meetings, held various responsibilities, and were missionaries to others. Bud could be deeply spiritual and humble at times, and the Church brought out the best in him. I gloried in my testimony of the Church and hungered for religious knowledge. The Church became my substitute for love and happiness, but it could not change my co-dependency or cure his crippled syndrome. It could not give Bud ambition or appease our abusive tempers. Although we were both happy in the gospel, we were unhappy together. Even so, we were sealed in the temple, believing that if we acted long enough, we would achieve happiness, like the other couples we saw in the church.

CHAPTER XVII

The Test of Time

During the seven years since our remarriage, Bud and I had two more children, Molly and Seth. Bud worked and did his church duties; I worked part time and was a good mother.

"Mommy, can I have some toast?" I pulled myself away from my reverie to listen to my daughter. Ben had already left for school.

"Yes, Molly, I'll make you some toast." My children were so beautiful. I determined to sacrifice my happiness and keep our family together at all costs. Bud squeezed his way into the small kitchen and poured a bowl of cereal. He sat with Molly and Seth and tried to look cheerful. We were waiting for a private time to have a discussion. I did not know what the outcome would be. Could I, should I leave him again?

My children had seen physical violence between Bud and me. When he worked the midnight shift, he was especially short-tempered. I was ashamed to expose my children to the parental fighting that plagued me. Bud practiced unrighteous dominion over me. When he attacked me, I fought back, but since he was twice my size, I didn't have much chance. I never discussed the abuse with the bishop because, like many abused women, I feared it was my fault. I discussed Bud's behavior with my mother, and she told me to forgive him seventy times seven. To be a good Christian I had to forgive him, which meant overlooking his assaults on my spirit. Further, it meant I was not entitled to my anger. Forgiveness cannot erase psychological and emotional wounds. I told my mother I didn't believe domestic violence was included in the biblical seventy times seven, since God never intended anyone to suffer physical and emotional indignity.

I tried to make myself happy in our family circle, but I knew I would never be complete, no matter how many children I had or how much I prayed or how much I was involved in the Church. None of those could make me love Bud. His dependency controlled my choices, and his salary controlled my loyalty. Since he had a good salary and I didn't, he thought he could treat me any way and suffer no consequences. Although I might fight back, yell and scream, I knew and he knew that with no means of support, I had to stay with him. Texas City was a dying town, and I was dying with it. All the businesses on Sixth Street closed, including the Showboat Theater. By the time I was excommunicated, I wanted to get away from Bud, the town, the Church, the neighborhood, everyone.

I dressed the children and sent them to the backyard with carrots to feed the rabbit. We kept many of the children's toys on the screened back porch, which had ice cream parlor chairs and tables. The children played there for hours. I watched them from the sliding glass door, wondering how much longer Bud and I could stay together. For the last seven years my social circle consisted of good, wholesome, Mormon women who were modest and chaste. I pretended to be happy while submerging my true self, but my true self wanted to know love. I might have continued that way if Pinky hadn't shown up unexpectedly.

I had not seen her for several years. Her hair was tinted a light red and cascaded down her shoulders. She was incredibly thin and wore jeans that zipped from her belly button, between her legs, and all the way up her backside. Unzipped they separated into two separate legs. The fit fascinated me. I couldn't imagine myself wearing such sexy jeans. We ate chocolates and visited like two kids in a candy store. She told me about her escapades modeling, dating famous people, and living it up generally. My life was boring compared to hers, so I loved hearing her stories.

"How long have you been bi-sexual Pinky?" I asked.

She gasped in surprise and bit her bottom lip, because she had never told me of her experiences. "How did you know?"

"I just know. Nobody told me, but if you're running with the crowd you say you are, I figure you're into bi-sexual stuff. While divorced, I met a bi-sexual girl and I know the kind of parties she went to. Your escapades with the rich and famous sound familiar." I recounted my experience with Leo Joiner and Leslie, the bi-sexual girl I met in New Orleans.

"Yes, I guess you can say I've had an experience or two. I have to be pretty lit to do it though," she confessed with a little shame.

Pinky had a perfect figure and worked part-time for a Clear Lake City architect who paid her generously. She drove a sports car, wore expensive clothes, and dripped diamonds. She invited me to lunch to meet her boss and some of her friends. I accepted eagerly, mainly because I wanted to see what she would do next. I awaited the next wild story or sexual innuendo during our luncheons. Nothing kept Pinky from doing exactly what she felt like doing. She was having a much better time than I was in life.

I began to emulate her, to tease the way she did, dress the way she dressed, and joke the way she joked. My suppressed personality begged to be free, but I suffered guilt, and scriptural quotes about modesty and righteousness flooded my thoughts. Eventually, I stifled my conscience and got into the spirit of Pinky's shenanigans and charades. Unlike my Mormon friends, Pinky wasn't modest or chaste, and I found her outlook liberating. She liked shocking people and loved to make me laugh. Pinky suffered neither guilt nor remorse and had no rules. She brought out the devil in me, and I encouraged the wickedness in her.

Once we were in the lady's room standing at the mirror when Pinky began massaging her breasts.

"What are you doing?" I asked.

"Massaging my boobs. Didn't I tell you? I had a boob job, and you're supposed to massage the silicone every day." She loved having great boobs. I had never known anyone with breast implants, and her openness about them amazed me. She asked if I wanted to see them. Before I could answer, she raised her blouse and exposed her pretty beige bra.

"Wow! I wish I had boobs like that!"

"You can," Pinky said proudly. "Just get a boob job!"

"Will you talk to Bud about it for me? I'm afraid he won't let me."

"Leave it to me, girl, and you'll get your implants!"

I became increasingly uninhibited and subconsciously emulated her style. I knew I turned heads. I was at the height of my beauty, and I wanted to flaunt it. Until then I always ignored those second glances men gave me, but I started looking back. Pinky talked to Bud about a boob job as she had promised, and we convinced him I should have the surgery. Before long, Pinky broke up with her boss and moved back to Dallas, but by the time she left, I was a changed person.

Just after Pinky left to go back to Dallas, my drafting teacher told me about a wonderful part-time job at the Johnson Space Center (JSC) working for FFS, the company with the utility and facility contract at NASA JSC. The teacher recommended me, and I got the job as an engineering aide. I was so proud to work at the Space Center. I left Texas City's blue-collar environment for a white-collar world with educated role models. Although the income was minimal, my family got free airline travel and could finally take vacations to exotic cities. I worked only three days a week, but I stopped taking college courses for a while so the schedule wouldn't strain the family. Awestruck when I drove by the huge space ship before the Johnson Space Center, I wondered if I might meet the astronauts. 'Where are the moon rocks stored?' I wondered. 'Will I ever see Mission Control?'

I loved the job. I accompanied engineers on inspections, surveys, and preventive maintenance checks. I climbed cooling towers, toured electrical substations, water treatment plants, and water towers, and checked boilers. I absorbed the environment like a sponge. Everyone wanted to know the name of the pretty lady at the drafting table. I felt pride in my job and believed my co-workers accepted me.

A man from my drafting class worked there, too. He dropped by my desk one afternoon to see how I enjoyed the job. Roy Lee was about forty-five, married, and the father of five girls. He wore a thick mustache and a blue uniform and always had a joke to tell. Since we both lived in Texas City, he invited me to join his carpool with two other men from Texas City. The idea sounded good to me, but I asked him to check with the other men. I discussed the carpool with Bud, and we thought it was a good idea. We met at McDonald's every morning and left our cars in the parking lot. On my first day in the carpool, I offered to drive. As I pulled into the parking lot, I spotted Roy Lee waving. He hopped in the front seat and started pointing out the other carpoolers. One was Glen Dunken, a tall grizzly man with an unkempt beard, thick glasses, and crooked teeth. Noticeably shy, he tried to hide his flushed face under the bill of his cap when Roy introduced us.

"Rose, this is Glen Dunken. He works in the landscape maintenance crew and drives on Fridays."

"N-N-N-Nice to meet you, M-M-M-Ma'am." Roy Lee grinned as Glen stuttered his reply.

"Isn't there one more, Roy?" I asked.

"Yes, he's coming. He's inside filling his coffee cup." We waited another minute for the final member of the quartet. "There he is. That's Cruze."

"Who?" I asked.

"Cruze," Roy Lee answered. "That's his nickname, but don't ask me why. His real name is Jose Ramos, but we like to call him a no good Mexican!" Glen joined Roy in a high-pitched giggle.

Cruze noticed his buddies in my car and waved an acknowledgment before locking his car. As he got into the backseat he said, "Good morning ladies!" We made eye contact, and he introduced himself, "I am Jose Ramos, the famous Jose Ramos."

Without missing a beat, Roy Lee corrected him. "You mean the infamous Jose Ramos." We all laughed.

"I'm Rose Murphy. Nice to meet you, Jose."

"Call me Cruze, Rose. Welcome to our traveling team."

Cruze was a pipe fitter, twenty-seven years old, married, with no children. The first few weeks, I paid little attention to my carpool partners. I told them to be themselves and not act differently just because a woman was in the car. I joked with and teased them during the twenty-five minute ride in the morning and afternoon. They enjoyed having a pretty, young woman with them. I laughed at their jokes and participated in irreverent teasing. Vacillating between the wayward and the virtuous, I was confused.

We picked Cruze up at his home a few times, because his car was in the shop. I noticed that he was a fanatic for neatness and organization. His garage was very tidy, his lawn manicured, and his cars were always clean. He served a tour of duty in the military and married his best friend's sister before being discharged. One afternoon when we dropped him off at his home we saw his wife washing the car. Although not overweight, she was a big woman. Roy Lee commented on her size.

"I guess your wife wears the pants in your family," he smirked.

"You better believe it. Look at the size of that woman. She can just about beat me in arm wrestling." His wife worked for the railroad and earned as much as Cruze. He measured the worth of a spouse by her ability to contribute financially. His wife's college degree intimidated him, since he didn't graduate from high school and had only a GED.

Cruze was amazed that I had three children and often reminded the gang there was no room for children in his busy life. He played racquetball after work every day and worked out at the civic center or went fishing in his boat. Cruze and his wife had matching Harley-Davidsons they rode together on weekends. How different his life was from mine! I spent my life wiping runny noses and picking up toys, while he cared only for himself.

About three months after joining the car pool something unexpected happened. One afternoon it was Glen's turn to drive home. Roy Lee sat in the front passenger seat, leaving Cruze in the back seat with me. Not thinking, I opened his lunch kit. He watched carefully, thinking I was a little intrusive, but he didn't stop me. I saw a tube of toothpaste, deodorant, and a small bottle of baby powder in the bottom of his lunch kit.

"What do you do, Cruze, take a bath at work?"

"If I could, I would. I always freshen up after lunch. I'm sort of a fanatic about cleanliness."

"Well, I'm impressed." We both laughed. I shut his lunch kit and looked out the window, but my eyes were drawn back to his side of the car. I tried to hide my sudden curiosity about his features. As if my eyes had opened for the first time, I saw him differently from before. His short, jet-black hair was neatly cut and combed straight back. A carefully trimmed mustache framed his lips and perfect white teeth. His unbuttoned shirt revealed his well-defined pectoral muscles, dashed with pixels of baby powder. Muscular biceps bulged from his sleeves, while the veins in his copper colored forearms jutted out a quarter of an inch. Cruze watched my roving observation of his physique from the corner of his eye and enjoyed the scrutiny. He was waiting for me to notice him the way he wanted me to. Why hadn't I noticed how truly stunning and desirable he was? He hadn't taken his eyes off me since I shut his lunch kit. He could see what was happening; he could feel it; I could feel it. My eyes roamed past his throat toward his face, and I flushed as our eyes met. We didn't need to say a word.

In March I took leave from work and had the boob job. I didn't tell my mother. She wouldn't have approved. The guys in the carpool knew about it and were eager to see the new me when I came back. They joked about it. Cruze and I started teasing each other, using the implants to camouflage flirtatious conversation. We were about to openly confront our attraction for the first time. I was driving Cruze home from work, and the other two men were not with us. I was wearing a loose-fitting short-sleeved sweater with a thin, silk skirt and sandals. It was late spring and I already had a tan. My golden hair shimmered in the sunlight passing through the window. Cruze watched as I dried the sweat from my chest with part of my loosely knit sweater. Aware of him, I reached between my breasts to wipe the dribble of sweat running down my chest.

"Uh, uh, uh. My, my, Rose. You sure are a beautiful woman. You're enough to drive a man wild–and you know it, don't you?"

"Do I drive you wild, Cruze?"

"Yes, Rose. You drive me insane." His lips quivered. "When are you going to let me feel those things?"

"What things, Cruze?" I asked coyly.

"Your breasts; your new breasts. Your boob job, as you call it."

I thought about Pinky. What would Pinky do? I knew exactly what she would do, but I didn't say anything. He touched me ever so gently, and we both melted into our seats. I wanted to pull to the side of the road and fall into his arms, kiss, and be devoured by him, but before we knew it we were in his driveway. His wife was working in the yard and guilt flashed across our faces. She had blonde hair and a nice smile and wore a two-piece swimsuit. She waved, and I waved back. He gave me a quick glance before opening the car door and said he enjoyed the ride home and looked forward to seeing me the next day. As he exited the car he placed his lunch kit in front of his lap.

I told myself it would be a one-time impropriety and wouldn't happen again, but I was kidding myself. His tender touch unleashed an uncontrollable desire in me. Over and over, I relived that interlude, savoring the memory. For the first time in my life I felt passion, the feeling I was missing, that I hungered for-passion, obsession, lust. I was crazed with desire. Could that be what love felt like? I wanted nothing more than to be in his arms.

We began finding excuses for driving alone to work together. Glen and Roy Lee were suspicious, but we didn't care. Cruze began calling me at work, asking me to meet him for lunch in a quiet park. One afternoon on the way home from work he pulled over under an over-pass, "I'm going to kiss you, Rose. I must kiss you. I can't wait another minute." He stopped the car, put the gear in park and left the air conditioner running. I didn't resist. We rushed into each other's arms. We couldn't get our lips together fast enough. I couldn't kiss him deeply enough or long enough. The passion was overwhelming. I loved the way he held me. I thrilled when he brushed my hair with his hand. We were mad with desire for each other! I licked the salty sweat from his chest. He bit my neck, and tasted the palms of my hands. The heat inside my body felt like a fever that was burning me up. The drama lasted only a few minutes, but I wanted it to go on forever. I had never experienced such emotion, such yearning, such passion, such desire. 'Do I feel this way because it is forbidden?' I asked myself.

We could not wait to be together. Sometimes we met in a building at the Space Center to talk, tease, hug, and kiss. We discussed our marriages. Neither of us was happy, but we knew what we were doing was wrong. He told me he thought his wife was having an affair. That they were in the last stages of their marriage didn't justify my involvement with Cruze.

Eventually, we went beyond kissing and made love. Ecstatic with passion, I didn't think about the consequences until it was all over. I had not planned to go so far. The chemistry between us charged the environment, and I am sure others noticed. But after a while, things with Cruze began to change. As my emotional investment escalated, he seemed to withdraw. He still wanted to spend romantic time with me, but I sensed resistance, because he knew it was getting complicated. I thought he was the answer to my unhappy marriage. I wanted him to tell me to leave Bud so we could be together. He never did. I was too proud to suggest it and lived in constant fear he would abandon me. Several times we tried to stop seeing each other, but we always broke the rules we set. He would call and I would run. I knew I loved him, but I wasn't sure how he felt about me. I knew he couldn't live with my children, so there was no hope of future union. I couldn't understand why he didn't love me and believed he rejected me because of the children. They were baggage that would impede his lifestyle.

I decided to quit the carpool. I wanted to leave him before he had a chance to abandon me. For two months I only caught occasional glimpses of him at work. I hungered and yearned for him. Sometimes I felt like I was dying. I missed him and longed to be with him; I couldn't sleep, eat, or be happy, not even around my children. Sinking into a deep depression, I sought medical help. The doctor gave me antidepressants that made me sleepy. I lost weight and became much too thin. I didn't want Bud to touch me. I thought only of Cruze and didn't feel worthy to go to church. Even breathing was difficult.

Bud knew I was depressed and had been to the doctor for pills. He saw me lose weight and could tell something was wrong. An open, honest, intimate relationship with Bud was impossible. Every moment of feigned happiness with him was forced. Throughout the entire marriage I faked affection, warmth, openness, sensitivity, and support. I felt nothing for Bud. He was more like a brother than a husband. I knew passion for the first time in my life. I told Bud what I had done, but I lied about my lover's identity. I told him the man had moved to another state and I would never see him again. We knew that I had to confess to the Bishop and that I would likely be excommunicated. He didn't leave me, though I secretly hoped he would, even though I couldn't make it financially without him. I am sure he felt used.

CHAPTER XVIII

The Tunnel

Curiously, the lesser requirements of sainthood, such as not smoking or drinking, were still important to me, even when I had committed adultery. In every other way, I was still committed to my Mormon beliefs but unable to be faithful to my husband. After my excommunication, we went back to church, and no one treated me differently. If anything, they were more nurturing and kinder than before. They wanted me to overcome whatever problem I had, and they let me know without saying a word that they loved me.

Bud and I tried to move beyond the troubles in my hollow marriage. We went to Cancun for a vacation using my flight benefits, but I was bored to death. Every Mexican in Cancun reminded me of Cruze. We went to Hawaii, but I saw my lover's face in every dark skinned islander. I couldn't forget him or be happy without him. I wanted only to return to work so I could catch a glimpse of the man I loved. I was going out of my mind. My obsession was ruining my life. I drove by Cruze's house almost every day to see if I could see him outside. I waved nonchalantly when I saw him, but I wanted to die. I was stalking him. I imagined being married to him. I wanted to live with him forever. I could hardly concentrate at work. Each time the phone rang; I prayed to hear his voice. Pretending everything was fine at home was difficult.

I had to talk to someone, so my sister became my confidante. She and Dean Ray had four children but her marriage was not happy. She listened to my story of Cruze sympathetically but cautioned me to stay away from him.

"He isn't worth it, Rose. I don't care how much you love him, he isn't worth losing your family." She felt sorry for Bud. I told her I did not plan to see Cruze again, but she was sure I would. "It isn't over yet, Rose. I can tell by your voice that you will see him again."

She was right. He called me at work a couple of weeks later, told me he missed me and wanted to see me. He asked if I could meet him during lunch near the mechanical room of Building 16. I knew exactly where that room was. I said I would be there. I could hardly wait for lunch. Just to kiss him once more would be worth everything. I brushed my teeth and went to meet him. He was waiting for me with the hamper to the tunnel opened. "Let's go down into the tunnel."

I had been through most of the dark, winding seven-mile tunnel on engineering surveys. I went down first, in a white and purple sundress with backless heels and no hose. An excommunicate, I no longer dressed like a respectable Mormon. I wanted to look good for Cruze. The wall mounted light cast a dim shadow on our faces. With my back pressed against the concrete wall, he leaned forward and kissed me tenderly, then passionately. I thought he would swallow me with passion. Were passion, sex, lust, and desire all we had? Had we nothing deeper, more meaningful, or binding? Should love be defined by passion or logic? Perhaps passion should yield to common sense when selecting a partner, but who would choose a mate on the basis of sober logic and passionless common sense? He lifted my right leg so he could lean closer. The encounter was costly. That day, in the tunnel of the Johnson Space Center, I got pregnant.

During the time we stayed apart, I mentally rehearsed our meetings. I tried to remember every conversation, every event, every kiss, laugh, hug, joke, smile. Women with a college degree impressed Cruze, since education translated into earning power. He wanted a woman whose salary was equal to or better than his own so he wouldn't have to support her. He wanted to spend his salary on himself and the things he wanted only. A woman who couldn't support herself was a burden. Although I had some college education I had no degree, and I worked part-time for a measly salary. In addition, I had three children. He would never agree to take on that responsibility. My circumstances would cramp his style.

I tried to hide my morning sickness from Bud, but I couldn't. Before leaving for work one morning he saw me throw up. At the breakfast table as I was eating my oatmeal he asked, "Rose, when is the last time you had a period?"

I paused, wiped my mouth with a napkin, and swallowed. "Longer than I care to admit, Bud"

He glared at me for a minute before asking the dreaded question. "Are you pregnant?"

Staring into my cereal, without looking up, I answered. "Yes, I think so."

He knew it wasn't his. He stood up in a rage and poured the bowl of oatmeal on my head, then headed to my dresser drawer. Finding the sexy lingerie I bought with Pinky, he took them to the back yard, poured gasoline, struck a match, and burned them. I did nothing. He deserved to feel rage. I didn't care what he did. I didn't care if I lived or died. I wanted him to hate me. I wanted him to leave. I took a shower and washed the cereal out of my hair, and smelt the faint odor of smoke coming from the backyard. I hated him. As I got out of the shower, he came back in, still in a rage, "I thought you quit seeing that bastard! You better tell me his name. I'm going to find him."

"There's no use. He came back to town to see me, and we met for lunch. That's when it happened. I didn't plan it. It just happened." Bud pushed me against the wall, and struck me several times. Pointing his finger at my face with the other hand doubled into a fist, he threatened, "Well, I'm leaving you this time and I won't be back!"

I didn't blame him. I didn't fight back. He could kill me if he wanted to. Death seemed easier than what I was dealing with. "I don't blame you. I don't care where you go. I want to be alone. Leave me, I want you to." After he left, I examined the bruises on my arms and legs.

Bud went to stay with his mother, but he told no one of my situation. He quickly found another woman to date. I kept the kids, and we became inactive in church. I quit the job at JSC, because I had to get away from Cruze. I wasn't sure how to tell him I was pregnant. When I did not hear from him for a while, I decided to call him. I asked him to meet me at the park that afternoon. When I drove up, he was waiting for me. He could tell by the look on my face I had something serious to discuss.

"Why did you quit your job, Rose?"

"I had to get away Cruze. This thing between us has become too painful. But that isn't why I asked you to meet me. I have to tell you something important. I'm pregnant, Cruze."

His eyes widened, and he threw his head back against the car seat. "Oh, no! Did you try to get pregnant with my child, Rose?"

"No, I didn't want to get pregnant. I didn't plan it. You called me that day, remember? I didn't call you. But I'm going to have this baby, no matter what."

"What about Bud? Does he know?"

"Yes, he left me. He's staying with his mother."

"Oh my gosh. I can imagine how he feels. Rose, this is a bad thing we've done. I just couldn't resist you."

"As I recall, the seduction was pretty mutual."

"I know. I felt it the first time I saw you, but I tried to hide it. I even tried not to like you. I thought you would never notice me. I have never felt so much passion for a woman. It was beyond my control. It was so wonderful, but so, so bad."

"I don't know what is going to happen, Cruze. At this point I won't even try to predict."

"Does he know it's me?"

"No, I won't tell him."

"He'll find out some day. I don't know how, but I'll be waiting for that call. He's a big guy, and I think he could cause some damage. I'd like to remain unknown, at least for now. I guess I should also tell you I am separating from my wife. It's been coming for a long time. She admitted she's in love with a man she works with. I suspected that. When she told me, I wanted to tell her I had an affair too, but I didn't. We'll probably get a divorce."

I didn't want to care more for him than he did for me. He wanted to be free and would not want the burden of four children and me. We were never to be and I knew it, although I didn't want to accept it. Yes, I will keep his secret for now. He can go and have his fun while I get big and pregnant with his child.' When we parted, I didn't know if I would ever see him again.

Bud stayed away for a couple of months, but by Christmas, he was tired of living with his parents and the shock of my condition started to fade. He felt bad about dating other women while he was married. He came over to the house with a noble proposal.

"I will stay with you until the baby is born and give it my name. After that, we will just see what happens."

I had no choice. I appreciated the offer, but I feared being in his debt because that would give him more control over me. He had a good side, and I knew he must love me if he volunteered to do something so chivalrous. I tried to be happy and make it up to him, but the more I tried the greater the act. I felt like I was in the last scene of a bad play. He didn't know the baby was part Hispanic, and I couldn't tell him. He said that he would try to treat the baby as his own. Regardless of his reason for staying with me, I commended him. Not many men would have done that.

During the entire pregnancy I worried about how the baby would look. My instinct told me it was a girl. Would she look different from my other children? Would she be dark? I heard from Cruze only once, right after Christmas. He called while Bud was at work, and I told him Bud had decided to stay until the baby was born. We agreed it would be best for him to stay out of my life. I told him Bud and I would try to make it together. He knew I didn't love Bud.

In the summer I learned the baby was breech. I would need a Caesarean section. She would be born under the sign of Gemini, the name of one of the space rockets in the early NASA days. Gemini–the sign of the twin; the split into two, which would be a symbol of the dichotomy of her life. I drove myself to the hospital the evening before the Caesarian after dropping the children off at my mother's house.

I told Mama the truth and she considered Bud the hero for staying with me. I suppose she was right. She was glad that even under the circumstances, I was going to keep the baby. I prayed to the Lord that if he would let this child blend in with my other children in color and features, I would not see Cruze or tell him about the baby. I was afraid the baby would be very brown. Cruze lived only a few blocks from my mother, and I had to pass his house to get to the hospital. He was in the front yard, alone. I fought the temptation to stop and tell him what I was doing. I wanted to tell him I loved him and would take good care of our baby, but I stood by my promise to the Lord. If I didn't, I thought I would be punished with a brown baby, and everyone would know. I looked straight ahead and kept driving.

The doctors arranged the surgery a week before my due date but I started labor that night at the hospital. They were not sure if they could hold off the Caesarean until the next morning, but they did. Bud came to the hospital early the next morning and was in the delivery room with me.

"It's a girl!" the doctor said, holding up a black-haired, seven-pound, crying baby. She was white with dark hair and didn't look Hispanic. The Lord had answered my prayer. Bud smiled when he saw her. Even under those conditions the cry of a newborn is a beautiful sound. How could anyone not love an innocent baby?' And we did love her. Bud loved her and treated her as his own. I could tell she was not quite the same as the others, but she blended. We named her Marbella.

The children greeted little Marbella with enthusiasm. She was special to me because she was my love child. When she was a month old Bud blessed her at church in front of the entire congregation. She wore a little, white bonnet and a long, white blessing gown. We sat in the back row of the church. While he was blessing her, I remembered a premonition I had at least three years earlier in church. It had flashed in my mind with such vivid impact that I gasped aloud. Bud looked at me and asked what was wrong. I told him I had seen a premonition.

"What kind of vision?" he whispered.

"I saw a vision of us in the future, sitting together at church with another child that was ours . . . but not ours."

"What is that supposed to mean?" Bud held my unique ability of personal revelation in esteem and recognized it as a gift.

"I don't know. I felt blood related to the child, yet there was something different about it. Maybe it means that we are going to raise one of our relatives' children as part of our family."

"Was it a boy or a girl?" Bud asked.

"I don't know. I only know it means something, but I don't know what."

We both pondered the premonition. I had not really thought about it again since that day, but when Bud brought Marbella back to the back row after blessing her, I saw the vision again. I had completely forgotten it until that moment. I gasped again.

"What is wrong with you?"

I leaned over and whispered, "Remember the vision I had a few years ago, Bud?"

"Which one?"

"The one where I saw us on the back pew of the church with a child that was ours but not ours."

Recollecting his thoughts he responded, "Yes. I remember...Hum."

I didn't need to say anything else. We both remembered the vision and knew its meaning. Bud never denied my gift of premonition, but we sometimes feared it.

Addie came to visit me, bringing a gift for my baby girl. She held her admiringly.

"Do you want to have children Addie?"

"Not before I am married!"

"Well, do you want to ever get married?"

"Rose, I'll consider marriage if I begin to see happily married people. As of now, I don't know anyone who is married and happy."

"You're probably right. But that means you may never be a mother!"

"Why should I? I feel like I've been a mother all my life. I'm always taking care of people."

"Yes, you are."

"Anyway, you have enough little rascals for both of us, don't you?" She laughed.

"I sure do."

I told her all I had been through with Cruze and about my excommunication. The expression in her big, blue eyes told me she was amazed. "This is something like you read in a novel, Rose. It's like *The Scarlet Letter!* Why did you put yourself through the humiliation of a disciplinary court?"

Addie had not changed a bit. She was still my protector.

"I guess I feel differently about the Church. I'm not angry with the Church. I understand the purpose of a disciplinary council. I would rather admit my mistakes now and pay the price than suffer the consequences later."

Addie rejected the Church because her father was a hypocrite who preached to everyone while breaking the commandments. He left her mother with nothing, and Addie resented the way he treated her in the divorce. She was angry at the Church for doing nothing about it. He gave his children nothing. Lamar had money to share with his children but never did. When Addie asked him for help, he refused.

After I confessed my love affair, she told me she was seeing someone special.

"Do you love him?" I asked.

"I'm not sure. I think so."

"Well, tell me about him. What is he like?"

"He has a PhD in psychology. I met him during an internship I did last semester. He's twelve years older than me, and we get along wonderfully."

Changing the subject, I asked how Matt was doing in San Francisco.

"He's doing great. His art is really starting to sell, and he's making lots of new friends."

"Is he gay?"

"No!"

But he *was* gay. Addie couldn't acknowledge it, and Matt had not told her. I knew she would think she had made him that way since she played with him when they were children. By now, Matt had developed a recognizable artistic style of his own.

"Why do Billy and Jessie still live at home with your parents? Addie asked

"Strangely enough," I explained, "after Mama was shot, she stopped working and started taking better care of them. They work, but they don't manage their money well enough to be independent."

I explained that if Billy liked a girl, Jessie and Mama teased him and talked badly about her, especially if they thought it was more than just a fling. They didn't want anyone else to interrupt their triage. If

Jessie liked a girl, Billy and Mama ganged up on her and treated her badly. They were so enmeshed in each other's lives that no one could come between them.

"That is really strange. Do you and your mom get along better now, Rose? What does she think of your situation... having a Hispanic baby?"

"Oh, you can imagine that she thinks I am dirt and Bud is a hero."

"Well, that is nothing new! She always treated you like dirt. Is she still dancing with Mary Jane in the living room?"

We laughed. "No, not really. I don't think she ever quite forgave Mary Jane for marrying Dean Ray!"

Within a month after Marbella was born, Pinky showed up with a short, well-built man named Andy Dull. With a big smile she announced that she and Andy were getting married. Pinky asked me to stand up with her at the wedding. Andy was a mechanic and had been married before. He had a son. A vegetarian, he was a few years older than Pinky and very much into physical fitness. He was definitely not a member of the jet set she had associated with for so many years. I don't know where she found him, but he was probably the best man that I had ever seen her date. Pinky with the last name of Dull was ironic; she was anything but. She had a small wedding in the Baptist Church across from her parents' home, and I was Matron of Honor. To hear the preacher address her as Patti Kaye instead of Pinky sounded funny.

Pinky and Andy married the morning of our ten-year high school reunion. She was not about to miss it; not even for a honeymoon. She was flying high as a kite that night, and Andy wasn't complaining. She came to the dance in a Dale Evans cowgirl get-up. I asked Andy where she found the outfit, and although they picked it up from a Houston store only two hours earlier, he said he couldn't remember. He said she wanted to get everyone's attention, and she certainly did. White, cowgirl boots with fringe around the top matched her short, black-and-white flared skirt with red can-can petticoats underneath. A red, silk western shirt, and a white patent leather belt, a fringed vest completed the get-up. Half the night her black and white cowboy hat was on backwards, its two little flashing lights making her easy to spot. Thank goodness, she couldn't find guns and holsters, or she would have been firing them off that night. She slung Andy all over the dance floor with one arm around his neck and one arm around anyone else she recognized. Andy followed her like an obedient pup. Everyone knew they were newlyweds. They danced the night away, and each time a song ended Pinky kicked her leg up in the air and yelled, "Yahoo!" By the end of the evening half the class was doing the same thing. I was glad to see Pinky enjoy herself. Andy and Pinky were the life of our ten-year reunion party.

After she married, Pinky's parents agreed to let her and Andy take Jobe to live with them. After several years of estrangement, her parents let Pinky back into their lives. They liked Andy and hoped his influence would settle her down. Jobe was nine-years-old, and nobody could have asked for a more beautiful, loving, well-adjusted son. Pinky tried to make a good life for Jobe after marrying Andy, but before long she was back to her tricks. Andy called me looking for her one night and told me that Pinky was still doing drugs, though she had sworn she would never touch them again. Pinky could be without drugs and booze for a while, but not for long. She often drank until she couldn't remember what happened.

She and Andy eventually separated, and Jobe went back to his grandparents. Pinky couldn't survive without a man to take care of her, since the drugs and alcohol kept her from holding a job. Andy was a good man, and I felt sorry for him. I knew Pinky would get bored with him and seek the bright lights again. They went back and forth for several years. I asked Andy why he put up with her and took her back time and again. I will never forget his answer.

"Well, when she's good, she's very, very good–and convincing. But when she's bad, she's real, real bad."

I thought about Bud. He was the same way, and so was I. At some point the bad in Pinky must have outweighed the good, because there came a time when good old boring Andy refused to take her back. I lost contact with her after that for several years, but I knew her pattern. She drifted from one man to another.

PART III, CHAPTER IXX

Another Break

My kids loved to dance to Michael Jackson's *Thriller* album and imitate his famous moonwalk. It was Christmas so we put up a tree and as was our tradition after the birth of each child, we bought a special first ornament for Marbella. We baked holiday cookies, attended Christmas socials, and wrapped presents. I tried to be strong for them and enjoy my time with them, but despondency overwhelmed me. The doctors worried about my deteriorating condition. Fighting my obsession made me weary, and living a lie was maddening. I was settling into my role as mother of four when I had a call from Cruze.

"Hello, Rose. It's me, Cruze. Can you talk?"

"I . . . ah . . . ah, yes. Yes, I suppose I can. How are you?"

"Well, as good as can be expected, I guess. How's the baby girl?"

"Oh, you know. How did you find out?"

"Let's just say I made it my business to find out."

I told him I saw him in his front yard on the way to the hospital.

"I wish you had stopped."

"I couldn't, Cruze, it would have made things worse. She's beautiful and healthy. She has a light complexion and dark hair. I had to have a Caesarean because she was breech."

"Are you healing well?"

"Yes, I'm doing okay. I'm pretty well back to normal."

"Can I see her?"

"I don't know how you can, Cruze. It would be too dangerous for you to come here. Besides, I'm not sure it's a good idea under the circumstances. It wouldn't be right. It wouldn't be fair to Bud."

He told me his divorce was final and he was dating a little. That crushed me. How could he date other women while I carried his baby? He was oblivious to my feelings, so I tried to hide them. He didn't know how deeply I hurt. I told him I was planning to go back to school in the fall. I didn't want to try to work with a new baby. By the time we got off the phone, he convinced me to meet him in a department store so he could see the baby. I knew I shouldn't do it, that it was wrong, that he didn't deserve to see the child ever, but with him I never chose logic over emotion.

The next day we met at Target. Christmas music played over the loud speaker. My heart melted when I saw him standing there in a black leather jacket, but I tried to act unimpressed. I reminded myself that he was dating other women and having a great time, while I raised his child and lived a lie. If he could date other women, I knew he did not love me the way I loved him. Perhaps he never loved me at all.

He took Marbella in his arms and held her tenderly, lovingly. She was in a soft, light green dress with lace and matching bonnet and shoes. I almost cried when I saw them together. Gently, he untied her bonnet and took it off her head so he could see her hair. It stuck up all over.

"She's like glass. I'm afraid I might break her. Oh, she's so pretty," he said adoringly. We talked a few minutes and he watched me change her wet diaper. He seemed in awe of her. To be her father and know she would never know him must have stirred his emotions. I tried to put myself in his place. He would have no input about how she was raised. He wouldn't hear her first words or see her first steps or watch her blow out the candles on her birthday cake. As difficult as my lot was, I wouldn't trade my situation for his. I couldn't stand to have someone else raise my baby. I wondered if he would ever have another child. Perhaps she would be his only offspring. Maybe he thought that he would have another opportunity to father a child. She curled her tiny fingers around his thumb and he kissed them.

Our visit ended too quickly. I watched him leave the store and drive away, wiping tears from his eyes. Each time our paths crossed, I thought it would be the last. On the way home, I asked the Lord why He gave me all the pain while Cruze was footloose and fancy-free, dancing and dating. "How can you let him be happy, Lord? He is as responsible for all of this as I am, yet you punish only me!" Then I heard that still small voice: "He will be happy only when he keeps my commandments. He will never be happy until then. If he keeps my commandments, wouldn't you want him to be happy?"

God seemed to be right next to me, answering my questions. I knew Cruze wasn't keeping the commandments, so he wasn't happy. If he kept the commandments, I would want him to be happy. Keeping the Lord's commandments was the only way I could find true happiness, but I knew I would never be happy without love. Being married to a man that I didn't love made keeping the commandments more difficult. 'I wouldn't be tempted if I were in love.'

Ironically, I saw Cruze again on Valentine's Day. Leaving my mother's house, I drove past his home. He was at the mailbox. I waved at him and stopped.

"Hi there, Rose. How are you? Where's the little girl?"

"She is with my mother. I'm taking cookies to Ben's school for their Valentine's Day party."

"Is there a time I can call you later?"

"Is anything wrong?"

"No, I just would like to talk to you. I'll call tonight."

After Bud left for work, I fed the children and made sure my evening was organized so I could take his call. I looked forward to talking with him. I wanted to tell him all the cute things Marbella could do. She was cutting teeth and performing little tricks I thought he would like to know about. I also wanted to know about his love life.

The children were asleep by nine o'clock, and I thought he would call soon. I waited until ten o'clock, and he still hadn't called. Had he forgotten? I would not be treated that way! He wasn't about to stand me up. I got angry. At 10:30 p. m., I called him.

"You'd better never again tell me you're going to call and forget about it. It doesn't set well with someone who has sacrificed so much for you. I don't think I deserve that from you. You don't deserve my love! You are not worthy of me!"

He apologized and said that a girl had dropped by unexpectedly. He added that he was sure he wasn't worthy of me and didn't deserve my love. We talked for at least an hour. He saw my wrath for the first time and didn't want to make me mad again. Being made a fool drives me over the edge quicker than anything.

Cruze had made new friends since his divorce. He met them at a League City pool hall and said a man named Frank was the ringleader. A sworn bachelor, Frank worked with the astronauts at NASA. He was forty-four and had two handsome sons; one was gay. The group included two nurses married to each other, James and Jan, and Darin, a foul-mouthed physician's assistant who cheated on his wife. They had motorcycles, went to wild parties and to the local country western dance hall at least twice a week.

Frank's assignment at NASA took him to Cape Canaveral in Florida two weeks each month, and he left his much younger girl-friend in Houston. Cruze took her to the dance hall while Frank was out of town, and before long they were doing more than dancing. Cruze felt guilty about it. "I guess I'll never learn," he said.

Though I hurt to hear those things, I tried to be nonchalant about his escapades. Inside, anger and jealousy seethed. I wanted to know Frank's last name so I could get in touch with him. I asked if Frank was Italian.

"Let's see, Fowler. Frank Fowler. No, I don't think Fowler is an Italian name," he replied innocently. I had all I needed and would fig-ure out a way to meet Mr. Fowler. I didn't know how or where or when, but I would find a way, and when I did, I would expose Cruze's dirty little secret.

A few weeks later Bud and I had a terrible fight. One Friday, at about 9:30 p. m. all the children were in bed except Marbella, who was eight months old. Bud was lying on the carpet with a pillow under his back, watching sports on TV as usual. He had not helped me get the kids fed or bathed, nor had he helped with the dishes or played with the children or read to them. He just watched TV hour after hour. I was holding Marbella while she finished a bottle. I had taken an anti-depressant pill and I was sleepy so I asked Bud to rock Marbella. He gave me an evil look and replied, "You shouldn't have taken your f__ing pill so soon."

In disgust, I threw the plastic bottle at him. Although I missed, he came at me like a werewolf. Having seen that look before, I knew that I was about to be attacked. His temper rendered him uncontrollable at times. When he got that look of rage, I knew I should run, but he usually cornered me before I could get away. Throwing the empty bottle put him over the edge. He started throwing me around although Marbella was still in my arms. "Let me put the baby down, Bud. Let me put her down!" I begged.

I was reliving my childhood, living as my parents did, fighting and crying. Soon there was broken glass everywhere, and a policeman was at the door. The neighbors heard the commotion and came outside to see what was going on. The children called Bud's mother, and she arrived just before the police. Clearly, it was time to end it. We could not do that to our children any more.

Bud moved to his mother's house again, but we sold our house to make it final. I didn't have a job, but I knew I would find a way to make it without him. I would die if I had to live with him another minute. He bought a mobile home on two acres in a nearby city, and I moved to Clear Lake near the Space Center. I knew I could not take care of four children by myself, so he took the boys and I took the girls.

The children were together every weekend but apart during the week. One weekend I had all four; he had them the next. Although Bud knew nothing about taking care of children, I was in no condition to take care of all four, plus hold down a job.

We both quit going to church and our divorce became final. Before long I had a job with a NASA contractor as a facilities planner, a good job with a compensation package worth almost as much as Bud's. My education was beginning to pay off. The job gave me the security I needed to get past needing a man for financial support. I could survive on my own. I was happy to be away from Bud and Texas City. I wanted to start over and make a new life that included happiness. Marbella stayed with a lady in our apartment complex while I worked, and Molly stayed there after school until I got home.

After things settled down, I decided to call Mr. Fowler. I looked up his name in the NASA directory and called him at work.

"Hello, Frank?"

"Yes, this is Frank Fowler. May I help you?"

"Frank, you don't know me, but I've heard a lot about you, and I want to meet you. Are you opposed to meeting a stranger for a drink?" I told him I had a story that would interest him. He was intrigued and said that he would meet me. I wouldn't tell him my name, because I didn't want it to get back to Cruze. We agreed to meet at the club in the Hilton Hotel across from NASA.

"How will I recognize you?" he asked.

"I'll be wearing a white jacket with a black carnation in the lapel."

"A black carnation? That sounds ominous."

"Maybe it is," I said. "I have never seen you, so I won't recognize you either. You'll have to find me." I could tell he enjoyed the game.

That weekend, I met Frank in the Hilton lobby wearing a black, strapless dress with white polka dots and a white jacket with a black carnation in the lapel. I was 5'3 and 107 pounds. My blonde, shoulder-length hair was layered, thick, and frosted, with just the right amount of curl. I was walking up the stairs when I met Frank. He stopped in his tracks and smiled. He had a thick mustache, beautiful eyes, and salt-and-pepper hair. He wore alligator boots and a western jacket, and he almost seemed to keep a rhythm as he walked. His expression showed he wasn't disappointed in the person wearing the black carnation.

"Well, well, you must be my mystery girl. I don't think I'll be sorry I came," he said.

"Frank," I said, putting my hand out to shake his, "I'm Rose Murphy."

"Very nice to meet you, Rose." He walked me to a table and pulled out a chair for me. "What would you like to drink?"

"Sprite."

"Sprite? You don't drink alcohol?"

"No, not at all." He smiled and ordered.

I wasn't nervous. We talked casually, but I wouldn't tell him how I got his name or why I wanted to meet him. I told him I was divorced, and we discussed our jobs at NASA. When I told him I had four children he looked surprised.

"You don't look like you have had any. You're beautiful!" he said. I didn't want to overstay my welcome, so after a while I told him I needed to leave.

"Well, when do I find out why you wanted to meet me or how you heard about me?"

"Maybe another time?" He asked me for a date the following night.

"But Frank, aren't you dating someone else?"

"Not any more," he replied.

Giving him the first hint of a mutual connection, I asked, "Aren't you dating a girl named Susan?"

"I was, but not any more."

"Oh, and when did you stop dating her?"

He looked at his watch and said, "About two hours ago–but how do you know about Susan?"

"I'll tell you all about that tomorrow night, Frank." I stood up and put my jacket on. "Where shall we meet?"

We arranged to meet for dinner at a Cajun restaurant. He walked me to my car and kissed my hand. He told me once more that I intrigued him.

Over dinner the next night, I told Frank all about my affair with Cruze. I told him about Marbella, and then I told him that Cruze and Susan saw each other behind his back when he went to the Cape. He said he didn't care about Cruze and Susan.

"He can have her for all I care. I would trade Susan for you any day. Cruze must be crazy if he could have had you and didn't take you, especially if you were carrying his baby. I can only surmise that those four children scared him away."

I wanted Frank to like me, but only so I could get back at Cruze. He became my link to Cruze. He confronted Cruze on the telephone the next day about dating Susan behind his back. Cruze apologized profusely.

"Look, don't worry about it, Cruze. These things happen. I'm gone two weeks out of every month, and I'm not married to her. You can have Susan. No hard feelings, okay? You see you're really doing me a favor because I found someone else."

"Someone you met at the Cape?"

"No, not at all. She lives right here near JSC." He told Cruze about our curious meeting and that surprisingly the woman turned out to be a beauty.

"You lucky dog, Frank. Why can't anything like that ever happen to me?" Cruze asked.

"Oh, I suppose it has happened to you, Cruze. You are just too dumb to recognize it!"

"Well, maybe so. How old is she?" Cruze asked.

"I think she's about your age. As a matter of fact, she's from Texas City."

"Well, maybe I know her."

"Yes, it would be pretty hard not to know the mother of your child!" Frank added.

Cruze was dumbfounded. "You aren't serious, are you?"

"Yes. You may have let her go, but I won't."

After that Cruze and Susan began to date openly. Dating Frank gave me the chance to shove a little bit of my hurt in Cruze's face and punish him for not wanting me. We went to dances and parties all together. Frank never trusted Cruze again–nor did the rest of their group. They didn't trust me either. They treated me well enough, but they found the awkward four-way relationship disconcerting. Cruze hardly spoke to me, but I didn't care. I wasn't really enjoying my new life of freedom, even though I had a good job and was away from Texas City. I missed my sons and hated the children being separated. I was not spending good quality time with my children, and I felt sadness.

Bud was dating, too. Because I was afraid of him, I tried not to see him when we exchanged the children. One evening when I dropped the boys off at his place after their weekend visit, he invited me inside his mobile home. He said he had something to give me. I told him I didn't want to go in, but he convinced me it would just be a minute. The children were playing in the back yard. As I opened the door, he grabbed my hand and pulled me in. I struggled to get loose, but he started hitting me and split my lip. The children heard my screams as I bolted from the door and ran back to the car. I took the girls with me, leaving my sons behind with their despicable father. I drove straight to

Frank's house.

Frank had seen Bud's temper once. After dating for three months, Frank and I drove up to a restaurant and were about to get out when I saw Bud, staring at us with that familiar look of rage. As he approached Frank's car, I slammed the door shut without explanation and told Frank to start the car. Fire-eyed, Bud chased the car two blocks, slipping and sliding in ditches, throwing rocks, and yelling profanities at the top of his lungs.

"Who is that madman?" Frank asked, looking in the rearview mirror.

"My soon-to-be ex-husband," I replied.

Bud thought I should love, honor, and obey him, especially since he stayed with me during my last pregnancy. If I could have loved him, I would have. I wanted to love him, but I couldn't. My busted lip did not surprise Frank. He was outraged and insisted I never go near Bud's again.

I dated Frank for about a year. Leaving him was hard, because leaving Frank also meant leaving Cruze. Cruze and Susan stopped dating before Frank and I did, so the link to Cruze was gone anyway. The game was over and reality set in. I wasn't being a good mother. Even though I loved my children, I was not caring for them the way I should. Nobody understood better than I did how a woman goes crazy in a loveless marriage and ruins the lives around her. I could now sympathize a little with my mother. She must have felt helpless and hopeless in her marriage. Being alone again gave me time to think about my life, to try to put it in perspective. I thought of my future, my children, my mortality, and I knew my life had to become more balanced, spiritual, and orderly. Once more I yearned for stability, and I was tired of dating and trying to find love.

One Sunday, I decided to take the children to church in my new city where nobody knew me. I met the bishop and explained my struggle. After listening a while he suggested I see a therapist who was a member of the Church. I had never been to a therapist, but I agreed I needed one. I arranged time off from work every week to visit with Dr. Hart, a frail man with very keen awareness and insight. We talked about my childhood and adolescence. He called me a defector.

"What is a defector?" I asked.

"Someone who tries to be the opposite of his example or environment. One who extricates himself from his boundaries, often forsaking his past and the people in it. Your family might think of you as a traitor because you defy your roots."

"Have I defied my roots?" I asked.

"In a way you have. You want to succeed, although you came from an environment that told you that you couldn't. For example, a girl defecting from an overly religious family may become a stripper. A child defecting from a ghetto may try to become a professional, like a doctor or a lawyer. Your acute memory of childhood events gives me another clue that you are a defector. Most people have vague recollections of childhood, but the defector makes it a point to remember. Memory serves the defector. It is the tool a defector uses to be strong and stay sane. But because the defector has likely been repeatedly hurt or humiliated, he finds it hard to trust anyone. I don't believe you have resolved those issues. You appear tough, but you bear permanent scars."

He was right, but I didn't want to concentrate on the past, since my immediate needs were for the present and future. "I can resolve the past later. Right now, I need help sorting out my life as it currently is." He agreed to put my past on the shelf and concentrate on the present and future, but he cautioned me that we must come back to my childhood.

His strategy was to determine my long-term goals and objectives and to help me reach them. I said that my goal in life was to have my children all together, raise them in the Church, and be married in the Mormon temple to a man I loved. He gradually made me realize that if I wanted those things, I had to stop doing certain things and start doing others. I had to stop dressing sexy, stop going to clubs, and start going to church.

"You can't reach your goals if you date men who have different goals." I met with him for at least six months before I felt my life begin to stabilize.

Another year passed. I started reading the scriptures, dressing modestly, and attending church regularly. I continued to work on my college degree, and I switched jobs where I worked. The new job did not go well, and I took a day off in January due to stress. That day the horrible Challenger accident occurred. Through Frank, I had met some of the astronauts who died in the accident, so I was especially sad. Later that week, I watched President Reagan's motorcade pass our building on its way to the Johnson Space Center for the memorial. I remember thinking that life is so fragile, unpredictable, and short.

CHAPTER XX
Return to the Familiar

After putting off facing the Church court as long as he could, Bud finally confessed his sins to the bishop and was excommunicated. He, too, was tired of the revolving door dating game and wanted to repair and stabilize his life. During the time we were divorced, he learned to run a household, manage finances, and have responsibility for children. He learned to cook, wash and fold clothes, pack lunch boxes, and buy groceries. Had he been free of children, he would never have understood or appreciated my role. Bud never let the children see the women he dated. They knew he dated, but he never brought his girlfriends around.

I dated a few men while I was trying to force stability into my life, but they were all temporary. I was no longer fooled that any of my relationships could be permanent. I knew my children were not in a healthy environment, and I couldn't create a sense of wholeness that simply wasn't there.

Soon after Bud was excommunicated he learned the identity of Marbella's father. My sister gave him the hints that helped him put it all together. I wasn't upset, since I knew he would find out some day. He called me and told me he knew. He was outraged.

"How could you do it with a dirty ol' Mexican?"

"I loved him. That's all I can tell you, Bud. I loved him."

"We're just lucky that Marbella doesn't look Mexican," he said. "You lied to me when you said that the man had moved away, didn't you?"

"Yes, Bud. I lied. I wanted to protect him."

"Well, why didn't he want to marry you?" he prodded.

"I don't know. It was too complicated, just too complicated. I guess if he loved me he would have married me. I would have married him."

"Do you still love him?"

"I don't know, but it doesn't matter because we'll never be together. He's selfish, and if he was ever going to care or show any commitment it would have happened by now."

He calmed down and lowered his voice. I was wrong to hide the truth from him, and I was relieved that he finally knew. Marbella was three years old. Her brown, shoulder length hair was straight and thick. Her large, aqua eyes and caramel skin always drew attention. Her face was a little rounder and her nose a little flatter than my other children's. Her lips were perfectly shaped, and her smile lit up the sky. She was petite and loved to shake her bubble butt to Madonna songs. At three she was teaching the latest dances to her sister, Molly. Even without obvious Hispanic characteristics, she resembled Cruze. Our genes produced an exotic beauty. My other children were just as beautiful, especially after they shed their baby fat, but Marbella never had baby fat. She was solid muscle—trim, fit, and athletic.

A couple of days later Cruze called me at work. Bud had phoned him, and they had an unexpectedly civil conversation. Bud accused him of breaking-up his marriage. Cruze apologized and told him he had had no idea of the damage we caused.

"Bud," he said, "even if I had known, I'm not sure I could have controlled what happened. All I can tell you is that it seemed beyond my control. For my weakness, I am very sorry. I wish you could understand that it's hard for me, too. Knowing that I can't raise my own child is hell for me, and that will haunt me for the rest of my life."

"Yes, it should haunt you. I know it would haunt me if I were in your place. Your haunting will be my blessing. Don't ever interfere with Marbella's life," Bud warned. "I am her father. Remember that. She's mine. She bears my last name, not yours. I was there in the delivery room when she was born, and she saw my face above her crib."

Cruze assured Bud that he would stay out of her life and was glad to know that his main concern was not the affair, but Marbella. Before they hung up, Bud told him, almost compassionately, "You might find consolation in knowing that I feel the same for her as I do for my other children."

Cruze ended our conversation by saying, "He's a better man that I!"

Hearing that he agreed to stay out of Marbella's life was hard. I knew he decided long before, but hearing him say it made it absolute. He never tried to be a part of my life or Marbella's. When I put the phone down I knew my affair with Cruze was finally over. I would no longer wonder where he was, whom he was with, or if he wept for the daughter he would never know. Bud did not tell me of his conversation with Cruze, so the next time I saw Bud I told him I knew of it. He did not respond. It was over for him, too.

Bud's demeanor changed. When he picked up the children or brought them home he was respectful, humble, and meek. That side of Bud set him apart from other men. He couldn't compete with other men when it came to looks, charisma, fortune, or intellect, but he stood above them when it came to having a humble heart. If he had been consistently humble in our marriage, things might have been different. Perhaps I brought out the worst in him. Our difficulties left him physically weak but spiritually stronger. Enormous pressure changes coal to diamonds, and so with Bud. He overcame a great trial by stumbling, faltering, falling, and rising again. He became a man.

Cautiously, we began talking about the children, the future, and spiritual matters. We knew we had let Satan affect our marriage. We rationalized that letting evil into our lives was why things went wrong. We forgot that there was never any intimacy or love in our marriage, even when we lived righteously. He was sorry for not being a better husband and father. He fasted and prayed often to nourish a righteous spirit. We were looking for the same thing at the same time. At first I found it hard to talk to him, but we became more comfortable with each other and began doing things with the children, who seemed happy when we were together. We took them fishing, camping, and riding bicycles. We forgave each other. He said he still loved me. He clearly wanted to reconcile, but I wasn't ready. I could not touch him without feeling strange.

I asked my therapist to talk to Bud. Dr. Hart met with Bud a few times and then with us together. We told him we might consider trying to get back together yet again. Dr. Hart's face looked the same as Bishop Smith's ten years earlier when I told him we were going to remarry. Bishop Smith didn't think it was a good idea then, and Dr. Hart didn't think it was a good idea now. Neither of them said it was a mistake, but their faces did. Dr. Hart said that he would have some real concerns with reconciliation. He cautioned us to move slowly, but we didn't. We fasted and prayed for direction, and soon we planned to remarry.

I felt like I was on a fast train that couldn't stop. I wanted someone to talk me out of it, so I called Addie.

"Don't do it, Rose. You're having a weak moment. You're listening to your mother. You're letting the Church paint a rosy picture that doesn't exist, at least not with Bud. Let Bud find someone who can love him. You will never love him, Rose. You deserve love, too. If you do this, you'll be sorry. You know what love is, and you know what it isn't. You want it, and you'll never be happy without it. Never settle for orange, when you want red!"

"I don't think red is my color."

"How do you know you won't find love some day? Give yourself more time," she begged. Addie was in love, and neither her psychologist boyfriend nor she thought marriage was important, especially since they never considered having children. I had just completed my bachelor's degree in architecture and she was working on her master's in behavioral science.

I didn't listen to Addie. Bud and I married the third time in March, and he and the boys moved into my home. I no longer thought of my own happiness; I focused on the children, church, and family. I did not have love and intimacy with Bud, but at least my children were together again. Neither of us would have found love and intimacy had we remained apart either. We tried to repair the damage, and the children were happy we were together. Our parents supported our decisions and seemed pleased that the nightmare was over. Ben was in high school. We bought a four-bedroom home on a golf course near the Space Center, just around the corner from Addie, in an ideal neighborhood. The elementary school was across the street. Soon Bud and I were re-baptized and brought back into the Church's full fellowship. Bud was more helpful around the house, more considerate, and we got along much better. I went to work for a NASA contractor; by that time, my salary equaled Bud's.

During the summer of 1989 the world watched the student protests in Tiananmen Square on CNN. I marveled at the lone student who stopped a tank. 'What bravery! What courage! How valiant!' While I watched and marveled, Mary Jane knocked at my door. Now over 200 pounds, she looked hopeless and downtrodden. Her weight gain resulted from the misery of living with a man she detested. She was ready to end the marriage but didn't have a job or a place to live.

"I have to get away from him, or I'll die. Every second I'm near him is torture. We have grown so far apart I can hardly stand to be in the room with him any more. I know Mama won't like it, but I'm leaving him."

More than anyone, I understood how she felt. Dean Ray always tried to get something for nothing. After military service, he had a successful career with the Police Department. He joined the Church, and from that moment on, my mother respected him, just as she did Bud. Unfortunately, Dean Ray left the police department after ten years and all his subsequent career moves were fruitless. Turning to gambling and bingo looking for a quick buck, he and his family became paupers. My sister couldn't take the stress any more.

"Well, don't feel like a failure, Mary Jane. I heard that even Little Miss Perfect is getting a divorce."

"You mean Sue Ellen? Impossible. I didn't think those people ever got divorced."

"Well, they do a good job of hiding their problems, but they have them. You and I are just a lot more open about ours."

"I can't believe it!" Mary Jane exclaimed. "I don't think she realizes how good she has it. After all, she's married to a good-looking, successful lawyer, and she lives in a mansion. Besides, don't they have six children?"

"Yes, I think so. It must be pretty hard to divorce with six children. Mama said Sue Ellen filed." Her husband didn't fall at her feet or adore her the way she thought he should, but like me, she acted the role of the happy Mormon wife. She had six children with a man she hated, but instead of seeking love elsewhere, she closed her legs to her husband for the last seven years of their marriage."

"I wonder how our children's lives will be affected by all the divorces?" she asked.

"Maybe it will make them stronger, maybe weaker," I responded, "But the effect is incalculable. We will never know the magnitude of change in their lives, since we have no way of knowing what would have occurred if we'd made different choices. We can only judge the effects in the aftermath."

As soon as Mary Jane left Dean Ray she got a job and began losing weight. She struggled financially, but she was happy to be free.

Once Bud and I were back together, I found favor in Mama's eyes again. I adjusted to a loveless life, and we got along better than we ever had before, except for a couple of setbacks. The first was on a boat. I could tell he was tired and acting like the old Bud that day, rude and cocky, so I reached over in anger to knock his cap into the water. He elbowed me in the eye almost hard enough to knock me out. I was furious. I didn't want to fight, but I wanted to retaliate.

"You gave me a black eye, you bastard wife beater!" I yelled. I scratched his face. My mind ricocheted back to all of the times in our previous marriage he had treated me badly. I wanted him dead.

"I didn't hit you! You fell on my elbow." Bud never admitted being abusive. Unless he hit me with his fist, I wasn't hit. He said if he ever really hit me I would be dead, because he was so much bigger. Everything he did to me was a result of my falling on his foot, running into his backhand, or jumping on his elbow. Every slap, kick, shove, push, and jolt was my doing. I gave myself busted lips, black eyes, and bruised limbs. He always denied his abuse. I fought back with words. In front of the children I blurted out that I hated him and that I was glad he was not Marbella's father.

He was stunned. Nobody said a word. We drove home. I packed the car and took the children to a resort about three hours away. A day or two later Molly and Ben asked me if Marbella really had a different father. I admitted it and asked them not to tell her or Seth. I didn't offer an explanation, and they didn't ask for one. By the time I returned, Bud was humble again, and I was ashamed of what I said in a fit of anger. We promised never to fight again, but I knew we would.

His temper flared again one night when I fussed at Seth about something insignificant. Bud came at me with clenched fists, but before he could catch me, I escaped through the sliding glass door onto the golf course. I stayed there for hours, praying to die. Looking at the darkened heavens, I said aloud, "Lord, I can no longer stay in this marriage. I have tried as hard as I could. I can't put my children, my parents, Bud, or myself through a divorce again. Please take me. Let me die. It's my only way out."

After I poured my heart out to the Lord, I knew that my life was about to change, but I had no idea how. When I went back into the house everyone was in to bed. I sat in front of the television and watched the celebration of the fall of the Berlin Wall. I saw people who had been divided for decades chip away at piles of concrete and barbed wire with hammers and axes. The wall crumbled, fell, disintegrated in destruction.

CHAPTER XXI

The Interview

Just before Thanksgiving break we learned that our company had lost the government contract on which I worked. Everyone in our organization who wanted employment with the new contractor had to interview with the new management team at BNV Inc. Typically, the interview is a required formality so the employees can change badges. I had a niche as an engineering specialist, and I felt secure. Still, I wanted to be prepared for my interview. My closest friend at work, Melody Ann, interviewed before me. She was tall, black, and rich. As a degreed professional in computer programming, she was one of the best-paid people in the department. She and her engineer husband enjoyed a life of luxury. Melody Ann drove a Jaguar and wore expensive clothes and diamonds in abundance. The other women in our department envied her, but she didn't care; she was above petty jealousies. We became good friends.

We were scheduled to interview with the prospective boss in December, though we would not report until February. When Melody returned to her desk after the interview, I asked her what the new manager was like.

"Well, he's in his mid-forties, wears glasses, is balding, and he's very direct. He doesn't pussyfoot around. He means business!"

"Do you think you did okay in the interview? Do you think he's going to keep you on the job?"

"Yes. I think I did fine. I don't let those things get to me. The way

I look at it, he needs me as much as I need this job. Oh yeah, I almost forgot. He talks with an accent, but I'm not sure what kind it is. I did not want to get too personal so I didn't ask."

When my time to interview came, I dressed professionally in a navy blue suit, offset by a pink blouse with a brooch at the neck. I waited in a large room with several other people. When Mr. Bradley came in and called my name, I felt an immediate reaction, not like a vision but a distinct feeling that either I had known him before or he was going to be special in my future. In the interviewing room, when he removed his jacket I noted his athletic physique. He had a dark tan, penetrating eyes, and a strange accent. He removed his watch, put it on the table, and said, "We have three minutes."

I don't remember what he asked me or how I answered, but I tried to be professional and confident. He watched my gestures, my face, and my body language. I left the interview feeling connected to the man. I tried to articulate my reaction to him but could not. Back at the office, I asked Melody if she felt anything strange when she interviewed.

"No, I didn't feel strange. Did you feel something strange?"

"Yes. I don't know why, but I have a peculiar feeling about him."

"What kind of feeling?"

"I don't know. I can't explain it."

"Girl, are you trying to tell me you're attracted to him?"

"No, it's not like a romantic attraction, I don't think. It's like a special chemistry." Melody didn't understand and neither did I.

On February 1, I started working for BNV Inc., and Dugan Bradley became my boss. Nothing changed except the building where I worked, the badge I wore, and my boss. I still shared an office with Melody and worked on the same project. Everyone wanted to know how Mr. Bradley would change things. He called a meeting the first week and said he would institute change slowly on an as-needed basis. His office was just down the hall from ours, and when I passed by, he always smiled and called me by name.

After a couple of weeks, he stopped by our office to chat. At first, the three of us talked about work and needed process changes. Eventually, the conversations became more personal. He told us he had three grown children and had recently divorced. He was a cyclist and had raced bicycles for years.

"I can beat any of the young bucks around here cycling or in running," he bragged. "I'm forty-eight-years-old and I will still be cycling when I'm ninety. I've been an athlete all my life, and I intend to stay fit until the day I die."

Melody looked at me and raised an eyebrow. He raised his pant leg above his sock to expose a calf muscle that protruded two inches as it pumped and pivoted when he moved his foot. "See what I mean? These are the legs of a cyclist!"

"Dugan, do you shave your legs?" Melody asked.

"Of course. All good bike riders shave their legs. Would you believe that I won a leg contest in Canada when I was younger?"

"Well, yes, I suppose I would believe it," Melody replied.

I had seen legs like those only on body builders, so I believed him when he said he had to wear special pants because his thighs were so muscular. I acted polite but unimpressed.

"What kind of accent is that?" I asked.

"Oh, I'm from Trinidad, West Indies." I had no idea where Trinidad was, but Melody did.

"Trinidad?" she looked perplexed. "I thought only black people lived in Trinidad?"

"Well, you're almost right. I was born when the population was only three percent white, and I made up part of that percentage." Still laughing he added, "Most people say my accent and protruding jaw remind them of Arnold Schwarzenegger."

"Well, Arnie doesn't have a cleft chin like you do," I replied.

"No, that's my Kirk Douglas," he said coyly as he left the room. When he was gone we looked at each other and laughed.

"Rose, I was afraid that he was going to drop his drawers and show us those thighs! I have to admit I wouldn't mind seeing them. I think he's kind of sexy, don't you?"

"I suppose so, but he' s a little too full of himself."

At the end of February, the company threw a big party with plenty of food and music at the Hilton Hotel to celebrate winning the contract. Once the formalities were over, everyone danced and had a great time. Dugan told everyone that this was a good opportunity to mingle with the staff and get to know them better. Bud was with me, and Melody's husband, Jerome, came with her. Earlier in the week, Melody and I had jokingly asked Dugan to save us a dance!

I was wearing a lovely blue dress that wrapped my body like a glove. I still didn't know if Dugan was a flirt or just supremely charismatic. Out of the corner of my eye, I noted his friendliness toward the good-looking women. When he came over to ask us to dance, Melody was already on the floor with Jerome. He asked Bud if he could dance with me, and Bud nodded politely.

"I won't keep her long."

We saw Melody on the floor, and he told her she would be his next partner. We danced fast, keeping the beat with perfect timing. He had good rhythm but not much style. The fast dance ended and a slow tune started almost without a break–*Endless Love,* one of my favorites. I started to walk away, but he gave me a gentle nudge and nod as if to say, "Shall we dance this one also?" Dancing fast was one thing, but to be in my boss' arms was a little intimidating. I paused, took his hand, and moved toward him. We positioned ourselves for the dance and waited for just the right beat to start. He swayed me back and forth, side-to-side, delicately moving, guiding, leading, rocking deliciously. Our bodies moved as one but kept a discreet distance.

"You are a good dancer," I said.

"You are too," he whispered, *"Two hearts, two hearts, that beat as one; our love has just begun."* The music was hypnotic, the atmosphere, mesmerizing.

"This is one of my favorite songs," I said.

"Mine too."

When the song was over we returned to the table, the band took a break, and Dugan excused himself, telling Melody he would be back for his dance. Bud seemed to be having a good time, but I think he was surprised that I had two dances instead of one. Melody leaned over and whispered, "Still have that strange feeling?" I smiled, but didn't answer.

Dugan came to our office every day to chat. I looked forward to his visits. One day he left a note on my desk, asking me to come to his office. When I saw the note, I went to see if he was still there. He was.

"Dugan, did you need me for something?"

"Yes. You look nice today."

"Thank you."

"I wanted to know if you would like to go to happy hour at the Hilton Hotel. Some friends are getting together tomorrow night, and I thought you and Melody might like to join us. The two of you could meet some other people in the company. I've been here a long time, and it helps to know the right people. I'm not inviting everyone. I thought about you and Melody because you are more senior."

"Senior as in old or....?"

"No, senior in your positions," he clarified. "I already mentioned it to Melody before lunch."

"Oh, well, I think that sounds like a good idea. Yes, thank you for inviting me."

"We'll meet there right after work. I thought you might need to arrange a sitter," he said. I was pleased he thought of my career and my children. When Melody came back from lunch, I asked her what she thought of the invitation.

"Rose, I think he likes you."

"What do you mean?"

"I mean, I think he *likes* you," she replied.

"Well, he must *like* you too, because he invited us both."

"You know it's not the same, Rose. I can tell he's got a thing for you. Anyway, I can't go, and I don't want you to go either. If I'm not there to protect you, he'll make a pass at you."

"Oh, Mel, that's ridiculous!"

"You must know that people notice how often he comes to our office?"

"Well, I haven't heard them say anything."

"But they do. I think his britches get tighter when he's around you."

"Melody! You aren't serious."

"Yes, I am, girl. I think he has a thing for you. Besides, what if there are people we know there? They'll start rumors about the two of you."

I was quiet for a minute. "I suppose you're right. Perhaps I won't go. I'll just make an excuse."

She waited for a minute and asked, "Rose, why don't I believe you?"

"I don't know, but I'm going to his office right now to decline."

"Good! I'll go with you. Anyway, I need to tell him I have relatives coming in tonight."

He wasn't in his office, so we left a note. He came to our office after he read it. Melody was already gone for the day.

"I'm sorry you can't make it. I'll be there if you change your mind." I nodded and smiled but gave no indication I would change my mind.

Bud worked that evening. Ben had a date with the girl he was in love with. I made dinner for the other kids and put the dishes up while they watched television. I went to my room and took a bath, but Dugan was all I could think of. I couldn't stand it. I decided to go for just a few minutes. I asked Molly to baby-sit her little brother and sister while I went to a meeting. I put on a red dress and left quickly.

Dugan spotted me the instant I entered. He signaled me over.

"I was hoping you would come."

"I can't stay long."

"That's all right. What do you want to drink?"

"A 7-UP will be fine."

"You don't drink?"

"No, I'm Mormon. It's against my religion."

"Are you religious?"

"Yes."

He smiled and introduced me to his friends.

Some people left once the happy hour was over, but a few stayed. The band started to play and the dance floor became crowded. We sat and talked for a while. I was treading on dangerous ground; getting personal with my boss was a bad idea. I wasn't naïve. I knew he was interested in me. I tried to seem indifferent, but he knew I enjoyed his company; he made me laugh. I learned that he had two daughters and a son, whom he adored. His older daughter had a child; a grandson was the sparkle in his eye.

When conversation lagged, I pushed back and excused myself to the ladies' room. He stood to pull my chair out. Looking into his eyes, I felt magnetically drawn to him. The air between us was electric as we stood face to face, only inches apart. I blushed. Regaining my composure in the ladies' room, I decided it was time for me to leave before my feelings developed further. When I returned he didn't let me sit. Taking my arm, he led me to the dance floor as the band played *Lady In Red*. "We must dance this song since you are wearing red." I followed him to the floor.

We danced close. I loved his scent, his movements, his body, his cleft, and his accent. He looked at me and smiled. "Every time I hear that song, I imagine myself dancing with a beautiful woman dressed in red. Tonight, I am."

"Do you like red?"

"Yes, it's my favorite color."

I thought about what Addie said: "Never settle for orange when you want red." We danced to one, two, three tunes without stopping and were oblivious to others. Our bodies fit together like two spoons. That night he was not my boss, and I was not his subordinate. That night we were one. We forgot where we were. We forgot who we were. We said very little. We just danced. The chemistry was undeniable. We didn't have to speak. We knew our feelings were mutual.

When the band took a break I said I had to go. He walked me to my car. I thanked him for the evening and said goodnight. I knew he wanted to kiss me, but I opened the door and got in without giving him a chance. I was fighting my feelings from the edge of danger. Without a word, I turned to meet his gaze once more, then drew my finger gradually toward his cleft and pressed deep into his dimpled chin. He smiled.

"I'll see you Monday. Thank you for inviting me." I closed the door and drove away while he stood staring at me until I was out of sight.

On the short drive home I tried talking sense to myself. 'How can you allow yourself to feel such emotion again?' I knew better than to walk into temptation's path and play with fire. I recognized my feelings as those I knew when I fell in love with Cruze, and nothing in my life had been more devastating. 'This is probably just another fling for Dugan. He doesn't know all I've been through, all I have to lose. He doesn't know the destruction I have caused or the sacrifices that have been made. I cannot and will not let myself love again. It will end just as my love for Cruze ended; ruining lives, breaking hearts and homes.' I screamed, "Oh, God! Please help me! Don't let me love again!"

Monday morning, Melody was eager to know if I went to the party. Guiltily, I said I had broken my promise.

"Well, did you meet some interesting people?" she asked suspiciously.

"Some, but I really didn't stay long."

"Was it fun?" she asked, hoping for more.

"Yes, it was fun." I replied.

"Did you dance with our boss?"

"You know I did. We danced several times."

"Rose, I don't want you to get involved with him. It won't be good for your career, not to mention your family."

"I know. I know. I am fighting it, but it's hard."

"You mean you really are starting to have feelings for him?"

"Yes, Melody. It's terrible. I can't control it. I'm really scared."

"Didn't you tell me that you and Bud have been through a lot and that you have been divorced and remarried?"

"Several times, but that alone should tell you how difficult life has been for us. We never should've been together in the first place. I'm not happy and never will be with Bud. I told myself a long time ago that my happiness didn't matter, but once it stares you in the face, it's hard to let go of it."

"But, girl, you have all those kids to consider, and Bud seems so nice."

"He is nice most of the time. He wasn't always nice, but he's come a long way. I don't want to hurt him. I didn't plan to fall in love."

"Love? Love? Is that what you're feeling? There is no way love has had time to develop. That's impossible, Rose! I thought we were talking about lust! Lust we can deal with. Love is something altogether different, girl. Now you have me worried."

"All I can tell you is that I have only been in love once in my life, and this feels very much like the beginnings of love to me."

"I have a feeling you're going to tell me that your love wasn't for

Bud."

"Right. I have never loved Bud, Melody. I think I trust you enough to tell you about it some day. It was the most painful thing for me, and I don't ever want to go through it again. Love hurts."

"Love doesn't hurt unless you fall in love with the wrong person."

"I don't feel comfortable talking about this stuff here. Why don't we go to lunch today?"

We took an early lunch, and I told her the story of my life. She sat amazed for an hour and began to understand what I was feeling. "I don't know where all this is going to lead, Rose. I should have known that first day when we interviewed with him that something would happen. You said you had a funny feeling, and now I know why."

Dugan and I talked every day. I told him where I lived and how many children I had, but I said nothing about my marriage or my divorces from Bud. I told him I married at fifteen and was reconciled to a loveless marriage. He confessed that he, too, had been unhappy and recognized how difficult it was to go through a divorce. I wondered if he was just looking to fool around. I was scared to be hurt again. I had too much to lose to entangle myself with a man who would not go the whole nine yards. I could not survive another one-sided love affair. The love would have to be mutual and strong enough to die for. I decided to stifle my feelings and let things cool-off. He didn't take long to notice my changed attitude. I made myself unavailable and tried to keep our conversations strictly professional.

One day, he stopped me in the hall and asked me to drive him to the airport. I concealed my aching heart and tried to be nonchalant, but I agreed to drive him. We hadn't gone far when he said, "Rose, you scare me."

Keeping my eyes on the road, I responded, "I do?"

"Yes," he repeated, "You scare me. The feelings I have for you are driving me crazy. It's like I am going insane. I don't know what to do." He punched his thighs in frustration. "Can you understand?"

"Yes, Dugan, I understand. I understand perfectly. I know those feelings. I have them for you, too. I have felt them only once before." I decided to be honest. If I scared him away, it was fine with me. I wanted him to know who I was and what I had been through. He had to know that I was beyond being a toy for his pleasure.

"Dugan, I've felt this way before, and it was the most painful, hurtful, and destructive experience I ever endured. To tell you the truth, after all of these years, I'm still recovering." I looked for his reaction.

"Please, go on. Tell me."

I told him about marrying at fifteen to get away from a horrible home. "I became a mother at sixteen, divorced at twenty, then remarried to a man I never loved because of pressure from my mother and my commitment to faith." He listened intently. "I had a love affair with a Hispanic man, was excommunicated, and gave birth to his child, Marbella." I summarized my second divorce, my children's separation, the three years of havoc, the fruitless dating, and finally the feigned reconciliation. "I am not doing it again. I can't! I can't go through it again and neither can my children! Don't put me in that position, please."

He reached for my arm and squeezed it. "I don't want you to go through it again. I'm sorry for what you've been through, and I would never want to hurt you." By that time, we were at the airport.

As I turned into the parking lot, he asked me to pull into the garage so we could talk a few minutes more. I parked and turned off the engine.

"I guess you think I'm a pretty sad case, don't you, Dugan? I bet you've never known anyone with a more screwed up life."

He sat sideways in the bucket seat of my van, facing me. "Rose, the things you have done, good or bad, are what make you who you are today, and I wouldn't want you to change one thing about who you are today. Let me just tell you that I don't have love affairs, and I don't have these feelings for other women. This is something new for me, a feeling so strong that it goes to the bone. I don't know what to do about it. It makes me want to cry."

When he said that I knew he was sincere. All I had said to convince myself and to convince him that we must not get involved was in vain. We moved toward each other and kissed, softly at first and then deeply. He pulled me into his lap and held me as if he wanted to take away all my past, all my pain.

"Oh, Rose. I can't let you go. I don't want to let you go."
We held each other so long he almost missed his plane.

CHAPTER XXII
Torrential Deluge

Dugan called me at work while he was away. "I've thought about all you told me, and nothing has changed my feelings for you."

Soon after he came back, Dugan was in an awful bicycle accident, suffered a concussion, and went to the hospital in an ambulance. He lost his memory temporarily, so the nurses searched his pockets and found a contact list of his employees. My address was nearest the place of the accident, so they called me to drive him home. I told Bud where I was going. He was surprised I would be called to do such a personal favor for my boss. Dugan was pretty banged up, so I took him inside his house to make sure he was comfortable before I left. My desire for him was greater than anything that I had ever felt, but we controlled our passion. That day we knew we wanted each other forever.

Over the next few weeks Dugan wrote me beautiful letters full of love and concern. We talked about our families, values, philosophies, and future. We shared our sky castles. We talked about our parents, our upbringing, and how we loved our children. He told me Marbella was my love child and especially precious. Melody knew everything and tried her best to dissuade me, but she finally gave up. There was no turning back.

I decided not to have a love affair behind Bud's back. I would be honest, up front, and willing to suffer the consequences. I could not love Bud, but he didn't deserve my cheating behind his back again. I felt bad enough for kissing Dugan. I was prepared to lose everything, and I would not allow my mother or my faith to influence my decision. I would cut all ties to my mother if need be, but I never considered leaving the Church. My biggest concern was the impact my actions would have on my children.

The last four years with Bud were not perfect, but they were the best four years of our lives together and important in our children's lives. Had we known that we would divorce again within forty-eight months, I would still have chosen to have the family together during that time. Bud and I didn't find love for each other, but I don't think we would have found love elsewhere had we stayed apart. Being married to a woman who didn't love him was not easy for Bud. He deserved love, and so did I. I phoned my sister and said I needed to talk. She must have sensed fear in my voice.

"Is there something wrong?"

"Yes, I'm falling in love with my boss."

"Oh, no, Rose. Not again? What about your kids? Think of them. Think of the heavens, and the hereafter, and eternity. Think of Bud. Think of yourself!"

"What am I going to do, Mary Jane? I wish I could just fast-forward my life to next year so I could see how this is going to turn out. I'm not sure I can survive it."

"Well, it's not going to be pretty. It's going to end in divorce, and this will be the third time! Perhaps you should transfer out of the department so you won't ever see him again. Why don't you talk to your bishop?"

Mary Jane couldn't help, console, or advise me. I was beyond advice.

"You don't want to get excommunicated again do you?"

"No. We have abstained, but the temptation is there." Dugan was all that mattered to me. He was worth risking everything. Nothing and no one could keep me from my one last chance for red.

Bud saw a change in me. He knew something wasn't right. He sat down on our bed while I was at the dressing table. "Rose, tell me what has happened. Something's wrong."

I turned to him and shook my head but said nothing. I looked down.

"There is something wrong, isn't there?"

"Yes. Bud, I don't love you and you know that." He said nothing. "That is what's wrong. It's wrong for two people to be married when they aren't in love. I think I should leave so you can find love, and I can have love."

"Do you think you've already found it somewhere?"

"Yes. I do."

"Is it your boss?"

"I am afraid so, Bud."

He looked frustrated and insulted. He stood and hit his fist in his hand. He got a look of rage on his face. "Well, I hope this works for you, because it'll be the last time for us. Have you done it with him?"

"No, Bud. I'm not going to do that."

He looked at me and shook his head.

"Bud, some day when you find a woman who really loves you, you will thank me. You deserve to know what it's like to be loved, and I want to be in love. I'm not sure you really love me anyway, Bud. I'm just a habit."

"I don't know any more. I guess you could say I love you enough to let you go, to let you find your selfish definition of happiness." That night he stayed at a hotel.

The days that followed are a blur. Telling the children. Splitting the furniture. Putting the house up for sale. Going through all the motions and emotions and tears. I can't remember the trauma. Bud leased a condo from Melody and Jerome. I kept the children with me until the school year was over and the house sold. Ben got his own apartment, and Seth went to stay with Bud for the summer. My mother called once to tell me I was a home wrecker. I said I didn't expect her to understand and didn't need her approval, now or ever. I was prepared for estrangement.

One evening after Bud moved out, Addie walked to my house. I was surprised to see Matt with her at the door. He was driving to Florida to see his mother and stopped in Texas for a couple of days to visit Addie. We sat in the back yard while the sun went down, looking over the golf course and drinking root beer. Matt was openly gay, and Addie no longer tried to hide it or blame herself for it. We talked candidly about his partner.

"Matt, have you ever even been with a woman?" I asked.

"Why, are you offering?" he riposted.

"No, just being nosy." He smiled and looked at the sky. He had no intention of answering. We laughed. He brought a couple of his art pieces for Addie and Mildred. I told him I wanted one of his paintings, too. He promised me one, some day. Matt said my kids were beautiful and that Marbella looked just like me when I was a child.

"How are the kids faring through another divorce?" Addie asked.

"How did you know? I mean . . . I haven't had time to tell you. It all happened so fast."

"Oh, you can just guess that your mother keeps my mother aware of all the latest news. I just found out last night."

"Well, aren't you going to say *I told you so?*"

"No, but I'm not surprised. I'm only sorry you all have it to go through again."

"Me too. The kids are holding up pretty well. Children are resilient, but I'll never know the whole effect this will have on them."

"Well, Rose, you have to admit it is a little unusual."

"Yes, I know. You should use me as a case study in one of your internship classes. Unfortunately, Ben is quite angry. He decided to get an apartment since he's in college. He didn't want to live with either of us, and I don't blame him."

Matt interrupted. "What is it with you, Rose? Why do you keep remarrying a man you don't love?"

"I think it has to do with the pressure from Mama and my wanting the blessings of the Church."

"Well, God never meant for you to be unhappy. You can't let your mother or your father or the church or society define happiness for you. You and only you can know what brings you happiness," he replied.

"Addie, is this going to happen to me for the rest of my life? What type of a sick, psychotic person am I? Why would I drag my family through tar and ice again?"

"As long as you're married to someone you don't love, you'll look for love, and that cycle will go on forever. If you were married to someone you love, you wouldn't be tempted to have an affair! The reason you get into these situations is that you don't love your husband. Just remember what I told you before you married Bud for the third time: you want red!"

"I should have listened to you. I believe that if I love my husband I can be faithful."

She smiled. "Yes. I know you can. That is the root cause of your problems. When you're in love, there's no other temptation! You won't even have the desire."

"Addie, I think you're right. I know you're right."

"Now, tell us, who is he?" Addie asked.

I looked at them and shook my head. "You figured it out?"

"Well, it would have been easy enough to figure out, but your mother told Mama that you had someone else. Isn't he your boss?"

"Yes, Addie. I really love him, and he loves me." I told Addie and Matt all about Dugan.

Dugan and I could not stay away from each other. From the beginning we shared an emotional intimacy that I had longed for all my life. We talked for hours about anything and everything. We both loved one another's children, even though he had not met mine, nor I his. I loved anything that was a part of him and he felt the same for me.

I got a job offer from another company. Leaving would remove the stress brought on from working together. Eventually we began to see each other more openly. We took long walks on the beach, visited museums, and danced together often. He taught me about different cultures, his culture, and ethnic food. I loved hearing him speak in different languages and telling me that he loved me in French, Je t'aime. He met my children, and they liked him. We included them in almost everything we did. From the beginning, he taught them gently, and I could tell he would be a wonderful influence. I met his mother and family. They seemed glad to see him happy. We were in love beyond measure. He was my knight and I was his princess. He said our love was like two trees growing near each other—not so near that the shadow of one stunts the growth of the other, but near enough that the roots intertwine and become one system. He sent a long, slim, white box to my office. I opened it privately and found one long stem red rose. Taking it from the box, I pressed the petals to my lips and smelled the fragrance. As I ran my fingers down the long stem, I noticed that all the thorns had been removed. In the card he had written the last stanza of that beautiful song made famous by Bette Midler.

When the night has been too lonely,
And the road has been too long,
And you think that love is only
For the lucky and the strong,
Just remember in the winter
Far beneath the bitter snows,
Lies the seed, that with the sun's love,
In the spring becomes the Rose...

If we could have married the day he moved into his apartment, we would have. Unable to marry before Thanksgiving, we were too weak to control our desire. Every moment with him was fulfilling. I once again found myself discussing my sin with a Mormon bishop and was excommunicated before we married. Second excommunications are rare. I was about to give up on having any real chance in heaven. I was unworthy of heaven anyway, unworthy to be there with people who kept the commandments, but I never lost my love for the gospel or my testimony of its truths. I just couldn't seem to live it. Dugan didn't criticize the Church. He said that when the time was right, he wanted to understand what I could believe so deeply, yet struggle with so intensely.

We had a friend at NASA, Conrad Boswell, who was about the same age as Dugan. Conrad was a little over six feet with thick salt and pepper hair and deep blue eyes. He was the senior executive responsible for site safety but he was a cowboy at heart. He ran two thousand head of cattle on his 1600-acre ranch outside of Waco. I never saw him wear any other shoes except alligator or snake-skinned boots. Conrad had a way with the ladies but never seemed to find a keeper. By choice, he wasn't married, and we wanted to find a date for him.

I don't know why, but I called my cousin Sue Ellen and asked if she was dating since her divorce. She was surprised to hear from me because, though we were first cousins, we had never been close. We knew very little about each other, and I suspect the little she did know about me, she liked about as much as I liked the little I knew about her. However, I decided to dismiss my lifelong notions of her. 'Perhaps she's really a very nice person, and I have had the wrong impression of her all these years.' I was probably more sympathetic toward her since, like me, she had experienced the heartache of divorce. Her ex-husband was already remarried to his secretary. She had been divorced about a year and said she was ready to start dating. She agreed to meet Conrad.

Just before Dugan and I married, I arranged the date between Conrad and Sue Ellen. She came to Houston and stayed at my house. She was forty-three, and I was thirty-six. Despite bearing six children, she looked great. We spoke briefly about her unhappy marriage although I didn't ask her many questions since I didn't want to pry. To my surprise she was very open about it.

"I was miserable for years and faked happiness in public. You know, I look around at other couples and I can see they are not happy. I guess most people just try to act happy, but it is easy to see through them." She told me that she cried a lot because her husband didn't respect her. Over the years, she had lost respect for him, too.

"During the last seven years of our marriage, I refused to have sex with him. It has been a long time since I have had intimacy in my life and I am ready!"

"Seven years! How did you manage that? Did you sleep in separate rooms?"

"No, in the same bed."

"What did you do if he tried to touch you?" I asked in amazement.

"I got stiff as a board!"

"Wow! Did your Bishop give you a hard time about divorce?"

"Not really. He worked with us a long time before he finally told me that the Lord never meant for us to be so unhappy."

I certainly related to her comments about feigned happiness. She dealt with her grief in her way and I dealt with mine in quite another. Either way, both of our responses to the pain of matrimony were wrong and only served to propel the doomed fate of our unions.

We went out for a seafood dinner at one of the nicer restaurants nearby. Afterwards, we took a long walk down the fishing pier. Considering that Conrad was the first man she had dated she seemed amazingly comfortable. They acted like they enjoyed the evening and planned another date together. Sue Ellen was pleasant enough and I hoped that this experience might put to rest any negative feelings between us. However, because of my earlier memories of her I moved cautiously in her presence.

CHAPTER XXIII

The Betrayal

On the day before Thanksgiving, Dugan and I married in Melody and Jerome's home. Melody stood by me through the divorce and never let me down. I broke my commitment to myself and called my mother to tell her I was marrying Dugan and invited her to the wedding. While she wasn't rude, she declined the invitation and offered no congratulations. She had not met Dugan and was determined not to accept him. She was concerned for the children and could never sanction divorce. She wanted me to be noble like her, denying myself love and intimacy forever. Addie was at the wedding, along with my sister and my children. Before the ceremony, Addie hugged me. "Everything is going to be okay now, Rose. You have finally found red!"

The children soon accepted Dugan and acclimated to their new environment. When my sister came to know Dugan she saw that he was a fine person and that we were unmistakably in love. We married as soon as possible, hoping for a quick return to stability for my children. We also understood that for the sake of his adult children, we should have waited. His prompt remarriage did not set well with them. Dugan went to church with us and everyone treated him kindly. Surprisingly, Bud would remarry within three months of my marriage to Dugan.

Conrad and Sue Ellen agreed to meet at a church conference in Houston. He rode with us to the meeting, but once we were there, we could not find Sue Ellen. My mother and Aunt Beverly had devised a plan for Sue Ellen and Bud to meet there also. That Sue Ellen and Bud would be interested in each other seemed unlikely because she was seven years his senior. I also remembered when Bud saw her a few years earlier at a family reunion; he said she was not his type. I was surprised to learn that Sue Ellen wanted to meet Bud. The secret meeting with Bud was insulting and deceptive. If she wanted to meet Bud she could have at least spared Conrad for being played a fool that day.

We searched for Sue Ellen to no avail, but found my mother, Aunt Beverly, and Uncle William sitting together. Since they had not met, I introduced Dugan and Conrad to them. My mother shook Dugan's hand and tacitly showed her disapproval while all three concealed the mystery of Sue Ellen's whereabouts. She finally showed up and airily acknowledged our presence at the end of the conference. She had been in her pre-arranged meeting with Bud.

Since we separated, Bud and I had moved past our regrets and had developed a civil relationship. Bud told me how my mother and Aunt Beverly had arranged the meeting with him and Sue Ellen at the conference. He went to a dance with Sue Ellen about three weeks later but didn't call her again. Conrad phoned and told me Sue Ellen broke a date with him because she didn't want to set a bad example for her children by dating a "heathen."

"I've been called plenty of things but never a heathen!"

I laughed. "Conrad, don't worry about it. I think I can explain what's going on. She called you heathen because you're not Mormon. But please don't think all Mormons are so judgmental." I told him about Bud and Sue Ellen. "My guess is that Sue Ellen likes Bud and doesn't want to make a sticky situation worse, so she's not going to date you. That way she can be more accessible for Bud. After all, he's not a heathen!"

I was naturally annoyed at the deception of my mother and Sue Ellen's family. The matchmaking scheme bothered me, because there was no need for secrecy. I phoned my mother to explain that I wanted Bud to be happy and didn't care who he dated, but the meeting in secret embarrassed me. She didn't understand and was smug and satisfied that she had perturbed me.

I then called Sue Ellen. "Sue Ellen, this is Rose." She didn't know what to say. "Sue Ellen, you know that I know. I am calling because I don't want bad feelings between us. I have no problem with your dating Bud. He knows I don't care who he dates; in fact, he is the one who told me. But, I don't appreciate the deception. There is simply no reason for it."

"But your mother said it would make you mad."

"No, Sue Ellen, my mother wants me to be mad or maybe jealous, but the fact is, I don't care and she wishes I did. If I thought you were interested, I would have gladly fixed you up with him myself! Put yourself in my position. How would you feel if your mother went behind your back to arrange a date between your ex-husband and me?" She said nothing. Sue Ellen didn't care about my feelings. True to her character, she thought only about herself. She admitted she was interested in Bud, but had lost hope since he had not called since their date three weeks earlier. I was of the spirit that I wanted everyone to be happy and if she and Bud could find it together then that was fine with me. I offered to tell Bud that she was very interested and she happily agreed.

A few days later, Bud came for the children and I asked him why he hadn't called Sue Ellen. He said he hadn't thought about it. I told him that I had spoken with her and she was waiting on pins and needles for his call.

"It sounds to me like she is already convinced that you are the one for her!" We both chuckled.

"Well, I guess I'll call her back then." He casually replied. Before Bud knew what hit him, Aunt Beverly was making Sue Ellen's wedding dress. Three days before the wedding, Bud told Molly and Seth that he had cold feet, but it was too late. They married five weeks after their second date in a civil ceremony with a big reception, my mother front and center at the festivities. She refused to come to my wedding but she attended the reception for Bud and Sue Ellen. The entertainment was a talent show by Sue Ellen's children. Bud's children were not included. That was the first sign of things to come.

From that point on, Sue Ellen wanted no communication between Bud and me, not even about the kids, which made life difficult. For her own security Bud had to hate me before she could believe he loved her.

My hope was that because she was blood related to my children that she would have a genuine inclination toward them, but my expectations were in vain. The passing years would prove her inability to adjust to them and their aversion to her.

During the first year, Seth and four of Sue Ellen's children lived with them; her other children were grown. Sue Ellen gave birth to a baby boy, so they could add *ours* to *yours* and *mine*. They decided not to treat the children the same. Sue Ellen didn't want Bud to discipline her children, only his. She disciplined her children far differently from how Bud disciplined his. Seth became the whipping post and was blamed for everything that went wrong. By the end of the school year, Seth looked like he had been in a POW camp. He lost twenty pounds, missed almost all his orthodontic appointments, and was an emotional wreck. I knew that I had to get him away. I told him that I wanted him to live with me.

"Can I? Can I really?"

"Of course you can! You could have lived with us from the beginning, but you never said you wanted to."

"I thought I had to live with dad since I lived with him when you were divorced before, but it's different now because Sue Ellen is there."

He came to live with us and told me that if I had not taken him out of that house, his rage at being mistreated would have ended him up in prison.

"Sue Ellen has convinced Dad that we are selfish little devils. When Dad isn't around she is rude and won't speak to us, but she puts on an angelic act for Dad." The children complained endlessly about Bud and Sue Ellen. They were happy with Dugan and me but miserable when they had to deal with Sue Ellen.

"Mom, she can't talk about anything except the church and her kids. She brags about her children constantly and ignores us. She even has pictures of her kid's displayed in their house, but none of us." Like a mother hen, I wanted to protect my chicks from the hurt she caused them, but there was nothing I could do. Bud the chameleon defended her.

Dugan and I treated everything equally: the money, the children, the property, and the responsibilities. We didn't try to replace the children's natural parents, but we didn't discriminate among them. We shared their lives as if they were our own. We tried to be fair with all of our children. They might not like us, but they could not say we were unfair. Eventually, we gained their respect and ultimately their love. They found there was room in their hearts to love us both.

Five months after we married, Dugan was baptized. The meetinghouse was packed, and I was thankful for the show of support. Clearly, the Church was less judgmental than my mother. When she heard Dugan was baptized, her attitude toward him changed. She accepted him solely because he joined the Church. I was still excommunicated when Dugan joined, but our bishop assured me that through repentance I could be baptized again, and once again enjoy the blessing of the Church.

Billy visited us after Dugan's baptism and saw the way I felt about Dugan. He told my mother he had never seen me so happy.

"Mama, Rose is a different person. For the first time in her life, she's happy. Dugan is the best thing that ever happened to her, but you may never get the chance to see her happy or congratulate Dugan for getting baptized–and it's your own fault. What you did to Rose was wrong! If you didn't go to their wedding, then you shouldn't have gone to Bud and Sue Ellen's. Rose is your daughter, not Sue Ellen!" My mother reluctantly accepted that I was in love, happy, and would never mourn for Bud. Billy and I spoke many times about the bizarre admiration Mama had toward Uncle William and his family. We couldn't understand it and were both embarrassed by it.

CHAPTER XXIV
Broken Silence

Dugan and I built our dream home near the Space Center on a lot in one of the nicest neighborhoods and moved in just before the November 1992 elections in which William Jefferson Clinton was elected the forty-second President. During Clinton's presidency the country enjoyed an unrivaled economic boom. But the company I worked for lost a bid for a major NASA contract, and I was laid off. We made plans for me to study for a MBA at the University of Houston.

One day, after I had returned to school full-time, I got a desperate call from Pinky. She had nowhere to live, no car, and nobody to take care of her. Pinky didn't know what to do without a man. She never supported herself. Her mother had not spoken to her since she broke up with Andy, so she couldn't go home, and she had burned her bridges with others. I felt sorry for her and asked Dugan if she could stay in the guest room a few weeks until she got a car and a job. Pinky swore she would not do any drugs and would get a job as soon as possible. She said that she would help me clean house and do some cooking. Since I was a student, I was glad to have Pinky's help. Soon she found a job at a catering company within walking distance of our house.

One of President Clinton's first challenges after becoming president was the 1993 Branch Davidian crisis in Waco, Texas. During a siege by government law officers, a fire in the complex killed all of the cult members and their leader, David Koresh. It was Pinky's birthday.

"Why is it that bad things always happen on my birthday, Rose?"

"It's just a coincidence, Pinky. Don't take it personally."

Pinky thought her birth brought a curse on the world. Her premise was reinforced two years later when Timothy McVeigh celebrated her birthday by blowing up the Federal Building in Oklahoma City to protest the siege on David Koresh. From that time Pinky maintained that her birth was an omen that unleashed catastrophe upon the universe. She eventually saved enough to afford an old car; that was the first step in getting back on her feet.

Pinky joined a class action lawsuit against the manufacturer of silicone implants; hers ruptured, and she became very sick. She was confident of the outcome and planned to have her implants removed and speculated on what she would do with her millions. I thought it was another of her dreams, but I hoped she would get a settlement. She observed that I suffered from bad headaches every week and frequently didn't feel well.

"Rose, your silicone implants are causing your headaches and making you sick."

"Oh Pinky, my implants are still intact, and if there isn't a silicone leak, it shouldn't affect me."

"That's not true, Rose! Just the fact that you have implants and the silicone is in your body can cause all kinds of negative reactions. You better start paying attention to what I'm telling you. You're sick far too often. You're forever on the couch with a headache." I hadn't thought about it, but she was right. I had horrible headaches all the time, and I was tired and listless.

"I wonder if you could be right?"

"I'm giving you the name of my lawyer. You should call him and get in on this suit before it's too late. The lawyers pay for all the medical tests, so you don't even have to front the money."

I went with Pinky to the attorney and joined the class action lawsuit. The tests for ailments related to silicone exposure came back positive, so I scheduled surgery to have them removed and replaced with saline implants. The surgery was on April 19, Pinky's birthday, and she drove me home. I felt bad that I could afford to have mine replaced and she couldn't. We heard of a woman who couldn't afford to have

ers taken out and was in such misery that she got drunk and cut hers
out with a knife. Pinky said she felt like doing the same thing.

Three weeks after the surgery Dugan asked, "Rose, when was your
last headache?"

I hadn't thought about my headaches until then. "Wow! I haven't
had a headache since I had surgery. In fact, I've felt wonderful since I
had the implants replaced. I never expected to feel better that quickly!" Feeling so much better immediately after the surgery convinced
me the lawsuit was justified. A few weeks later, Pinky moved into her
own apartment.

In their mid-thirties, Billy and Jessie still lived with Mama and
Dad. They both married briefly, and Billy had a son who lived with his
ex-wife's parents. Much like Pinky, Billy was incapable of caring for his
son permanently. Billy disliked Jessie's wife and vice-versa. Both were
alcoholics, Jessie functioning better than Billy. They looked like outlaw
motorcycle-gangsters, tuff as steel, but their appearance was a facade
that covered scars.

Over the years Billy and Jessie lost several close friends to drug
overdoses, suicide, and gang fights, and I sometimes wondered if they
would be next. Nothing could have prepared them for the loss of their
lifetime friend, Ricky, who was like a brother to them. Ricky fought
every fight with them, was arrested with them, shared women with
them, was expelled with them, drank and drugged with them, and
pulled every prank with them. But, Ricky was pulling his life together.
He had a good job and almost entirely gave up drinking. For the first
time in his life, Ricky was in love and about to be married. Billy and
Jessie both liked Ricky's fiancée, and everyone looked forward to the
wedding. Two weeks before the wedding, Billy got a call from the
bride-to-be.

"Billy, Is Ricky with you?"

"No, he's at work, isn't he?"

"No, I'm worried. I've been trying to reach him at work all day,
and they say he never made it in. He left here at seven this morning
headed for work, and I know he wouldn't go anywhere else."

Billy knew she was right. "I'll find out and let you know."

Billy grabbed Jessie and took off down the highway. They contacted anyone who might have seen Ricky and retraced his path to the job-site. They searched for hours but found nothing. They both thought something bad had happened. While they were looking for Ricky, the coroner called his parents, asking them to come to the morgue to identify Ricky's body. He was in an accident on the way to work. By the time Billy and Jessie returned, the family had been to the morgue and identified the body. As soon as Billy and Jessie drove into the driveway the family walked out of the house to meet them. Seeing the anguish in their faces, Billy and Jessie froze in their tracks.

"Is he dead?" Billy asked the question whose answer he feared.

With no way to soften the blow, Ricky's father answered, "Yes Billy, he's dead. We've just come from the morgue. He was in an acci-dent on his way to work this morning." Telling Billy and Jessie was as hard as telling his own daughters. He crumbled explaining Ricky's death to the only brothers he had known.

Billy dropped prostrate on the ground, groaning. Jessie fell over him. Burying his face in the clover, Billy clawed at the ground as if try-ing to dig his own grave. Unabashed in sorrow, they refused to be comforted. Billy turned to Jessie and sobbed, "I never even told him I loved him. I never told him . . . " He couldn't finish. The macho trio too masculine for expressions of the heart, parted without avowing their devotion to each other. Each would have given his life for the other gladly.

My mother broke her boycott to call and let me know about the loss. Anyone who knew Billy and Jessie also knew Ricky, for they were inseparable. As she explained the scene of Ricky's family breaking the news to my brothers, I imagined Ricky's spirit being there at that very moment in time. I visualized him standing by the mailbox, watching the woeful reaction of his dear brothers who had shared the best and worst parts of their lives with him. He must have wanted to tell them himself that he was gone, that he must be away for a short season, that he didn't want to go, but he had greater work to do, and that he would miss them, and think of them, and that he loved them.

After the funeral, my mother and I got back on speaking terms. She regretted the way she treated her family and grieved aloud with my father sometimes. She knew they were ignorant parents and made mistakes. Like me, she also knew they could not turn back the clock. She was glad Dugan had been baptized. She also knew that attending Bud's wedding reception and not mine was wrong.

"Mama, I don't ask you to treat us better than Bud and Sue Ellen. I only ask to be treated as well. Why have you always treated Sue Ellen better than your own children?"

Adamantly, she denied the accusation.

"Can't you see that Sue Ellen enjoys your flattery, especially when I am there to witness it? She feels superior knowing you worship her. You know she treats both my children and me badly, yet you don't disapprove of her. She thrives on your loyalty considering it a confirmation that she is upstanding. If my niece treated my grandchildren or my daughter badly I certainly wouldn't fall at her feet."

"But she is my niece."

"Yes, and I am your daughter! I am also Uncle William's niece and he ignores me when he sees me. Ask Mary Jane or the boys if you've been partial, and they'll say you have. It didn't start when Bud married Sue Ellen. You've held Uncle William's family above yourself and your children all your life."

She repeated emphatically, "I don't love anyone better than my own children!"

"I never said you did. I said you treated them with more respect. Perception is reality, and it's embarrassing. Uncle William and Aunt Beverly would never put another child above Sue Ellen. It's just not normal. It goes against human nature."

"Okay. You've made your point. I am not perfect." She admitted.

"Look. I haven't been a perfect mother either and am sorry for putting my children's needs aside at times to indulge myself. If they can forgive me my trespasses as a mother, I must forgive you yours. But, I want to understand why have you treated me so badly all my life? Why did you praise the other children but never me? And why did you rebuke anyone who tried to pay me a compliment? Why did you treat Mary Jane so much better? Were you jealous of me? That's the only conclusion I can come to. You must have been jealous of me."

Guiltily she replied, "Relatives, strangers, and friends always complimented you. Everyone paid attention to you. Your Aunt Paula once said you were so pretty, because you looked like her children. I didn't want you to get the big head. I didn't want my other children to feel left out."

"So you overcompensated for the other children by ignoring me?" I asked.

"Yes, that's what I did. When everyone googooed over you while poor little Mary Jane stood by watching, I took up for her and shamed others for being partial."

"Do you think that was right?"

"I don't know if it was right. I only know that's why I did it."

"But didn't you see that Mary Jane got her own compliments? She never competed with me nor I with her."

"Yes, she got compliments on her voice, but you got attention," she said hesitantly.

So it was not just my imagination or Addie's. It was true. Mama always let people praise Mary Jane and did everything to draw attention to her, but she rebuked any approval for me. Her rejection of me was punishment for what I represented, and I had to find out what I personified in her mind that made her treat me so badly.

Ten more years passed before I discovered what I signified to my mother. To get beyond the despair of my childhood, I needed the answer. Maturity and freedom from my past hinged on my understanding what drove my mother. Perhaps my temperament, indestructibility, resiliency, or defiance set her off, but those characteristics were the effects of her treatment, not the cause. I believed I might never discover what provoked her wrath. Having studied psychology all through school, I thought my coursework might enlighten me, but the answer did not come in the classroom but in the form of inspiration and personal revelation. It was revealed through my gift of vision.

CHAPTER XXV

Graduation and Discovery

Ben and I graduated from the University of Houston the same day, he with a bachelor's degree and I with a master's. Only because of the unplanned coincidence did we decide to participate in the graduation ceremony. The dean announced that a mother and son were graduating simultaneously and asked us to stand and take a bow. Afterward we posed in our caps and gowns as Dugan snapped pictures.

Bud almost missed his son's graduation. He was at the beach with Sue Ellen. Ben called to remind him just before the ceremony. He rushed from his picnic with sand between his toes just in time to see Ben walk across the stage.

Having completed my educational goals, I was ready to return to the job market. The first opportunity was a teaching assignment with the Institute of Engineering Management at Arizona State University where I had completed a certification while with NASA. The Institute's founder, Vince Quest, offered me the position, and I was the first female instructor. My picture in the Institute's brochure and a write-up on my education and experience in architecture and engineering management opened up the opportunities I needed. By the end of the summer I was receiving unsolicited interview requests from companies all over the United States. After exploring several of the companies and receiving offers from some of them, I accepted an offer to manage the facilities at PCs Inc. in Austin, Texas. Relocating to Austin meant Dugan would have to give up his job of thirty years. We had no qualms about the offer or the relocation, and we knew it was the right thing for us.

Just before moving to Austin, Dugan and I watched twelve-year-old Marbella play in a soccer competition in Texas City. The route home took us past Cruze's house. We stopped at the stop sign on the corner by his house. The garage door was open.

"Dugan, that's Cruze's house. There he is in the garage." Marbella had not seen him for almost ten years, and hearing his name, she looked in the garage and somehow remembered him. I couldn't believe the excitement in her voice.

"That's Cruze?" she exclaimed opening the car door as if she were going to jump out.

"Marbella, what are you doing?" I asked.

"Let her go." Dugan answered.

She bolted from the car and ran into his garage, her face full of glee and enthusiasm.

"Cruze, do you remember me? I'm Rose's daughter, Marbella."

He swallowed. "Marbella . . .Marbella . . . What a surprise! What a wonderful, wonderful surprise!" He glanced at our car. "Well, aren't you the prettiest thing I have ever seen?" He grabbed her and hugged her before he asked who was in the car.

"That's my mom and step-dad, Dugan."

Cruze had no idea I had married Dugan. He gathered his composure before approaching the car. Dugan was eager to meet the only other man I ever loved. As Cruze and Marbella walked to the car, his long time girlfriend came out of the house and followed. Cruze disclosed his life's secret to her long ago; she knew Cruze had come face to face with his clandestine love child. Dugan introduced himself, and they shook hands while we nodded and smiled. Cruze wasn't sure if Dugan knew about our affair, so he was cautious. He introduced his girlfriend. They observed Marbella's obvious resemblance to Cruze.

I told him that we were moving to Austin where I would work for PC's Inc. He lingered by the car until dusk. He couldn't take his eyes off his daughter. She was still wearing her soccer uniform, socks to the knees, and cleats, with a mouth full of braces, thick brown hair, dark tan, cute figure, and neon eyes. She looked at him lovingly as if she wanted him to kiss her, as if she sensed the relation. That was impossible, since she knew nothing. We drove home in silence, reflecting on the impromptu encounter. Addie was right. My temptation for other men was gone. The love I once had for Cruze paled in comparison to my love for Dugan.

Before I left for Austin, I was baptized again. I moved into a company apartment and stayed until my family joined me at the end of the semester. Dugan stayed behind with the children, sold the house, and took an early retirement package from BNV.

In the Mormon Church, a couple who has been sealed in the temple and subsequently decide to divorce, they must get a temple divorce in addition to a civil divorce before being sealed to someone else. Since Dugan and I wanted to be married in the temple, I petitioned the highest church office for a temple divorce from Bud. During our twenty-year on-again off-again marriage, I kept Bud's mistreatment of me secret from all of my bishops. I needed to protect him-part of my codependency. I was ashamed to admit that I showed some of my parents' disgusting behavior of domestic violence. When I petitioned the first presidency of the Mormon Church, I decided to be honest. I admitted to having an affair, and I described Bud's abuse as one reason for annulling the temple sealing.

When Bud learned of the petition, he was furious. I had blown his cover, so he asked the bishop to referee a confrontation with me. He denied being a wife beater and accused me of moving to Austin to estrange the children from him. I agreed to meet with him and the bishop.

Sue Ellen came with Bud and waited outside, glaring. Bud claimed that I took the Austin job to keep him from seeing the children. He accused me of poisoning his relationship with them.

"First of all, Bud, it's ridiculous to imagine I would take a job based on how far I could take the kids away from you. Tell me, was Sue Ellen accused of that when she married you? Didn't she take her children away from the city where their father lived?"

Bud looked stumped. The bishop awaited his response. He offered none. Although Dugan and I were happy to know our path would cross Bud and Sue Ellen's less often, that had nothing to do with our decision to move.

"Bud, it's time you quit blaming me for your horrible relations with the children and start taking responsibility for it yourself. I wish they liked to visit you, but they don't. Maybe you should take a realistic look at why!"

"It's because you put ideas in their heads, and you don't want them to like Sue Ellen."

"Bud, the kids are too old for me to brainwash them. They draw their own conclusions. I am outraged at the way you allow her to treat them and the way you treat them yourself. How would I even know how they're treated if they didn't tell me themselves? She treats them differently when you're not around. She won't even speak to them. I don't tell them how they should feel about you. They tell me how they're treated. It has been very hard to deal with."

"Well, why don't you encourage them to like Sue Ellen?"

"I don't encourage them not to, Bud! I know why they don't like her, because I listen to them and I believe them. You only listen to Sue Ellen."

The bishop remained silent. Since Bud's arguments weren't holding up, he changed the subject and went to the next item on his list.

"Well, I've heard that you are saying I beat you, and that's not true."

"Bud, you are not really going to deny that you've hit me, are you?"

He pounced on the opportunity to shame me in front of the bishop.

"I only hit you when you told me you were pregnant with another man's child!" Bud thought the bishop would side with him if he revealed that secret. The bishop didn't stir, so I answered.

"That was perhaps the only time I deserved it, Bud, but your abuse predated that by a decade. Why do you lie? Don't you remember kicking me with steel-toed boots, pushing me, busting my lip, blacking my eye, and knocking me down too many times to count? Shall I give the bishop a copy of the police report from one of our family disturbances? Perhaps the bishop should ask our children if you beat me. They were eye witnesses!"

He didn't want the children summoned, because he knew what

hey would say.

"Oh, you've told them to say they saw me hit you."

"Do you really think they would lie? Do you know that Sue Ellen told Molly that I lied in the letter to the first presidency about your abuse? Molly told her it was not a lie, because she saw it herself." Bud was not convincing the bishop.

"Well, what about all the times you hit me? How many times have you hit me?"

"I don't know, Bud, probably a lot. Although I weigh 110 pounds, and you are twice my size, I fought back. I am not denying the fights Bud, you are! I have never denied hitting you. You say you didn't hit me, and you know that's the real lie."

The bishop looked at him and said, "So, will you admit that you fought with each other, Bud?"

"Yes," he replied reluctantly, hanging his head.

It was over. I left the room before Bud. Sue Ellen sat in a chair outside the office with a snide look on her face. I looked her in the eyes as I passed but didn't say a word. I heard her sarcastic voice behind me, "Well, Hello!"

I stopped, stepped back, and faced her. "Congratulations, Sue Ellen. That is quite possibly the first time you ever spoke first to someone in your entire life. Maybe there's hope for you yet!"

"At least I'm not a liar!"

"A liar?"

"Yes. You lie to say Bud beat you. He never beat you."

"How do you know? You weren't there."

"I don't believe you. I will never believe you."

"You don't have to, but you weren't there, my dear. I was!"

Although Bud admitted in the bishop's office that he fought with me, he continued to dispute it on record. Luckily, our bishop in Austin had watched the documentary of the O.J. Simpson trial on the day we sat together to discuss the dispute. Even with the evidence of police reports, recorded hysterical phone calls from Nicole, and pictures of her bruised face, Simpson never admitted that he beat his wife. The documentary claimed that a perpetrator could convince himself of his innocence and believe the abuse never happened. Such was the case with Simpson, and such was the case with Bud. I was thankful he saw the documentary. I asked him to interview one of the children about the facts. He called Ben, who confirmed that he had seen us fight on numerous occasions. "They both hit each other. He hit my mother and my mother hit him. But he was twice her size."

The Church authorities had all they needed. They documented Ben's statement along with their own comments and sent the letters appealing for a temple divorce. The divorce was granted and cleared the way for my sealing to Dugan. I wanted Dugan for eternity, and we were sealed together in the temple. I put the past behind me and allowed my mother to attend the special temple ceremony. I concluded that if I didn't forgive my mother, my children wouldn't forgive me. I suppose I would have forgiven her completely, had she not continued to insult and humiliate me.

CHAPTER XXVI
Truth Revealed

Dugan and the children joined me in Austin in January and he enjoyed the first break in employment he ever had. Dugan taught the children by precept and example, discussing things with them, never raising his voice or lifting his hand. They were not accustomed to lectures, and they didn't always like them. Sometimes they thought it would be less painful if he yelled at them and got it over with rather than endure his logical *do's* and *don'ts* and *why's* and *why nots.*

He was particular about manners and protocol. He taught them social behavior, reminding them to say *please* and *thank you,* and to cover their mouths when they coughed. Bud and I had been unforgivably lax about teaching manners, but Dugan, having been raised in a culture with British influence, understood the importance of good manners and social behavior.

"When you visit your friends at their homes, always find the parents, introduce yourself, and let them know you're there. When you leave, find the parents, thank them for the visit, and tell them you're leaving."

The responsibility for raising his own children Dugan often left to his former wife, since he traveled extensively with his job and sometimes had long-term assignments in other countries. At home, he turned to athletic activities, training on the bicycle after work and weekends. He acknowledged how difficult managing without him must have been for his wife and admitted that his selfishness with his own time had probably harmed his family's relationships. The opportunity to rear a second generation of children was a blessing in his life. He did all he could to influence their lives for the better and make our union a gift for them. He earned their respect, and the children grew to love him. His children had come to accept our marriage and treated me well, too.

We bought five acres of land on a hill just west of Austin and built a Mediterranean style stucco house with a swimming pool in front so we could enjoy the forward view. It had an open terrace for dining and a barn and stable for horses. Not large originally, we expanded and remodeled the house over the next six years until it became our *Casa Grande.*

PC's Inc. hired Dugan three months after he arrived. It was an exciting time to be employed by a young company positioned for exponential growth. Working at the same company proved prosperous for us; we were about to be catapulted to multi-millionaire status almost over-night.

Molly remained in Houston to finish the last semester of high school. She lived with her father briefly, but she couldn't stand the conditions and moved in with Bud's mother. Molly said Sue Ellen and Bud were religious fanatics and had such rigid rules they made living there impossible. The children discovered a baby monitor microphone in a bedroom closet so Sue Ellen could listen to their private conversations. Molly suggested to Sue Ellen that her rules were fanatical.

"The leaders of the Church say you can't be too fanatical about our religion," Sue Ellen retorted. Sue Ellen took the admonition out of context. I explained to Molly that one can never be too fanatical about following Christ's example, but he never had a *holier than thou* attitude. Christ came to heal sinners, not saints. He loved unconditionally, ate with unbelievers, comforted the broken hearted, associated with believers and non-believers alike, cured the sick, and loved everyone.

Sue Ellen's own children were unhappy. Of the four children she brought with her to the marriage, two dropped out of high school to get away, and one left immediately after graduation to live with her father. Only one girl remained at her mother's new home. Of the six children from her first marriage, she favored two girls over the others.

One of them she thought her most beautiful and the other her most talented. She gave those two almost all of the attention. She fantasized that they would be famous and live with bright lights and paparazzi. She did to them what her mother had done to her.

Marbella, now in junior high, hated her visits with Bud and Sue Ellen, and confronted Sue Ellen face-to-face or tattled to Bud about how terribly she treated them. Marbella asked me if she was old enough to have her legal visitation commitments terminated. I wasn't sure, but I encouraged her to avoid confrontations. Although I sympathized, I explained how much it would hurt Bud if she stopped visiting.

Marbella told me she felt something was missing within her, but she couldn't understand it or give an explanation for it. "Mom, I don't understand this constant, aching emptiness that keeps chewing at me. Is there something I should know, that I don't know? It's like a piece of me that I can't find, and I don't know where to look for it. I won't feel whole until I find it. Is it normal to feel this way?"

What she described was instinct. "No, I wouldn't say it's normal, Marbella. The only way that I can relate is my desire to know why my mother treated me so badly. I won't feel whole until I understand."

The next day, I came upon Marbella in my bedroom, looking through the yellow pages, crying. "What are you doing, Marbella? Why are you crying?"

"I am trying to find an attorney, so I can find out what my rights are."

"What rights?"

"My legal rights for visitations with Dad. I don't want to have to go to Dad and Sue Ellen's any more. I can't stand her, and I hate going there. I have gotten to where I even hate Dad. He acts just like Sue Ellen."

I took a deep breath and sat on the edge of the bed. I had not planned for this moment, and I didn't know exactly what to say–but it was time she knew. I put my hand on her back and tried to console her.

"Marbella, what if I told you that you *are* different, that there is a reason for all those feelings about not being whole, that you have described to me?"

"What do you mean, I *am* different?"

"What if I told you that Bud is not your real father?"

"He isn't?"

"I didn't say he isn't. I asked you a question. What if I told you he isn't?"

"Then I'd be glad. I don't want him to be my dad!" I felt bad when she said that. I wasn't sure I should say more, but it was too late. Knowing the past might change her feelings for Bud.

"Well, he *isn't* your real dad. He is Ben, Molly, and Seth's father but not yours. While I was married to your dad I fell in love with someone else and got pregnant. Your dad knew it and we separated, but he decided to stay with the marriage. We divorced after you were born. It was noble of him to stay with me until you were born. He always treated you like you were truly his, and he gave you his name. Remember that."

"Wow! That must have made him feel real bad."

"Yes, Marbella. It was a difficult time."

"Does that mean I'm not related to Ben, Molly, and Seth?"

"You are their half-sister. You all have the same mother but a different father."

"Do they know it?"

"Ben and Molly know. Seth doesn't."

"Now do you understand why you shouldn't stop your visits with Bud? It isn't fair after all he did. It just isn't fair, Marbella."

She closed the phone book and put it aside. A tear dropped from her cheek as she took in what I told her. She almost forgot to ask her father's identity. Suddenly, she looked at me fearfully and said, "But then who? Who is my father?"

Knowing that, she would also know she was Hispanic. "What if I told you that it was Cruze?" She grinned and grabbed my shoulders.

"You mean it? Is it really true? Cruze is my father! I would be so happy if you told me he is my father. I love him. I think he's wonderful, Mom. I just saw him last year remember? I wanted to hug and kiss him for some reason. Now I know why!"

"Yes, Marbella. It is true. His real name is Jose Ramos."

"Then am I a Mexican?"

"Well, you're Hispanic. But Marbella, Cruze has never tried to be part of your life. He could have been, but he never tried. I'm not sure he would be happy if this got out, and I'm sure Bud wouldn't. I never planned to tell you, never."

"But it isn't fair not to tell me. Everyone deserves to know who their real parents are, even adopted kids. Even if their dad is in prison or a gangster or something really bad, they deserve to know. I'm glad you told me."

"Promise not to do anything about it right now. I realize that some day you'll want to confront this knowledge, but not now. The time isn't right."

"When will the time ever be right?"

"I don't know."

I told Dugan about the conversation. He said it was bound to come out some day. He told Marbella that if she wanted to talk about her feelings he would be there for her. I went to work the next day, and Marbella asked if she could stay home. Knowing that she was trying to sort out her feelings, I agreed. That afternoon, she phoned me at work, "Mom, I called his house."

"What do you mean you called his house? How did you get the number?"

"I called information and asked for Jose Ramos. His recording is on, but I didn't leave a message. Do you realize my name should be Marbella Ramos? Doesn't that sound funny?"

"Yes, it sounds funny. It sounds ethnic. Remember, your last name is Murphy. It will never be Ramos. He is not your dad. He never nurtured you. Bud is your dad, Marbella." I had no idea what she was feeling. I knew her situation must be difficult. "Perhaps I should call him. Do you want me to call him and let him know?"

"Yes. Tell him I know."

I found the number where Cruze was employed and phoned his department. I was afraid. "Cruze, this is Rose."

"Well, hello. What a surprise. What's going on?"

Without hesitation I answered. "Cruze, she knows."

"She does? Little Marble knows." He called her Marble. He said she had to have a nickname, because all the children in his family had nicknames. I thought that it was fitting because refined marble is shiny and bright, and looks like a mixture of two colors. "How did she find out? Who told her?"

"I did, although I never planned to. I was going to take it to my grave."

I explained what happened. He listened patiently while I brought him up-to-date on all the events in our lives. He wasn't sorry she knew. He always thought she would find out and anticipated the day with mixed emotions. I told him Bud didn't know yet.

"She's been trying to phone you. I was afraid she would get in touch with you and you wouldn't be prepared. She was exuberant when she found out you are her biological father."

"May I see her?" I was surprised that he wanted to. "Can you send her here on a plane and let her spend the weekend with me? Do you think she'll want to come?"

"Yes, I think she will. I want to handle this the best way for her, Cruze. Perhaps letting her spend some time with you is the right thing to do." He never told his family he had a child, and I wondered how he could keep the secret if she became part of his life.

Marbella was eager to visit him. Cruze arranged her ticket, and I took her to the airport Friday afternoon. As she entered the boarding gate she turned and gave me a big grin. I waved, afraid I had opened Pandora's box. I didn't hear from her all weekend. When I picked her up Sunday, she greeted me with mixed emotions. She didn't want to tell me what a wonderful weekend she had, until she chastised me for having kept her from Cruze all her life. Without hesitation or denial, Marbella accepted that she had a different father. At first, she was angry for not knowing that part of her family. She now knew the answer to her feelings of being incomplete.

The weekend with Cruze was wonderful. After he picked her up at the airport, they went out to eat. Afterwards, they talked all night. He tried to explain his feelings for her and how hard it was to deny her all those years. He wanted to make her feel wanted. His absence was due to circumstances we had to accept. He invited his mother, brothers, and sisters to a party the next day without telling them its purpose; he aid it was a surprise. As they arrived, they noticed Marbella and were curious, but Marbella and Cruze told them nothing until everyone was there. Then, in the backyard next to the grill, he took Marbella's hand and said, "I want you to meet my daughter." Marbella smiled and blushed with pride. A barrage of questions overwhelmed them, and his mother almost passed out. Marbella said she had just learned her father's identity; Cruze said he had lived with his secret for thirteen years.

Marbella's new grandmother welcomed her with a kiss. "Why have you kept her from me? I would have loved to watch her grow up. I never thought I would live to see Cruze's child." She loved Marbella immediately.

I told Ben and Molly that Marbella knew about Cruze and had visited him, but Seth didn't know anything. I told them I had to endure yet another trial because of a choice I made long ago. "Nobody escapes trials, but some people seem to have more than others. If every blessing we receive is predicated upon the commandments we keep, perhaps every reprisal is predicated upon the commandments we break." I recalled that in the Bible Jesus was asked about the misfortune of a man born blind.

"Master, who did sin, this man or his parents, that he was born blind?" Jesus answered. "Neither hath this man sinned nor his parents, but that the works of God should be made manifest in him." Different spirits need different tests. It is all part of the Divine Plan. Trials and blessings are given not only to those directly affected, but also to test the actions and reactions of those who deal with that person.

I knew Bud would soon find out that Marbella knew the truth. I told Seth because he started asking questions about the strange man who called for Marbella. When I told him Marbella was his half-sister, he convulsed as if he had been hit in the chest. He dropped his head and said, "Our family is so screwed up."

"I suppose it is, Seth, I suppose it is. But good things can come from bad beginnings. From David and Bathsheba came Solomon, the wisest king of the Jews. I am not sorry I have Marbella. I can't erase what happened. I know it was wrong, and I have paid the price. I continue to pay the price for that precious piece of marble."

My sin and the sins of others caused my trials. God gave me only blessings. Certainly, my childhood, punctuated with pain and hurt, was not a blessing, but my response to that pain irrevocably shaped my will and destiny. The lives of some of my friends amazed me. I pondered the relative ease of their childhoods compared to mine and thought the Lord favored them. Then I realized that perhaps the most difficult part of my life was over, whereas others, who may have had easier childhoods, would meet their trials as adults or in old age. I hoped for an easier fate in the second half of my life.

Those thoughts really hit home when Melody and Jerome came to Austin to visit us. We cooked steaks on the grill and sat beneath the oaks, discussing life and sharing philosophies. She admitted to having a relatively easy life. My life was cluttered with complications and misgivings, while she breezed through life effortlessly and without consequences. We mused over her many privileges and my lack of them. She, a black girl growing up before and during the civil rights movement, had a much easier life than I. We concluded that my childhood problems did not result from my sins or my choices.

"Why do you think that some children are blessed with better treatment, better parents, better environments than other children?" she asked.

I thought carefully before answering. "I don't know the answer, Mel. I only know that nobody escapes it. We don't know what lies ahead. Maybe my greatest trials are over while yours have yet to appear."

My words were prophetic. A month after that conversation, Melody encountered a trial I would not trade for my own. She was diagnosed with cancer and underwent a double mastectomy. I visited her during her convalescence and stayed with her for a weekend.

"Rose, remember that day we sat under the oak trees talking about trials?"

"Yes, of course I do."

"You were right. Nobody escapes it. Nothing I did caused this trial of mine. It's not a punishment for a choice I made." A tear rolled down her cheek.

I held her hand and replied, "No. Some trials are given and are not a consequence of our own choices. Although we probably wouldn't trade our trials for someone else's, we are not given more than we can endure."

By the time she healed and returned to work, her favorite brother was also diagnosed with cancer. He died a slow death thirteen months later. He held the highest position of any black man at the Johnson Space Center, and Melody admired him.

In May while I was attending a company conference in Washington, Addie called me from Galveston where she now lived. "Rose, Matt is dying from AIDS."

I was shocked. "But he doesn't even have AIDS. He couldn't be dying."

Through tears, she responded, "He does have AIDS, Rose. He had full-blown AIDS and we have known it for years, but he didn't want you to know. I promised I wouldn't tell you." I couldn't believe that they had kept it from me.

"How much longer does he have, Addie? When I come home from this trip I'll go see him."

"It's too late. He's on his last breath."

Matt died in Addie's home with the windows open to let the warm ocean breeze blow against the curtains. I was still in Washington when Matt's body was cremated and his life was celebrated at an informal gathering. By the time I visited Addie in Galveston, Matt's ashes were spread in his rose garden. He and his partner lived only two houses from Addie in a historical home they had renovated. I wanted to cry when I hugged Addie, but my emotions remained buried. I cried inside but was unable to demonstrate my utter empathy and feelings of loss. I had been unable to cry since my childhood. Afraid she would think me callous, I hid my face. I wanted desperately to openly express the depth of my sorrow. 'If only my tears could speak!'

Addie took a framed piece of Matt's art from her closet, an oil painting of an Egyptian princess wearing a beautiful multi-colored headdress.

"Did Matt do that?"

"Yes, who does she look like?"

I took it from her hands and looked at it closely. "I think she looks a little like me."

"That's what I think, too. He must have had you in mind when he drew her, Rose. I know he would want you to have it."

"Oh, Addie, thank you so much. He promised to give me a piece of his work. I'll treasure it forever." I hung it over the fireplace in my bedroom. Addie's mother, Mildred, moved into Addie's downstairs apartment shortly after Matt died. She now walked with a cane and was shaped like a question mark. Addie, always the mother, became her keeper. Two years later, her father died from emphysema. Addie made peace with him before he died and, true to her character, was a pallbearer at his funeral. Her life was forever changed. Losing both her father and brother so quickly left her in a state of depression and she came out of it only after a brush with death.

That summer I took Marbella to Texas City and dropped her off for a couple of days with Cruze. I gave him an album of her pictures as she grew from baby to teen. When we arrived, he invited me in. I told him my life had changed a great deal and I was no longer the same confused person he knew. I told him all about Dugan, my love for him, and our devotion to each another. Cruze did not remarry and had no other children, and I knew he wasn't happy. The Lord told me before that Cruze would not be happy until he kept the commandments. The Lord blessed me in spite of my shortcomings, but I endured repentance, accepted the consequences of my actions, acknowledged the atonement, was re-baptized, and went forward, keeping God's commandments. I was always more restricted and less successful when I did not live gospel principles.

I didn't know what lessons Cruze learned or what wisdom he gained over the years, but his life had not progressed very far. He lived in the same house, had the same furniture, and worked at the same company doing the same job. No longer physically fit, his athletic build had softened. He had a beer belly, his hair was thin, and his lustrous appeal was gone. He still took road trips on his Harley, went to dance halls and played pool, and fished in the same boat on weekends. The only thing different in his life was Marbella. At one time I wished that he were as miserable as he made me, but that was all gone. I hoped he could find love, marry, and be happy. I was not as appealing as I had een thirteen years earlier either, but my life was very different.

In due course, Cruze came to visit Marbella in Austin, and he found something he would never have predicted while I was hopelessly in love with him. I had moved beyond my once doomed station in life. I had completed a college education and I was positioned well in a great company with almost a hundred employees reporting to me. I was raising his daughter in a home he considered to be a mansion. I loved Dugan's children and he loved mine, and neither of us ever considered them baggage. We were active in church, happily married, getting rich, and had healthy grandchildren.

"Wow, Rose, you're lucky to have married a rich man."

Aware that pride precedes a fall, I cautioned him gingerly. "Cruze, didn't marry a rich man. Dugan and I have independently earned what we have. We found wealth after we met, not before."

Marbella returned from a visit with her dad and Sue Ellen that summer and confessed that she told Bud about Cruze. She thanked him for accepting her as his own, and they had a long talk about how hard that was for him. She said she would always think of him as her dad and that the new revelation only made her love him more. Her attitude humbled him and reassured him that he had done the right thing. She told him she wanted some kind of relationship with Cruze, but she didn't know what that would entail since she didn't know him yet.

"No matter who he is or what I find out about him, good or bad, I want to know it. I may be disappointed, but I want to know what kind of man he is. I deserve to know." Bud let it be.

On a hot August day, my sister married a police detective from Galveston. His wife died the previous year, and Mary Jane was the answer to his prayers, while he was her Godsend. Never before had she been happier or treated better. She lost all the weight she had gained. Although a grandmother, she was a lovely bride.

That same month I became a grandmother. My grandson, born in South Dakota, arrived a month early and struggled for life. Underdeveloped lungs put him in intensive care for three weeks where he was tube-fed and given antibiotics intravenously. He eventually recovered and came home, but we were worried and called every day.

I visited them shortly after the baby came home and realized that the best reward of motherhood is becoming a grandmother.

Sue Ellen did not call to check on the baby nor did she send a message of congratulation. Bud called once. They sent a pair of overalls, something appropriate for a baby shower. Six months later, Ben confronted his dad in a heated telephone conversation from my home one evening. Ben listed all the complaints his brother and sisters had and let Bud know in detail why they rejected him and Sue Ellen.

"Dad, you're either blind or stupid, I don't know which. But if you can't see why we feel the way we do, there's something wrong." Bud defended, denied, and justified Sue Ellen's behavior and rationalized his own. He said Sue Ellen loved them and wanted to be a grandmother to their child, that she tried to get along, but they rejected her.

"Well, if she loves us, she has a strange way of showing it. She never asks us about our lives because she simply doesn't care. She did not congratulate us when the baby was born, or call when he was in intensive care. Half the time when you're not there, she doesn't even speak to your children." Raising his voice, Bud interrupted with a defensive posture several times, but Ben continued.

"Don't you see Dad? She has you convinced that we're the worst kids on the face of the earth. The woman can talk about nothing except the Church and her kids, so how you can expect us to like her when we can barely tolerate her. How can you allow it to go on?" The conversation ended when Bud hung up the phone. Ben figured he probably wasted his breath but felt better after getting his resentment off his chest.

CHAPTER XXVII

Adding Insult to Injury

When Seth turned nineteen he was called to serve a religious mission in Utah. Since he would be away for two years, we decided to take all my children to the Cayman Islands for a week together before he left. We swam with the stingrays and walked along the white sand of Seven Mile Beach enjoying the clear water and warm sunshine, one of the best vacations we had ever had.

At his missionary farewell Seth and I spoke to the congregation. Bud and Sue Ellen attended the meeting. My mother did not, although she had attended the missionary farewell for Sue Ellen's favorite daughter a few weeks earlier. I overlooked her ongoing insults and at times tried to rationalize her behavior with flimsy excuses.

My mother was admitted to the hospital with high blood pressure and underwent quintuple bypass surgery. Dad treated her like a queen after that, but it was too late for an apology. Even after he changed, Mama could not forgive him for treating her badly through the years. He did not blame her for treating him badly. I suppose he believed that if he hadn't treated her so badly, she wouldn't have treated him maliciously.

I didn't feel good about living in relative luxury while my parents' living conditions were deplorable. They had made no improvements to their dilapidated house since my childhood. Dugan noticed he could see the ground through their bathroom floor. We offered to buy them a new house, but they didn't want to leave their home of forty-three years. Instead, we decided to remodel their home. We paid for the project, and my brothers provided some of the construction labor. Billy and Jessie bought a house across the street from them so Mama and Dad moved into their house for six weeks. The house was gutted, plumbed, rewired, textured, and painted. Central air and heat, new kitchen cabinets, new bathroom fixtures, wooden floors, carpet, and appliances were installed. The outside was painted and trimmed and a front porch big enough for two rocking chairs was added. We arranged to meet them there the afternoon it was finished. On our way down, we stopped and bought a kitchen table, couches with tables and lamps, and a bedroom suite. It didn't look like the same house. They were grateful.

Mama later ruined the effect of the gift when she told me that Bud and Sue Ellen dropped by to see the renovation. Suspecting the answer, I asked if she told them that we paid for everything. Perturbed, she said, "No, you know I can't mention your name in front of them."

"Isn't that something? You're afraid to mention your own daughter's name in your home. If I couldn't mention my child's name in someone's presence, that someone wouldn't be welcome in my home. You were ashamed to name the daughter who gave you this gift. Think about it. You should be ashamed!"

She didn't apologize and didn't think what she had done was wrong. I phoned Mary Jane and told her what had happened. She agreed that our mother's behavior was insulting. We knew of no other mother who would do such a thing. Her behavior embarrassed me. I didn't want my mother's ignorance to reflect on me, but I was often left with the fallout from her foolish deeds. Although my mother knew Bud let Sue Ellen ignore my children, she still gave her preferential treatment.

A few days later Mary Jane phoned me. "I confronted Mama about not mentioning your name in Sue Ellen's presence and reminded her that without you, she wouldn't have a beautiful, new home. I reminded her that you are her daughter, not Sue Ellen. I asked why she could tell others you paid for the remodeling but could not give you credit in Sue Ellen's presence."

"What did she say?"

"She said she didn't want to offend Sue Ellen. I don't know the answer, Rose, but she has a problem where Sue Ellen is concerned. Her priorities are warped or something."

"Mary, I'm convinced there's a psychological explanation for her behavior. I'm not sure what it is, but some day I'm going to find the answer."

I tried not to think about my mother's partiality and went on about my life, which was defined almost totally by my job. My responsibilities grew as my department doubled, then tripled and quadrupled in size. The company was growing in leaps and bounds and was NASDAQ's sweetheart stock. Dugan and I were both positioned well, and the company awarded us bonuses and stock options during every review cycle. We both were promoted, but we never stopped to calculate the incredible luck we had as owners of the fastest growing stock in the market. The awards came so frequently we paid no attention to the impact on our financial portfolio. We just kept accumulating stock options and invested our bonuses in the company stock plan. Before we knew it, we were millionaires, and a few months later, multimillionaires. Fortunately, we had no time to spend the money and did not diversify our portfolio, since PC's Inc.'s stock was the best to own. If the stock stayed strong and we stayed with the company until our stock options were vested, we would be set for life. We were realistic, though, and knew the stresses of our work environment would offset the value of our vested stock. We knew we would leave before all our options were vested, but we hoped to time our departure to our advantage.

My sister planned my parent's fiftieth wedding anniversary with a celebration in her back yard. Although I wanted to avoid my mother, I agreed to attend. When Billy arrived, his appearance concerned me. He was emaciated and looked like he was back on drugs. We sat together and chatted while we ate and listened to country-western music playing in the background. He told me he lost weight because he missed his girlfriend.

"Why did she leave?"

"Oh, you know how Jessie and Mama are. They did everything they could to drive a wedge between us. They gave me such a hard time about Tina that I couldn't take the stress any more, so I told her to leave."

"You mean you chose Jessie and Mama over Tina?"

"Yeah, I guess I did. They put so much stress on me that I just couldn't take it any more."

"Maybe I need to teach you a few things I've learned over the years. Mama practices conditional love. If you do what I want you to do, I'll accept you; if you don't, I'll make your life miserable. She did it to me with Bud, and she tried to do it again with Dugan. If you can get to the point where you don't care if you ever see her again, you can be free of her clutches, but not until then."

"Yeah, I shouldn't have let them control me like that."

"She doesn't want anyone to be more important in your life than she is. She wants to feel needed, maybe because she feels guilty for neglecting you when you were young and is trying to make up for it now."

"Well, I know I made a mistake by letting Tina go, because she was a good woman, and I love her. I can't be happy without her. Mama would never meet her or talk to her. She called her every name in the book without ever giving her a chance. One day, I took Tina and went over there and I told Mama it was time to stop badgering her and that it was important to me that she accepted her and treated her nicely. She was cordial, but as soon as Tina left, Mama was back at it and told me not to bring her over again. She refused to give her a chance."

"Well, that was a mistake. You should never tell Mama it's important to you that she accepts Tina, because that gives her control over you. You have to say the opposite, Billy. Tell her you don't care what she thinks or how she feels about Tina. Tell her that you choose Tina over her, and you don't give a damn about what she thinks. That's the only way you can take back control. You have to be ready to let Mama go. When you come to the point that you don't care if you ever see her again, then she won't be able to hurt you or control you. Do you understand?"

"You are right! I never thought of it that way," he replied.

"My advice to you is to follow your heart and get Mama out of your life."

"I will. If I can find Tina, I am not going to let her go for Mama or anyone again."

After the party, Billy found Tina and she moved into the house across the street with him. The rejection, bullying, condemning, cursing, criticizing, and insults continued. Tina was a freeloader. Tina was a whore. Tina was a crack-head. Tina was a bartender. Tina had a Mexican child. Tina was filthy. Tina was fat. Tina was an Amazon. Tina was a bad influence on Billy. I hate that woman. It could have been called The Never-Ending Story.

Billy and Jessie never let a woman come between them. Both of their ex-wives said being married to one is like being married to both. Billy was torn not only between Tina and Mama, but suddenly he had to consider Jessie, since choosing Tina meant losing not only a mother, but also a brother. Tina wasn't perfect, but much that was said about her was exaggerated. By Thanksgiving, Billy had had enough of Mama's taunting. He was on the verge of a nervous breakdown caused by his love for Tina and his need for Mama's approval.

That same Thanksgiving, my mother turned down an invitation to dine with Mary Jane and her family, since Bud said they might stop by to visit her after dinner at his mother's house in Texas City. Billy was drunk and went to talk to Mama once more about how awfully she treated Tina. Listening to her, he became enraged, cursed, threw things, and threatened to be there when Sue Ellen and Bud came. He said he couldn't stand Sue Ellen because she looks down her nose at us. He added, "You have always made us feel like that bitch and her family were better than us. You treat us like dogs, but you treat them like they are f__ing royalty! I hate the whole damn bunch of those bastards, and so does Jessie!"

My mother was mortified that Sue Ellen might see Billy drunk. She told him to get out and never to come back. She was so afraid Billy would make good his threat and cause a scene that she got into her car and drove to Bud's mother's house to visit them there. Once I heard of that episode, I quit calling her and decided that it would be better to stay away. It was hard to believe she turned down Thanksgiving dinner with her own children to await the possible arrival of her honored guests – Bud and Sue Ellen. I was sickened by her abnormal behavior.

CHAPTER XXVIII

Thou Shalt

As Marbella and Cruze spent more time together they learned many things they didn't like about each other. By the time she was sixteen he realized he was not prepared to deal with adolescent behavior. At the same time, she considered him selfish, intolerant, and backward. She thought he never married or took responsibility because of his concern for himself. Cruze phoned me after a difficult weekend visit with Marbella to tell me she was selfish and spoiled, and he did not really like her.

"That's funny. Those are the words she used to describe you. Perhaps some characteristics are indeed inherited!" She stopped visiting him and told me she was glad she had learned his true character.

I had finally arrived at a place where I thought I would never go. I would have given anything to have never met him. I never loved Cruze. In fact, I never even liked him. The only thing we had was lust. Although we enjoyed magnificent passion on occasion, my relation with him was never emotionally fulfilling or sexually gratifying. Neither Marbella or I have heard from him again.

Dugan and I began to plan our retirement for the summer of 2000. Many feared a major catastrophe caused by the failure of date algorithms in computer systems. Before the millennium changed, every computer system worldwide had to be evaluated and, in most cases, updated. Dugan was one of the key people responsible for the company's Y2K project and was committed to see it through to completion. We wanted to retire, but the earliest I could close out my projects was late summer. We set August 1st as our retirement date.

Several years of marriage changed our relationship, and the adjustment was difficult. At first, I was afraid our love was vanishing, but, once we figured out what had happened, things were better than before. We needed three and a half years to understand the changes, accept them, and adjust our behavior. Our feelings had always been so intense, and I didn't want them to change for fear that our love would diminish. In the beginning, Dugan was my knight in shining armor, my salvation, my mentor, and my beacon! I esteemed him above everyone, including myself. He earned more, was more sophisticated, learned, and well traveled–experienced, astute, knowledgeable, and suave, than I. Over time, everyone and everything changes.

I married Dugan at the beginning of what I call my great expansion. He had just completed his, causing unexpected consequences. I believe that during the decade before becoming middle-aged, people go through a period of great expansion. Typically, we accept who we are, realize the greatest fulfillment of our careers, and gain superior understanding of life and human emotions. We accept mortality, are more perceptive and selfless, dislodge past ghosts and unearth new freedoms, understand our own spirituality and sexuality, and appreciate the priority in our lives. It is our period of enlightenment, of peak performance. Prior to the great expansion, life is prologue and after it, epilogue. During the prologue we discover and develop. The great expansion augments, intensifies, and escalates the discoveries and development to the greatest extent in the shortest time. In the epilogue, growth goes slower, and assimilation, absorption, and incorporation are less dramatic. That is not to say further refinement does not take place during our epilogue, but the greatest impact occurs during the decade between approximately thirty-seven and forty-seven years of age.

Dugan was functioning at his peak when I met him. Since I was thirteen years younger, I was just entering the onset of enlightenment. By the time I reached middle age, I had become his equal in most things and his better in some. I no longer had him on a pedestal. When two people are equals, the scale is balanced and a more mature and healthier state of rapport results. The change is not easy to recognize or define, especially when an imbalance prevailed for a long time. My love for him was not less, and I struggled to understand the metamorphosis. Balance and equality changed our interaction. He did not step down the ladder; I climbed up to meet him. Our expectations of each other altered, the scale no longer tilted, and we needed to adjust. When Dugan understood me as his equal and he adjusted to the change, I no longer rebelled. The adjustment to a more mature relationship resulted in a richer bond of mutual respect and a deeper love. I have imagined losing him, and at those times I am overcome with heartache. I never want to draw one breath without him. Should I lose him and linger alone for a season, I would gladly give all I have to be in his presence for one more day.

In due course, the time came for us to leave our business careers and move on to other interests. Our financial security enabled us to become active in charitable organizations and fund raising. We began to travel, take dance lessons, do missionary work, do church work, write books, and spend time with our grandchildren, the greatest satisfaction of all. New grandchildren came almost every year. We loved spoiling them. Wealth changed our lives, but we lived more simply than we could have. Although we drove expensive cars and had a beautiful estate, we had no debt. We were humbled that the Lord poured blessings upon us more bountifully than we could ever deserve.

My sister kept me informed about the ongoing feud between Billy, Tina, Jessie, and Mama. I went to visit my parents. I had not talked to either of them since the anniversary party a year earlier. My mother's left eye was blood-shot. She should have gone to the emergency room but instead had scheduled a doctor's appointment for a few days later.

"Where are Billy and Tina?" I asked.

"I don't know where he went with that woman," she replied. She knew I didn't approve of her condemnation of Tina, so she was somewhat cool.

"Well it's too bad you don't get along with her. If you give her a chance you might find that you like her. You never gave Dugan a chance, and after insulting and rejecting him, you found out he'd terrific, didn't you?"

"Well, this woman is not like Dugan. She's horrible."

"What's so horrible about her?"

"For one thing, she's a bartender."

"Oh, really? Well, Dugan's son is a bartender, and we don't reject him for that."

"Well, she is a filthy house keeper, too."

"As I remember, you were not always a good house keeper yourself, were you?"

"Now, Rose, don't try to defend her when you know nothing about her. She has to prove herself to me, and she hasn't yet. Besides, that woman has a Mexican baby!"

"So do I." My voice intensified. "So do I! I have a Mexican baby, and she's your granddaughter, and she's beautiful! Who are you that she should have to prove herself to you? What kind of mother are you? I'll tell you what kind you are. You're a mother who practices conditional love, giving approval only if it is what you want, and rejecting your children completely if they don't follow your wishes. Billy chose Tina over you, and you feel rejected. You neglected the babies as children and now you insist on controlling them as adults. Let them have their own lives, will you? You pretend to be a saint, going to church every Sunday, but you're not a saint. Jesus didn't treat people the way you do. Tina probably has a better heart than you will ever have. You are not a saint. You're Sybil's Mother! That's who you are. You are like Sybil's mother! I will never forgive you for the way you treated Dugan or for the way you treated me as a child!" Her face twisted as she snarled, "If you don't forgive me, your children will never forgive you, because you weren't a perfect mother either."

"I know I wasn't a perfect mother, but I didn't intentionally harm them like you did. I could forgive you for the mistreatment during my childhood if you didn't continue it into my adult life. Whatever mistakes I made with my children when I divorced, I have corrected. But you! With you it's never-ending. The only difference is that, since you can no longer be physically abusive, you have changed to emotional torture. You're sick!" My father didn't say a word.

She tried to interrupt, but I didn't let her. I had my say with all the anger and hatred built up inside me. I came to Billy's defense like he came to mine so long ago when he confessed to taking the gold watch. I turned and walked away, leaving the two of them speechless. I finally told her what I thought of her, and I was not sorry. The commandment to love mother and father that your days may be long upon the earth does not mean, Thou shalt love thy mother no matter how lousily she treateth thee. I let my mother know I blamed her. I wanted her to digest it, feel it, and mourn the sin of it. Eighteen months passed before I spoke to my mother again, but before then I had the answer to my life-long quest to know what I represented to her that fueled her disdain and partiality.

I recounted the confrontation to Billy and Tina and told them if they didn't move away from her, she would always have control and would treat Tina outrageously. "You have to move to another town if you want freedom from her. When you move, she'll know she has lost, and once she accepts that, she will accept Tina."

Billy knew I was right, but he struggled another year to get his life together enough to move away. When he did, the war stopped. They moved into a tiny travel trailer unfit for animals, but it was better than being subject to Mama's badgering. Eventually, Mama began to talk nicely to Tina even allowing visits and ultimately she invited them for dinner. She vacillated occasionally, but she warmed to Tina somewhat, just as I predicted.

Pinky's mother died and Pinky mourned her. I didn't think her mother deserved mourning. Although they were closer after her mother was diagnosed with cancer, they never confronted the issues between them, and nothing was resolved when she died. Pinky never made sense of her past, so it would always affect her future. Reliving an unpleasant past and exhuming the pain is agonizing, but that enables us to get beyond it. Unless Pinky can mourn the child she was never allowed to be, her pain would never disappear. Pinky's mother treated her badly all of her life and never listened to her daughter's accusations or accepted the possibility they might be true. Whether she believed her, she should have sent Pinky for psychiatric help instead of discarding her. Her mother lived in a constant state of denial. I didn't like her when she was alive and I did not console Pinky

t her death. She called me in great sadness, saying her mother was an
angel.

"She was never an angel, Pinky! Is that what happens to us when
our negligent mothers die? We make them into angelic martyrs? Not
me. I won't do it when my mother dies, and I won't let you either. It
isn't true. She was a huge source of pain, and as far as I am concerned,
she abdicated her responsibility for you."

Pinky hurt to hear me say that, but I didn't believe in whitewash-
ing behavior. Pinky was better than I. She could forgive and forget. She
unconditionally loved the father who molested her and the mother
who abandoned her.

Shortly after her mother died, Pinky's ship came in. Luckily for us,
we never withdrew from the silicone breast implant claims, and finally there was a settlement. I had forgotten about it entirely and was
happy to receive a sizable windfall, but for Pinky, it was like winning
the lottery. She held out and negotiated a greater settlement than I got.
I was happy for her. For the first time in her life she had money she
didn't get from a man, and she was careful not to spend it foolishly.
Her mother's death opened the door for a miraculous revelation that
could never have been realized while her mother was alive.

CHAPTER XXIX

Unearthing...

A year after her mother died Pinky called me. She thought I had forsaken her since I had offered her no comfort for the distress of losing her mother. She was crying. "Rose, I wish you were here. I need you so badly right now. I am so upset."

"What's wrong Pinky? What has happened?"

"Rose, all of these years I wanted to believe that J.D. was Jobe's father, and I convinced myself he was, even though J.D. denied it."

"Yes, I know that, Pinky. You convinced everyone that J.D. was Jobe's father."

"Well, I went to dinner with Jobe and my dad on the anniversary of my mother's death, and Jobe told me that he and J.D. had DNA tests."

"You're kidding me."

"No, that's why I'm crying. The test confirmed that J.D. is not his dad. Jobe wants to know who it is."

"Pinky, every child wants to know who his parents are. Jobe is almost thirty years old, and he deserves to know. It's not easy for him. Think of Marbella. She was almost thirteen when I told her about her real father, and she said she would never have forgiven me if I had waited any longer to tell her. It's just normal for them to want to know. Even if they are disappointed, they still want to know. Are you afraid to tell him that you don't know who his father is?"

"No, Rose. I am afraid to tell him that if his father is not J.D. . . . "

There was a long pause.

"Yes, Pinky. What were you saying?"

"If his father is not J.D., it can only be one other person. Rose, his father . . . is my father."

"Oh, no! Oh, I had no idea. I am so sorry, Pinky. But you told me a long time ago your father never penetrated you. You told me that he only fondled you. Did you lie?"

"Yeah, I lied. I never wanted to believe he was my baby's father, because it was too much to bear."

"Pinky, your father knows he's Jobe's father and he has kept that awful secret too. This could never have come out while your mother was alive, but it's time. Jobe needs to know."

"Oh, Rose, why did this have to happen to me? Why do I have to go through this? I am such a sinner. I am the lowliest of the low. What will Jesus say to me when I die?"

I told her Billy's story. "When Billy was a child he was in a diving competition. His dives were much more difficult than the other boys', who had perfect form but easier dives. Billy won the contest because the degree of difficulty was a factor in determining a winner. You see, Pinky, some dives get extra credit for greater difficulty. People who think their scores as wife or mother or just as a person aren't very high needn't worry. There are some things that we couldn't do because of our circumstances. Where there is no choice, there is no condemnation. I have no doubt that when the degree of difficulty is factored in for your life, your crown will shine brighter than many others. God always factors in the degree of difficulty."[1]

"That's a beautiful story. I'm going to remember it. I hope you're right, Rose. I hope God factors in my degree of difficulty. I hope he can forgive me. I am going to have lunch with Jobe on Tuesday, and I will tell him the truth. Pray for me."

Jobe was eager to meet with his mother. She had promised to reveal his father's identity over lunch on Tuesday, September 11th, the fortieth anniversary of Hurricane Carla's destruction of Texas City. He awoke early in the morning and went to work, counting the minutes until his mother's arrival. She was afraid, but she mustered her strength and courage and began the drive to Houston. Suddenly, on the car radio, she heard the news of the attack on America. Terrorists had crashed airplanes into the World Trade Center in New York and the Pentagon in Washington. For the first time in history United States airspace was shut down and President Bush's location was undisclosed. Commerce stood still as America and the world watched the death toll rise as two of the most acclaimed buildings in the world disintegrated before their eyes. Pinky thought she should turn around and use the attack as an excuse to avoid the burden that lay ahead of her, but she drove on. When she arrived, Jobe met her at the door and gave her a hug.

"Mom, one of my clients is here visiting from New York, and he's in the back office right now. His wife was a flight attendant on one of the planes that hit the World Trade Center, and he's devastated. We have to pray for everyone who died."

"Oh, Jobe, this is the most horrible thing our nation has ever been through. This is worse than Pearl Harbor! Perhaps we should put our lunch off for another day, Jobe."

"Yeah, I don't feel right about leaving my client now. I think I should stay with him to help him through this. I'll walk you back to your car."

As they walked, he brought up the subject of his father's identity. "Why don't you just tell me, Mom? Let's not make this hard. If my father isn't J.D., then who is he?"

Tears welled in Pinky's eyes as they approached her car. He opened the door for her and stood waiting for a reply. She looked at him and started to speak, still not knowing what would come out, the truth or another lie.

"Your father is . . . is . . . .." She couldn't say it. "He's . . . "

Jobe waited and finally finished the sentence for her. "My father is your father! My father is my grandfather. He's my father and my grandfather. Does it help if I say it for you, Mom?"

Shocked, she asked, "How did you know, Jobe?"

"I'll never forget when I was ten years old and you were visiting me. You were so drunk Andy and Grandpa had to hold you down. You yelled at Grandpa and told him that you hated him for molesting you. You said it again and again and again. That stuck in my mind. I always wondered if you were telling the truth. People say that when you're drunk, the truth comes out."

"It's true, Jobe. I never wanted to admit he was your father, so I blamed it on J.D. I thought there might be a remote chance it was true. But in my heart I feared it was your Grandpa all along."

"He must have known it, too."

"Maybe, but he wouldn't admit it, even if I had confronted him."

"Isn't it ironic? All my life I've wished for a dad, while all along I lived with him under the same roof? My dad is the one who raised me after all."

"Yes, Jobe. I'm sorry. It's all my fault."

"No, Mom. None of this was your fault. You have to get over that. You were a child. You were not responsible. It's okay. You're okay, and I love you so much," he told her through tears. Jobe found it hard to believe that his wonderful, old, humble, religious Grandpa could have committed incest with his daughter.

"Jobe, this could never have come out before your grandmother died. The time is ripe for the truth to surface. Why don't you take a sample of your grandpa's hair to the clinic that performed your DNA analysis to get positive confirmation?"

"I will, Mom. I'm going to do just that. But I don't know if I will ever tell him I know."

The next month, Pinky called and said Jobe had given her father a birthday card, which read "Happy Birthday, Dad." That was the first card Jobe had given her father that said "Dad." The other Birthday, Christmas, and Father's Day cards from Jobe addressed him as Grandfather. Either way, all the cards spoke the truth.

Delaying the treatment of her bloodshot eye had disastrous consequences for my mother; she lost sight in that eye. Before the doctor's appointment, she almost had a stroke, and her dangerously high blood pressure burst the blood vessels behind the retina, resulting in total blindness in her eye. She was also diagnosed with diabetes and began to lose sight in the other eye. She was hospitalized a couple of times but I made no contact with her.

Addie was now a professor at the college where we both started our college education. She underwent a simple surgery for a deviated septum. I phoned to see how she was feeling and was shocked to hear that she had a rare reaction to the anesthesia and flat-lined on the operating table.

"Addie, are you telling me that you basically died?"

"Sort of, but they were able to bring me back. The great thing is that I saw Matt!"

"What do you mean?"

"Well, I guess all that stuff we were taught in church about eternal life is really true. Now I know for sure that when we die our family meets us on the other side. There is life after life!"

"Oh, Addie. I am so sorry that happened to you."

"Don't be sorry, Rose. I got to see my brother. We held hands and ran together in circles. And there were rainbows everywhere. Brilliant rainbows. Then he let go of my hands, and I heard the doctors calling my name. I didn't want him to leave me; it was so beautiful."

"Addie, I'm glad Matt let you come back. Maybe you're coming out of your depression."

"Yeah, maybe I am. I have lost fifteen pounds since then, and I feel great. I have something else to tell you. I just read a book I want you to get. It's about a child abuse case in California."

"I can't read about child abuse, Addie!"

"Why not?"

"Because when I read a book, I put myself into the story and become the character. I feel the character's pain, and it hurts for days. Sometimes, I can't shake it."

"Well, you have to read this book, because it's about you."

"Me?"

"Yes, Rose. I discovered you in the pages. Y-O-U!"

"Really?"

"Absolutely! The author, one of five children, was singled out and mistreated by his mother. She didn't abuse the other boys, just him. He was rescued from her as a young teen and put in foster care. He lived to overcome the abuse and later was a decorated military hero and got awards from several presidents. He went on to become a famous author, speaker, and advocate for child protection. He didn't abuse his children but was a loving husband and father."

"I'm not sure I understand."

"She singled him out, Rose, just like your mother singled you out! Remember when we were little and I always asked why Wanda gave Mary Jane everything and gave you nothing?"

"Yes, I remember." I hadn't thought of myself as 'singled out'. While all my siblings had undergone some degree of mistreatment, none had it like I did. Maybe that is why I felt differently than my siblings when Mama was shot.

"Addie, you're right. I never thought of it before, but you are so right. But tell me why? Why, Addie?"

"I don't know, Rose. I think she was jealous of you. Mothers can be jealous of their daughters, you know. It probably goes back to her childhood. You must represent something to your mother that she detested, something your brothers and sister didn't. You'll probably have to go back to her childhood to find the cause."

"Addie, a few years ago I asked Mama if she was jealous of me, but she denied it. I also asked her why she never praised me, and she admitted to withholding praise on purpose since I got praise from others. She thought Mary Jane got less, so she overcompensated."

"Of course she wouldn't admit to being jealous of you, but you went all of your life without any praise from her. After all she put you through, you rose above it, didn't perpetuate it, and became successful in spite of her, just like the author I just mentioned. She set you up for failure and you defied her. You were indestructible. You achieved in spite of her."

Pausing to digest her statement, I replied, "Yes, I suppose I did. I suppose I did."

I bought the book and read it. Addie was right. Although my mistreatment didn't compare to the horror of the boy's in the book, I felt an uncanny kinship to him.

When I finished the book, I contemplated my mother's childhood, which I knew of from the stories she told us while we were growing up. I realized that she, too, was a victim of neglect and humiliation. I vividly recollected stories she told about her sisters, brothers, teachers, friends, and parents, and it was clear she had suffered greatly. As a child she overheard neighbors say they felt sorry for her, because she never got any attention. Mama always described her sisters as having great talent and beauty, but she never said anything positive about herself. I heard her tell the stories a million times, but she never described how badly the neglect hurt her. She didn't blame her mother. She felt unworthy of praise or compliments. She thought if she hadn't been a bad child, a bad seed, a bad egg, she would have been treated better. She esteemed everyone in her family higher than herself and could not believe them capable of purposeful mistreatment. Consequently, she absolved them and blamed only herself, thinking she deserved to be ignored.

Again, I meditated on her surroundings as a child and thought of stories she told us. I closed my eyes and hypnotically went into her mind. Once again, I became little Wanda, Wanda the child. I regressed to her childhood in the Great Depression. I lived in her house, ate supper with her family, played in her yard, wore her clothes–an aviator cap and Crumley's shoes–attended her school, and slept in her bed. I was transformed into her body and mind, and for a few dramatic moments, I was Wanda.

I sit alone in the corner with wet panties, idly playing jax and ball. The only time I get attention is in the morning when I have to strip my bed and wash the sheets by hand before I go to school. Pearl refuses to sleep with me, because she doesn't want me to pee on her. I should pee on her on purpose. I see my mother bragging and laughing with my sisters dressed in lace and bows. My mother adoringly combs Pearl's curls, braids my older sister's hair, and gossips with her about her boyfriends and dates. Nobody notices me or combs my hair. There is nothing to comb, because my dad shaved my head. Crumley comes in and takes my ball.

"D've it back!" I shout. "It ain't yours!" Nobody tells him to give it back to me. He mashes my face in the floor, but Mom ignores us until I begin to cry. Now Mom laughs and tells Crumley to leave me alone. He looks at my tear-drenched face smugly and throws the ball and hits me on my nose, making Mom chuckle harder. Crumley giggles and disappears.

I hate my dad for cutting my hair like Crumley's. I tried to avoid the boyish haircut that he threatened me with. But Crumley found me and dragged me kicking and screaming all the way to the barber's chair. Dad laughs when the others see my shaved head. He doesn't cut Pearl's hair, because she has pretty curls. "I'll wear this old cap until my hair grows back. I'll even sleep in it." They laughed even more when they saw me wear the cap to bed. To punish him for shaming me I began to call my dad Mr. Young instead of Dad.

Yippee! Today is my lucky day. I have a penny sack of candy. Today, I have some friends to play with! But when the candy is gone, my playmates disappear. Nobody wants to play with me, not even Pearl. She thinks she's too cute to play with me. I can't stand how everyone adores her. Nobody laughs at the way she pronounces her words. I hate it when Mom makes me repeat things, pretending not to understand me. She chuckles as I try to make myself clear. I keep saying, "The fuwy wabbit can outwun de tuwtle," as she makes me repeat myself until I almost cry. Finally, when I am at the brink of tears, she acts like she finally understands, and says, "Oh, now I understand. You are trying to say that the furry rabbit can outrun the turtle." Everyone laughs. I want to hit someone. I want to fight. I'm angry. When I get big, I will never let anyone treat me like this and get away with it. I'm the forgotten one.

They don't know I exist. That is, everyone except William, my dear older brother William. He never teases me, because he knows what it's like to be unable to talk plain. "Would you like a piece of cake, Wanda? How about some milk? Do you need help with that wagon? Let me fix it for you. Come sit here next to me. Let's read together. I'll pronounce the words you have trouble with. But first let's wash your face and comb your hair." Oh, how I enjoy the comfort of his voice. He's big and handsome and strong. All that matters is that he loves me. He never laughs at me. I wish he didn't have to be gone so much selling vegetables from the garden, but I love it when he comes home. He whistles like a bird to entertain me. Mr. Young is hardly ever home because he's out with his girlfriend. I don't miss Mr. Young at all because William is here.

No matter how hard she tried she could not impress her parents, could not gain commendation from her siblings. Uncle William was kindest to her because when he was little, he was tongue-tied too. He

225

replaced the father who abandoned her and inflicted one of her most painful childhood memories, and she lived forever in his debt. Her gratitude to him surpassed normal admiration and overflowed to his entire family.

Finally, that day, all the pieces of the puzzle came together. I was Pearl, the adorable one, the one who replaced her as the baby of the family, the one who got all the attention and compliments, and the one during her childhood who made her jealous. My mother relived the neglect of her childhood during my childhood. She identified Mary Jane with her childhood self. Just like she was four years older than Pearl, Mary Jane was four years older than I. Fearing that in deference to me Mary Jane would know the same self-doubt, resentment and neglect she knew, she tried to protect her by reversing the victimization—hers for mine. She didn't want Mary Jane to feel left out when her little sister was born like she felt left out. She sought retribution for the mistreatment she suffered and was incapable of distinguishing between her sister Pearl and me. Suppressed feelings surfaced when she saw the circumstances recreated with her own children. The admiration she saw in the faces of strangers smiling at me ignited her memory and fueled her cruelty as she sought to repay the oppression of her own childhood. She relived the hurt, jealousy, and anger, but this time she was in control. All the vengeance she suppressed during her childhood was unleashed on me.

My search was over.

CHAPTER XXX

...Moving Forward and Beyond

Near Christmas I came home from a dinner party to find a message from Addie on my phone recorder.

"Rose, it's Addie. I'm sorry to bother you, but I just spoke with your mother. Billy is very sick, and I think he may be dying. You'd better call your mother."

Mama had called Mildred to tell her that Tina brought Billy to her house, because he was sick and their sardine can trailer was too cold for them. He hadn't eaten for days, was dehydrated, and had a terrible pain in the stomach. My first thought was a drug reaction or perhaps his liver was finally reacting to his lifelong struggle with alcohol. I phoned my mother's home to speak to Billy. He was too weak to talk, so I asked my distraught mother about his condition. Instantly our silent feud vanished.

"I am afraid he's dying, Rose. I've never seen him like this before. Jessie will take him to John Sealy Hospital in the morning if he isn't better, but I don't know if he will make it 'til morning," she said.

Billy always seemed to be in catastrophe mode. Friends and family grew tired of being drawn into his troubles, feuds, and drug rages. After discussing Billy's condition, we talked about our last encounter, my childhood, and hers. As I probed, she confirmed what I already knew.

"Yes, yes, yes," she answered. "Everyone said they felt sorry for me because I never got any attention. Pearl was the pet. There was an old black woman who used to pass our house every morning on her way to work. She always said hello to Pearl and called her "pretty little thing," but she never even recognized me. Sarah's boyfriend gave me a dollar once, because he told her he felt sorry for me because nobody ever said anything nice about me." She admitted again that she discounted compliments to me so Mary Jane wouldn't feel left out. On and on she explained her childhood humiliation, jealousy, anger, neglect, and her love for William. I knew I had found the cause of my mother's behavior toward me. I did it with Addie's help and inspiration from God.

I phoned to thank Addie for leaving me the message about Billy. I told her about the conversation with my mother, unraveling those unanswered questions. When I explained my conclusions based on my mother's childhood, Addie agreed it all made sense but cautioned me that Mama had likely blocked many things from her mind. "She does not understand that her behavior toward you was a result of her childhood anguish. She would probably deny it if you confronted her. She's the sum of her history, trapped by emotional demons she unleashed on you."

The next morning, Jessie took Billy to the hospital, and he was admitted immediately. He was severely dehydrated and could barely walk. His blood pressure was dangerously low. The doctors told him that if he wanted to live he must never drink or take drugs again. A few days later he was released to go home to recover.

That Christmas I sent my parents a grandfather's clock. I wanted to send a message that the feud was ended. Mama called me several times in the next few weeks, and I felt a compassion for her I had not known before, the compassion saved for a terminally ill person unaware of the illness. I knew the trials she knew. I was there. I lived them. I felt them. I had been transported through time into her childhood. God had let me feel her feelings, know her surroundings, and suffer her pain with all my senses and my spirit to give me compassion for a person who inflicted so much pain on me. I had to walk in her shoes to understand, to sympathize, and ultimately to forgive.

On my mother's seventy-sixth birthday, two months after Billy was released from the hospital, my sister had surgery. I drove to

Galveston to be with her. Her husband stayed by her side and took care of her. I was comforted to know that she, too, would have a better second half of life.

I stayed in a new hotel not far from the College where I used that first $200 scholarship. Driving past the campus brought back fond memories, yet a time of struggle. I thought about Addie inside her office, secure in her successful career, giving herself to so many who needed her.

Before returning home, I visited my parents. It was the coldest day of the year and I wore a black winter overcoat, fur trimmed Russian hat, and black gloves. Billy was there. He had lost a lot of weight since I last saw him. He was a shell of the brother I knew: toothless, too depressed to bother to wear his dentures, thin, disheveled, weak, teary, with sunken cheeks, recessed eyes, and filthy clothes–unable to work, broken, and distraught. He and Tina slept in his truck during the cold spell, because it was warmer than the travel trailer they lived in. In the truck they could start the engine every few hours to be warmed by the heater. It was all too much for Tina, and that morning, depressed and suicidal, she checked herself into the mental hospital.

I had been so busy in my own world that I was unaware of their dismal state. I had to do something to help. I went into the bedroom I once called mine and locked the door so I could phone Dugan and speak privately. As I explained Billy's condition, I broke down and cried uncontrollably at my failure to rescue him earlier. When Dugan heard my sobs, feelings of compassion overwhelmed him.

"This is the first time I've ever heard you cry, darling." He spoke softly.

"Yes, Dugan, It was here, within these walls, that my tears stopped almost forty years ago and now for some reason I can't seem to hold them back." Shedding tears again after so many years was medicine to my soul.

"Before you come back to Austin find Billy a new brick house with a double garage in Texas City. Tell him we will furnish it completely and that he can live there rent-free for the rest of his life." Dugan ordered.

"I was hoping you would say that! Thanks for understanding."

After hanging up the phone, I dried my face and took a few deep breaths before opening the door. I told Billy of my conversation with Dugan and asked him to get dressed so we could go house hunting. He hung his head in humble gratitude and sobbed silently before he spoke. When he stood, he put his arms around me and said, "I love you, Rose. Thank you."

Both of my parents cried as they witnessed the compassionate scene. Never again would Billy feel as he did that day when I saw him sitting in my mother's kitchen.

My mother thanked me for her birthday gift and for being with Mary Jane during her surgery, but especially for offering to help Billy. Her voice breaking, she said she could now go to her grave in peace knowing that Billy would always have a place to lay his head. She said she wanted Jessie, who still lived with them, to inherit their home when they died so he would have a place he could call his own. Dad rocked, shoeless and smiling, teary-eyed with gratitude, suspenders stretched over his swollen belly, a glass of ice water in his hand. Mama ate breakfast in her nightgown, reassuring herself she could still see well enough to cook. Her skin, thin as rice paper, covered with age spots and bruised, hung in wrinkles like a hound dog's cheeks. Sitting next to her I looked around at their tidy home. 'I wish it could have looked this way when I was growing up,' I thought. She noticed my gaze and interjected tearfully, "You know, Rose, everything we have in this house came from you. If it weren't for you we wouldn't have anything. You and Dugan have made us comfortable in our old age."

A lump in my throat kept me from responding. I just looked at her and nodded. She didn't know that I understood that her adult actions stemmed from childhood mistreatment. I decided to approach the subject. "Mama, haven't you written some poems and short stories about your childhood?"

She responded enthusiastically. "Oh, yes, I have a book of poems and short stories about my life. Would you like to see them?"

"Yes, I would."

She went to her closet and brought out two bound folders in a plastic bag. Handing me one and said, "This one is the short stories"–then passing the other–"and this one is the poems."

"Have you ever thought about publishing your poetry?"

"Yes, I'd like to have my writings published or at least duplicated and bound, so my children can all have a copy."

I thumbed through the poetry and realized that many of the poems described the circumstances in my vision of her past. Poem after poem, story after story...it was all there in black and white.

"Mama, why haven't you ever shown us these poems before?"

"Oh, we were all too busy." She didn't want us to criticize her most precious possession, so the books remained locked in her bedroom closet.

Paging through her poetry, I stopped at one that caught my eye. "What's this one about?"

"Which one?"

"The Clown."

"Oh, that's my favorite!" Without missing a beat, she began to recite the poem as my eyes followed across the page before me.

The Clown

My mother started me to school when I was five years old
I couldn't speak one word that could be understood I'm told.
I liked my first grade teacher . . . her name was Mrs. Knight
She didn't have a special pet so I was treated right.
I recall so vividly a fact that I'll relate
One morning Mother said to me, "Hurry, you'll be late!
The bus will soon be coming, Wanda how could you lose
Your little brand new shiny black patent-leather shoes?"
"Oh, Mother, must I go to school? May I please just stay?"
"No you cannot stay here because you'll just get in my way!
You can wear these tennis shoes that belong to your older brother,
There's nothing wrong with wearing them if they are clean,"
said Mother.
I could not hide the shame I felt whenever I looked down
To see myself dressed up to look just like BOZO the clown.
During recess time at school, I was playing jax and ball
Sitting on the sidewalk with my feet so big and tall.
"Ha Ha, He He, I heard this laugh, so I looked up then to see

Three high school girls were giggling and staring down at me.
"That little girl is pitiful," I heard one of them say
"I wonder who would send a little child to school this way."
I heard another girl ask, "Who's that poor neglected child?"
My sister Sarah answered, still laughing all the while.
"I do not know, Ha Ha, He He," Sarah let me down
She didn't want her friends to know . . . her sister was the clown.

As she spoke the last five words of the poem, her voice broke, she closed her eyes, and tears rolled down her cheeks as she strained to say, "the clown." Tears filled my eyes and compassion filled my heart as I embraced her and said, "It was painful. Your childhood memories are painful. I understand." We began to discuss her mother's mistreatment and neglect. We talked about her bed-wetting, her jealousy of Pearl, and her anguish–and about William, whom she loved.

"Mama, Grandma was mean to you."

"No, she wasn't mean, she was ignorant. I begged her not to make me go to school with those tennis shoes."

"I don't think she was ignorant. She should have cared more for you. Your parents allowed excessive partiality between you and Pearl and it was devastating... not only for you, but for me. Don't you understand? Mama, in your mind, I represented Pearl, and you identified Mary Jane with your childhood self. You tried to reverse the victimization of your childhood by treating Mary Jane the way you wanted to be treated as a child, and you treated me the way you wanted your mother to treat Pearl."

She listened intently and showed tacit acceptance of what I was telling her. She shook her head in recognition of a truth she had never heard before.

"Yes, what you are saying is true, Rose, even though I've never thought of it that way. Before Pearl was born I was babied and pampered by my family. Although I loved Pearl, I was jealous of her. She talked right, obeyed every rule, never peed in her pants, had pretty dark hair with curls, and she got every compliment. I used to wet my hair and comb it back so it would look darker because I hated my white hair. I thought I was ugly because of my hair. I wanted curls like Pearl."

"Such extreme partiality was emotionally cruel. It was mean!"

"My parents weren't mean, but they were partial. I was always dressed in coveralls until I went to school. When Mom made me my first dress I was six years old. I was so happy to have a dress so I could look like a girl. I climbed upon an old trunk and jumped off to see my dress flare up like a parachute. Then I twirled 'round and 'round to watch my skirt spin."

"Did Pearl wear coveralls 'till she went to school?"

"Oh, no. She always wore dresses from the time she was born. It is strange that I have never really thought about Mom being partial, but I suppose she was. But she didn't protect me, like I protected Mary Jane. I wouldn't let Mary Jane be ignored while you got the compliments."

My mother was still convinced she had done a noble thing. Perhaps I never received more compliments than Mary and it was all her imagination. Ironically, she didn't understand that in her effort to do the right thing, she committed the same crime as her mother. She treated Mary Jane the way her mother treated Pearl, and I became 'the Wanda'.

My mother was off balance, because what she had learned as a child was all she knew when she had her own children. The psychological imperatives of my mother's history affected me in turn. Although I defected from my upbringing, my mistaken choices affected my children. Never was it more real to me that a child's future depends on the way its parent's treat it in the privacy of the home. Parental maiming of a child's spirit endures far beyond the cradle.

"I want you to have my writings, Rose. You'll appreciate them more than the other children."

"Thank you. I will cherish these books forever."

I knew her writings would confirm my revelation of her childhood. I was no longer angry with her for what she did to me. I focused on all she had been through and all she had given me: the gospel, wonderful grandparents for my children, my brothers and sister, and my character. She provided those elements that make me who I am—my sense of humor, my determination, my fortitude, my inner strength, my resilience, my drive to be successful, my love of poetry, and my need to love and be loved. To be sure, they were accountable for my difficult childhood, but I was responsible in spite of my upbringing for the choices I made as an adult.

I hugged them both before leaving, not knowing when I would see them again. Walking to my car I stopped once more to look at the street, the neighborhood, the environment where I gained part of my biography, and I felt a strange ambivalence. I carefully put the book of her writings in the back seat of my car. They stood on the porch waving and watching as I drove out of sight.

I passed the narrow streets and tiny houses, thinking back to the games I played in those alleys. I came to the field where Pinky and I first met and dueled. Passing the house where she grew up, I saw her father's truck in the driveway, and I thought of him sitting inside his home, alone with his own memories, penitent, and forgiven. Glancing toward the house where Addie and Matt lived during those years, I saw three blond, barefoot children, two girls and a boy, running in the street, holding hands, laughing, jumping, squealing. I stopped to look closer, to stare into their faces, into their future. Gazing back at me though destiny's eyes, they paused but for a minute before disappearing, but in those sixty seconds, I recognized the alpha trio. They were Artist, Analyst, and Architect.

I drove slowly through Texas City and out onto the dike, reabsorbing my heritage and remembering my roots. I observed the changes that occurred over the years. The once barren town now had palm-lined streets, plants, flowers, sculptures, a lavish convention center, manicured parks, a betting racetrack, and shopping malls with new hotels. Extravagant recreation facilities rejuvenated the area, and Sixth Street was being restored to its original glory. At the end of the man-made fishing peninsula, I got out of my car to inhale the unfamiliar scent of salt air.

The bay waters were calm and smooth, the day, clear and cool. I could see Galveston in the distance, just a boat ride away. A lone seagull looking for food appeared above the waters, its wings spread wide

Boosted by the wind it seemed to hang in midair, patiently waiting, searching, hunting, and seeking with a determined, unyielding spirit. The gull lingered in the sky, riding the gentle breeze up and down, up and down. I stood mesmerized for several minutes. Finally, just beneath the surface of the sea, the gull spotted its prey. It swooped with unerring aim and snatched its reward from the watery hideaway. Content, the gull soared up and away from view until it was a tiny white spot, eventually fading from sight.

My gaze moved across the bay toward the eastern horizon where endless rows of smoke stacks, oil refineries, and chemical plants marked the skyline of a safe and refurbished city. No one would believe the town had been victimized by hurricanes, tidal waves, floods, and nitrate explosions. The land had not succumbed. *The City That Would Not Die* had prevailed and moved forward and beyond.

1.   The story about the dive competition was derived in part from a LDS Sunday School manual. Author unknown.

Printed in the United States
785400005B

9 780972 380621